Stories
MY FATHER TOLD US

*... That His Grandchildren
and Their Children Might Know*

Translated from *Der kleine Africa Bote*
compiled by Karl Bartsch

STORIES MY FATHER TOLD US

Copyright © 2006

by
Karl Bartsch
1001 University Drive
State College, PA 16801

Library of Congress Number: 2006931462
International Standard Book Number: 1-932864-98-9

Published by
Masthof Press
219 Mill Road
Morgantown, PA 19543-9516

Acknowledgments

The translation from German of the writings of Henry G. Bartsch occurred with the encouragement of many people. First and foremost I express gratitude to Evelyn for her continued encouragement to devote time and energy to the translation and for her reading of the manuscript and suggestions for improvement.

Our children, James and Terri Bartsch, Mark and Stephanie Bartsch, Craig and Christine Stutman, and Jonathan and Julliette Bartsch, also expressed interest in reading the writings of their grandfather in English.

My sister Erna Reimer, my sister Lydia and her husband Bill Reimer, and my brother Arthur Bartsch and his wife Helen, contributed pictures and corrections to the early drafts of this translation. I also drew on Arthur's translation of our mother's book, *Die Verborgene Hand (The Hidden Hand)*, to fill in and provide context to the writings of our father.

I gratefully acknowledge the editing contribution of Virginia Horst Loewen.

Contents

Preface   x

Chapter 1: Rescue and Promise, 1918-1923   1
- Life in Russia Before World War I
- The Day I Did Something Very Foolish
- My Near Death Experience
- My Recovery: God's Loving Presence
- Some Further Ordeals and My Exit to Canada

Chapter 2: Call and Response, 1930-1932   17
- Canada, Land of Opportunity
- God's Surprising Call
- First Steps in Response
- Faith and Doubt and Faith for a Year-and-a-half
- Preparations to Go
- The Visa Ordeal
- An Angel Arrives
- Two Lessons I Learned
- Visa Resolution and Deposit Concerns
- Kafumba Mission

Chapter 3: Adversity and Faith, 1933-1935   34
- Leaving Kafumba
- Finding Direction
- Our Trip from Kafumba to Bololo by Anna Bartsch
- Travel to the Sankuru River: Dad's Report
- First Contact with the Dengese People
- Arrival in Bololo
- Travel to Dekese
- Building the Mission
- Waiting for My Family
- Unexpected Help in Our Adversity

Chapter 4: Beginnings and Hope, 1933-1935   **59**
- A Child is Born: God Lives Here
- The Sorcerer's Magic Is Overcome
- A Summary Report of the Mission Work
- Evangelism
- The School
- Medical Services
- Our Plans and the Turn of Events
- Canadian Citizenship Problems
- The Mission in Henry's Absence
- Dad's Return from America
- Significance of the Trip to North America

Chapter 5: Challenges and Perseverance, 1936   **82**
- Events in Bololo
- Medical Conditions Among the Dengese
- Travel to a Village
- A Congo Village
- My Experience in Bisongonda Village
- The Difficulties I Face in Travel
- Do We Relocate the Mission?
- Work Among Girls of the Villages
- A Serious Catastrophe Averted
- My Reactions and Advice Regarding Another Mission
- Summary Report, January 4, 1937
- Christmas in the Jungle, 1936
- Margaret Siemens' Reflections

Chapter 6: Adversities and Fatigue, 1937   **107**
- Help Arrives on Time
- March 8, 1937 Our Family's Adjustment to the Congo
- Reports by Katherine Harder and Margaret Siemens
- Opposition to Our Work
- My Recent Trip to Port Francqui
- Experiences in Bolombo
- Conditions Among the Dengese People
- Care for the Body and Care for the Soul

- The Africa Committee Reports on Replacements
- Some Trials We Experience Here
- June, 1937: Dad's Sermon
- Mother's Medical Condition
- Mother's Report
- September 26, 1937: Report on Our Condition
- October 27, 1937: Mother's Condition
- Some Remarkable Events on the Mission
- Margaret Siemens Writes About the Same Incident
- When Replacements Come
- October 21, 1937: Update on Our Condition
- October 1937: Katherine Harder's Report
- November 7, 1937: Travel with Brother Lenzmann
- November 25, 1937: Last Travels
- December 9, 1937: Some Parting Comments
- Farewell to Bololo: Mother's Comments

Chapter 7: Furlough and Recovery, 1938-1939   142
- June 28, 1938: Reflections About Our Work in Bololo
- Our Approach to Mission Work in Bololo
- Our Trip to Germany and Canada
- Executive Committee Report of the Africa Bund
- Letters from Students in Bololo
- Report from Bololo
- Our Activities During Furlough
- Suffering of the Dengese Children

Chapter 8: Recall and Recommitment, 1939   153
- Events in the Summer of 1939
- Africa Committee's Response to the Crisis
- Chairman H.H. Janzen's Report
- On Board the *Empress of Britain*
- Lenzmanns and Katherine Harder Leave Bololo
- I Leave Europe August 12, 1939
- From Hotel Aletti Alger
- Letter from Gabo
- I Arrive in Leopoldville August 18, 1939

- I'm in Bololo, August 25
- Editor's Note: Lenzmanns Arrive in Winnipeg

Chapter 9: Obstacles and Isolation, 1940   168
- Conditions in Bololo
- Africa Mission Board's Attempt to Send the Bartsch Family Back to Africa
- A Year After Separation from My Family
- Travel to Lodi to Negotiate with the Commissioner
- Starting up School Again
- Isolated after the Kramers' Exile to Luebo in May
- My Visit to the Kramers in Luebo in July
- Conditions in Bololo after My Return
- My Loneliness (Notes from a Private Letter in July)
- My Thoughts on the Dengese People
- Turmoil in the Dengese Region
- There are Signs of Progress in Bololo but I am Lonely
- The Work Is Going Well but I am Lonely for My Family
- I am Lonely on a Sunday Morning
- I Get Frustrated in My Work
- There Is Trouble in the Lives of My Dear Teachers
- I Experience Some Replenishing Events in Difficult Circumstances
- I am Concerned for the Kramers and Experience a Fortuitous Event
- At the End of the Year: Hope and Confidence Though the Outlook Is Bleak

Chapter 10: Obstacles and Fatigue, 1941-1942   197
- Travel to Dekese and Kole
- February Report of the Meeting of the Directors of the African Mission
- A Family Letter
- The Voice of God Regarding the Zam Zam
- A Note in the *African Bote*
- Attack on the Zam Zam

- July, 1941: Africa Committee Notes on Conditions In Bololo
- A Letter to Constituents from Anna Bartsch
- News About the Mission in the Summer of 1941
- Events on the Mission in the Summer of 1941
- The Kramers' Child Is Ill and Dies
- The King Is Imprisoned and I Help Get Him Released
- We Get Permission to Place Itinerant Teachers in Villages
- Mid summer 1941: How I Feel Here Now
- I Met with Government Officials and with Father Alphonse
- Difficulties I Face on My Travels in the North
- A Note from the Kramers
- A Report from the Editor of *Der kleine Africa Bote*, November, 1941
- A Private Note: Conditions are Bleak Here in Early January 1942

Chapter 11: Return and Reflections, 1942　　　　229
- The Africa Committee Considers Possible Closure of the Mission
- Brother Bartsch Has Returned in May 1942
- June 1942: My Return to Canada and Reflections on the Status of the Mission
- Welcome to Brother Bartsch from the Executive Committee
- My Last Days on the Mission Field and My Views on Doing Mission Work
- Committee Affirmation of the Mission Work
- A Reflective Report on a Mission Trip in the Dengese Region
- My Last Days in Bololo, Written from Canada
- Questions About Where We Settle
- Committee Report of the Africa Mission Program
- My Travels in Canada in the Spring of 1943

- Farewell to Brother and Sister Bartsch
- The Final Status of the Bololo Mission Program

Epilogue: The Influence of My Father's Life on Me   255
- My Father's Influence on Me at the Crossroads of My Life
- What I Learned About My Father Through the Writings I Translated

Preface

"We had just passed Mr. Braun's yard, when two soldiers on horseback came up beside the wagon. Till then they had been behind us. I drove the two horses at full speed again. The commander laid his rifle down, pulled out his revolver and pressed it against my left ear. He roared at me, "I'll teach you to feed White soldiers. I'm a Red Officer and you're not getting away this time." Two of the riders came right next to the wagon. They drew their sabers. The other two riders behind us cocked their rifles so they were ready to shoot….

"The commander shrieked in my ear. He threatened to blow my brains out any minute. There was no way to escape: I felt the revolver next to my left ear, on either side and above me were sabers threatening to cut me to pieces, behind me were two soldiers that could shoot me down in case I tried to get away. I had only one way to go. That was to go to God, the Lord of life and death. If I should die at the hand of these murderers, I would be with Him."

I was eight or ten years old, growing up in Yarrow, British Columbia, Canada, when on cold winter evenings, with candles lit because the power was out, my father told stories such as this of his escape from Russia and God's leading in mission work. Sitting next to the radiator, he spoke slowly in a deep voice, cautiously relaying what he called "holy events." I imagined how God had rescued him from the Reds in Russia and led him in exciting ways in Africa. As I retell his stories I feel his voice, his pauses, his fears and his daring, deep within me. And I also feel his deep sense of God's presence. I want to share these stories with you, his children, grandchildren and great-grandchildren.

While I had always known these stories, remembering them as I do from my childhood, I recently received his stories in his own writing. Der kleine Africa Bote *(The Little Africa*

Messenger) *was a (Gothic) German publication printed in monthly installments in Winnipeg, Manitoba, from 1936 to 1943. It was to promote financial and prayer support for the work that Henry and Anna Bartsch were doing in Africa. Father wrote articles about his work in Africa in this publication. He also wrote of his early experiences in Russia.[1] I want to pass on these stories to you since you will not likely be able to read them directly in German. I will do so as accurately as I can, but also provide additional information about the circumstances in which he found himself. I will seek to provide a context or additional information, not found in his notes, but helpful in understanding his story. When I do I will italicize to distinguish my voice from his or from others. Some of this information comes from the writings of Anna Bartsch, my mother, about the same events.[2]*

Years later, as he remembered the loaded pistol behind his left ear, and his rescue from sure death, Henry Bartsch renewed the commitments he had made in the wheat field, to serve God for the rest of his life. His rescue from the "claws of death" during and after the 1917 Russian Revolution meant God had saved him for a reason; there was no doubt of that in his mind. When he obtained permission to leave Russia at the age of 24, he obtained an entry visa to Canada. The certainty that God had opened the path for him gave him a purpose. Surely his purpose was to do more than to farm, get settled and maybe to get rich in Saskatchewan, Canada!

He married Anna, my mother, on May 20, 1928. They sold their farm in 1930, shortly after the economic crash of 1929. With Anna's full consent, they sold their farm and livestock and paid for their trip to the Belgian Congo. They had a two-year-old daughter, my oldest sister, Erna. The ship took them to Germany, where my second sister, Lydia, was born. They ran out of money but an anonymous donor sent them enough to get to Africa.

---

[1] My mother wrote about her escape from Russia and her perspective on events in Africa in *Die Verborgene Hand*, translated by Arthur Bartsch, *The Hidden Hand*. Winnipeg, Manitoba: The Christian Press, 1987.

[2] Anna Bartsch, The *Hidden Hand*. Winnipeg, Manitoba: The Christian Press, 1987.

Arriving in the Belgian Congo in late 1931, they made their way into the heart of the Congo to a district called Dengese, made up of 40,000 Dengese people, scattered in a number of villages, ruled by King Ikongo-Samu. Belgian colonialists had exploited and brutalized the Congolese people.[3] The colonists had extracted taxes, abused women and taken ivory tusks and rubber from the Congo at will.[4] The Dengese people were naturally very suspicious of white people. Little wonder that, as was widely believed, the last white person to have entered the Dengese region was cannibalized.

Mother gave birth to my brother, Arthur, soon after they arrived in the Dengese region. The King came to see the white child born in his district. He was so impressed that a white child was born on his soil he said, "The great God lives here." He continued to look at the child and repeated, "The great God lives here." The King gave his own name, Ikongo-Samu, to my brother. He gave my parents a goat to provide milk and ordered the hunters to bring the white family antelope meat from the forest. My parents considered this an affirmation of God's call.

They began a school for boys. The King commanded children (boys) to go to the school to learn to read in their own language. Anna, my mother, put the language into writing and wrote Bible stories for the children to read in the Dengese language. She also translated many songs into Dengese. My father oversaw the school and the clinic, along with two nurses, and preached in the villages that God was a God of love and not of fear or

---

[3] Adam Hochschild, *King Leopold's Ghost*. New York: Houghton Mifflin Co., 1998.

[4] See Joseph Conrad, *Heart of Darkness: An Authoritative Text; Backgrounds and Sources; Criticism*. Ed. Robert Kimbrough. Norton Critical Edition; 3d ed. New York: W.W. Norton and Co., 1988.

hate. Henry had committed himself to follow God wherever God would lead him and his family. This commitment led them to the Belgian Congo. It was a decision he reached with the full support of his wife and an association of Mennonite brothers and sisters in Canada who promised to continue to support him as they were able. They arrived in central Africa in 1931, eight years after he escaped Soviet Russia and four years after my mother, Anna, had also left Russia.

Henry Bartsch, my father, wrote about his escapes "from the claws of death," as he put it, at other people's request. I'm sure he did so to praise the God who had rescued him rather than to point to his own exploits. I admit, however, that I did not think of God when I heard these stories from him, at about age eight or ten. As we sat around the hot air vent on cold winter evenings and listened to him talk, I thought he was a fantastic adventurer. I thought of him as an early Harrison Ford in the Raiders of the Lost Ark, *dodging bullets, escaping from prisons in Russia, slaying dragons (pythons), freeing the king from Belgian prisons, and on and on. He would never, I say never, have permitted such references. (Sorry, Dad!) These were holy events to him. He was only doing his part, being an instrument of the loving God of the universe, the one who had saved him. He was deeply committed to doing God's will.*

Thank you Dad, for sharing your perspective on life with me and for having lived it so fully. And thank you for writing about your life, the ways God was your very present help in time of trouble. You enrich my life as I read and remember the stories you told. I want to pass them on to your grandchildren and their children, children you have never seen. They need to hear from you. Against all odds, God saved and led you to serve others. May your God be their God, and may they learn to know the God of love in Jesus of Nazareth as you knew him.

Karl Bartsch
7/1/06

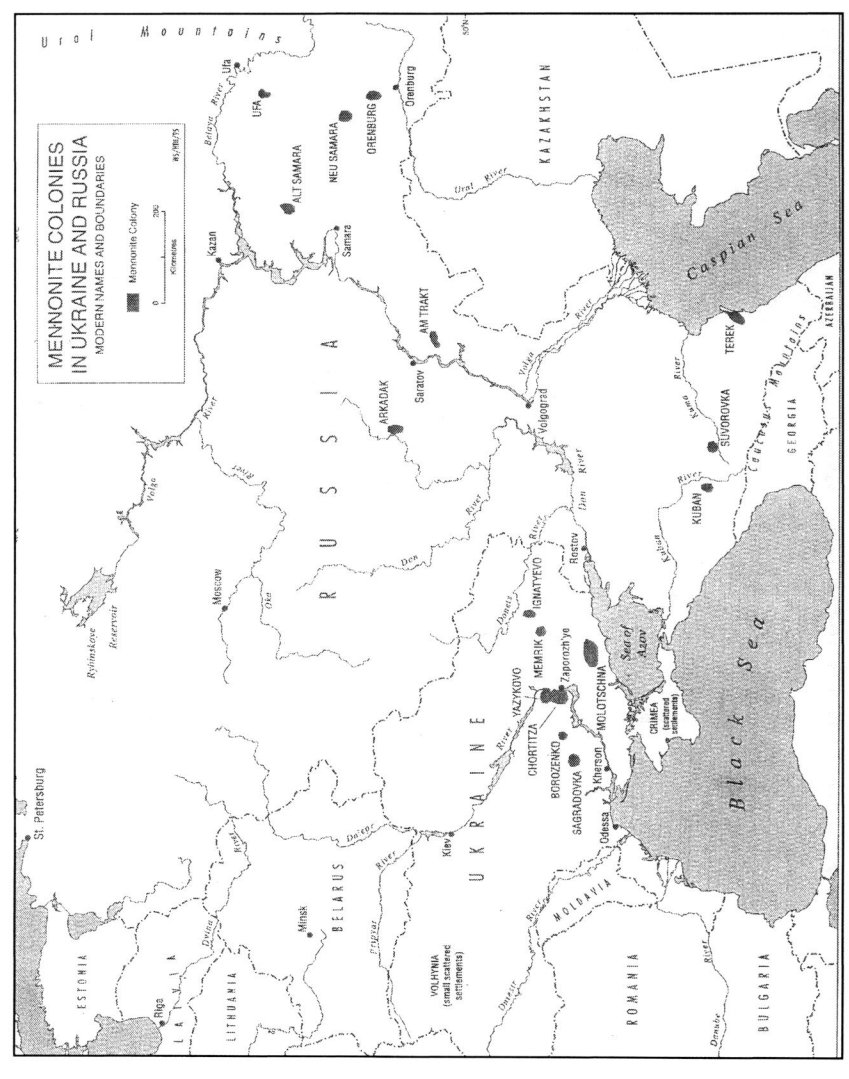

— Chapter 1 —

Rescue and Promise
1918-1923

Life in Russia Before World War I

Henry Bartsch, my father, was born in 1896, just over a hundred years ago, in a little town of Sparrau, located in South Russia, present-day Ukraine. If you look on the map on the preceeding page, you can see the city of Kiev. Sparrau was about 100 miles south of Kiev.

Everything was calm and peaceful in the little town. His family knew everyone. People were friendly. Everyone went to church, where children played in the yard and where adults sang and worshipped God. The railroad and train station did not come through Sparrau, so to catch the train, people had to take a short trip to Werknij Tockmack, the nearest train station. But they didn't do that very often; mostly they stayed in town. They walked, rode on horseback or hitched horses up to wagons. Although they had heard about and seen cars and trucks, there were none in the town of Sparrau. Henry loved horses and often hitched them to a wagon and rode full tilt down the dirt roads.

The Czar was the head of all of Russia. He was like a king or supreme ruler. His soldiers, the Cossacks, didn't come to Sparrau often because the Mennonites were given the right to take care of themselves and to manage their own villages. When Cossacks came to town, they came riding on horses, in full, bright, uniforms, tall fur hats, with long shiny sabers at their side. Everyone, including the kids, ran to the main street to see them. They usually visited with the mayor of the town, a Mennonite, who could speak Russian and handle things with the Russian government officials.

The Mennonites spoke German to each other because their forefathers came from Germany and Holland. Most of them had also learned to speak some Russian.

How did German-speaking Mennonites get to Russia? An earlier Russian Czarina (like a queen) invited Mennonites to Russia. This was Catherine II, (1729-1796) also known as Catherine the Great, empress of Russia from 1762-1796. She expanded her vast country's borders south to the Black Sea, as you can see on the map on page xiv. She wanted to westernize her people and so invited progressive farmers from Europe to settle her newly conquered territory.

Mennonites had lived in Germany and Holland and so they spoke German and Low German. Low German is a combination of Dutch and German. Czarina Catherine invited Mennonites because they were good farmers. She promised them land and freedom of religion. One of my forefathers, Johann Bartsch, along with Hoeppner, actually negotiated with Czarina Catherine to let Mennonites into Russia. That was in the 1780s, over a hundred and fifteen years before Henry was born.

Mennonites are Christian people who follow the teachings of Menno Simons. They got their name from his name Menno. Like Martin Luther, Menno Simons had been a Catholic priest. He parted from the Catholic Church because he saw that the Bible taught that God's grace was free, that it didn't have to be earned. He also saw that at the center of the Bible teachings is Jesus' Sermon on the Mount which teaches people how to live, that God is love and that we must love our neighbors as we love ourselves. This meant that people should join the church only after they voluntarily become Christians, that is, after they accept God's grace in Jesus. Mennonites believed that Jesus taught them to love their enemy and therefore they should not go to war.

Many people in Germany and Holland did not like what the Mennonites believed, so they fought against them. The result was a bloody persecution. Many Mennonites were killed. Others fled Holland to go to Prussia. Then in the 1750s-60s they were being conscripted, forced to join the army in Prussia, so it was a welcome opportunity for them to go to Russia under Czarina Catherine to settle newly conquered territory. They worked hard to cultivate the wilderness.

By the time of the beginning of World War I in 1914, there were 389 Mennonite villages in Southern Russia. Many of the farms were very large and prosperous. These Mennonites became very wealthy, had big barns, huge cow herds, and big fields of golden wheat and rye. They employed Russian servants and also had their own schools. Henry completed only three years of high school because as the eldest son, he had to assist his parents on the farm. His father died soon after that.

Life was good for Mennonite people before World War I. However it was not good for the Russian people. Those who lived next to Mennonite villages were often very poor. When people are very poor and see others who are very wealthy they become very angry. Since the wealthy people were foreigners, German-speaking Mennonites but living on Russian land, the native Russians became both jealous and resentful.

Before WWI, no one could imagine that anything could change in the peaceful little town of Sparrau. But everything changed when the war began.

WWI was fought between Great Britain, France, United States, Canada and Russia against Germany and Austria. When the German army defeated the Russian army, led by Czar Nicholas II, many Russian people felt very angry with the Czar. The soldiers felt terrible after they were defeated and many turned against the Czar. They started a revolution. Others were loyal to the Czar.

Mennonites did not believe that they should carry a gun and kill other people. But they did want to do their part in service to the country. The Czar's Russia had given them a home. So, many of the Mennonite men became orderlies or forest workers. Henry was 18 when WWI began in 1914. He went into the medical service of the Russian army where he was exposed to the dangers, cruelties and horrors of the Caucasian battlefields. He became an orderly. Because his family had horses and wagons, he had *the responsibility to pick up wounded soldiers returning from the battlefield and bring them to a hospital. He often heard the soldiers' stories. At first, soldiers returning from the battlefront were optimistic. They hoped Russia would win against the Germans. After a number of defeats, more and more wounded soldiers came back. He heard how angry they were with the Czar and his officers. He could sense that a rebellion was coming.*

The Russian revolution started in 1917 when Henry was 20 years old. It brought him release from the medical corps, but just after his arrival at home, his father, as well as many others, died of the flu epidemic that swept through Europe and North America.

In the Russian Revolution of 1917 the Reds (Communists, sometimes called the Bolsheviks) fought against Czar Nicholas, his officers and his government. The soldiers who were loyal to the Czar were called the Whites. People in the Mennonite towns were loyal to the Czar and his Whites. As the revolution progressed, the Red Army camped on one side of the village while the Czar's White Army (Cossacks) camped on the other side. Mennonite villages lay in between the two. People in the villages were very scared because sometimes the Red or White soldiers would raid the town. They would take horses, steal food and money, and often hurt or rape women and children. Since neither the Reds nor the Whites had full military control, Mennonite villages were overrun by one or the other side. When neither side occupied the villages, disgruntled groups of men, who had previously worked for Mennonite farmers, would ride into town to take what they wanted. These hordes of bandits roamed the Mennonite villages, killing people at will.

The Day I Did Something Very Foolish[5]

It was a bright and beautiful day in May 1919, about one-and-a-half years after the revolution began. The blossoms were out on the trees, the rye was high in the fields, the sun shone brightly. But people were scared. They rushed through back alleys, looked down the street and dashed into their homes. No one felt at ease. When a horse rode through town people looked out of their windows, from behind curtains, so as not to be noticed. They were worried. Only a few went to church. They were afraid that Red soldiers would come into town, burn their houses, and kill or maim their children and wives.

Our mayor, the main administrator, was Mr. George Braun. He was a very careful and thoughtful man. He didn't show his emotions very easily. He didn't get excited over little things. Whenever he said something, I knew that he had thought about it carefully.

Somehow the story spread through the town that a Cossack soldier, a scout, had visited Mr. Braun early that morning. Although we did not have telephones then, news spread quickly if anything important happened. At 10 o'clock that morning, I and some of my friends hung around my uncle's gate, waiting to see what was happening. We discussed the danger our town was in. That's what everyone talked about. We wondered what that Cossack commander had told Mr. Braun. We heard cannon fire to the east where the sun had come up. White Cossacks and Red communists were fighting there.

Then we saw Mr. Braun running/walking through town. His face beamed good news. I knew that something good was happening. Although the war between the Whites (Czar's soldiers or Cossacks) and the Reds (Communists, Bolsheviks or rebels) was close to our village, he seemed to be bringing good news.

He said to me, "Well, Henry, now you can relax and enjoy yourself. We'll be free of the Red dangers very soon."

I was surprised by the news. Mr. Braun was not usually this excitable. When I asked him for more details, he motioned

---

[5]*Der kleine Africa Bote*, August 1938.

me to his brother Peter's house, across the street, where a group of us met. He signaled to me. I knew what this meant. He wanted me to join him across the street. He did not want to share more of the news in public. I felt honored to be invited to hear his story along with a few others. Although he was an older man and the most important man in our town, he liked to have me by his side. I knew he liked me and that felt good. I went across the street with him.

Mr. Braun, the one who seldom smiled, sat in a chair, grinning from ear to ear. He didn't speak right away. He enjoyed seeing us eager to hear what he had to say. He was the center of our attention. Then he told us about his conversation with the Cossack commander early that morning on his yard. We paid close attention. No one stirred. Everyone was quiet. He said that the army of White Cossack soldiers were only a few miles from us and would come to free our town of danger from the Reds. "So today, things can change for the good in Sparrau," he said. Everyone agreed. We were excited and enthusiastic.

Der Mensch denkt, aber Gott lenkt.
We human beings make plans, but God directs events.

When Mr. Braun had finished the good news of the coming White army, he made a request. Everyone in the community should show their welcome to the coming White soldiers by offering them bread and ham. This was special food that we Mennonites ate and the Russians knew that we ate this kind of food around holidays. Mr. Braun said the Cossack commander had requested that we prepare food for 25 soldiers. We should also provide supplies for the horses as well. Everyone at the meeting was happy to help because we wanted to support the White Cossacks against the dreaded Reds.

I asked Mr. Braun who would pick up the food from the various homes, hoping that he would ask me. Mr. Braun pointed to himself and two other neighbors. I was disappointed. I wanted to greet the incoming White troop of 25 men with the food. Why didn't Mr. Braun select me to join him? I had always been at his side when he wanted something done! But this time Mr. Braun looked at me with a friendly smile and told me to go back to my house. I felt as though he was keeping a secret.

As I left the house where Mr. Braun had told us the good news, two of my friends followed me to the gate. As we talked we decided that we would go to see the White troops ourselves. We wanted to see them even before they came to our village to free us of the Red threat. We quickly hitched up our best horses and took off. Rather than take the main road, we took the wagon trail through the fields, where we might not be noticed easily, and where we could act as if we were checking on the grain fields. Maybe no one would see us behind the high grain. I know now that we were doing something very dangerous, but we did not feel that then. We were taking risks we should not have taken.

When we came to the edge of the grain field, to the open grassland, we saw two Cossack soldiers on horseback up on the hill. Even though they were far away, we could tell that they were Cossacks because of their large fur caps. We were excited because we thought we were close to the rescuers Mr. Braun had talked about. We thought we were out of danger. They were our friends and would help liberate our town. The soldiers on horseback were sentries. Sentries are soldiers who keep watch to see if any danger is approaching their camp.

However, things changed quickly. We saw that one Cossack had his rifle aimed at us as he rode toward us at full gallop. He shouted at us, "Stop, don't move." When he got closer and saw that we had no guns, he put his rifle down, and demanded to know where we were from and where we were heading. We explained the nature of our ride in a very calm tone and voice. In fact, we acted as calm as innocent little children.

This very experienced and skilled Cossack said, "My, you are crazy kids. (I was 22 years old.) Don't you know that the Reds carry their cannons on wagons just like the one you have? You are lucky I didn't shoot you." They let us go.

Only then did we realize the danger we were in. We were scared. We had no further interest in going any farther. We wanted the safety of our home. We turned the horses and wagons around and headed toward our town of Sparrau. Instead of taking the wagon trail in the fields we took the main road. We did not want to be suspected of carrying guns. We could get shot before they even saw that we were not carrying weapons.

We were about a mile-and-a-half from our town when we noticed a horse-drawn wagon with 15 soldiers coming towards us on the road. They were coming out of our town of Sparrau. Were these Reds? Surely they couldn't be Whites! My two friends got very pale with fright. I probably did too. We could not get out of their way because they had already seen us. To try to escape would have made us look suspicious. So we stayed on the road and tried to fake being calm. We gave the impression that we had come from a joyride.

But we were worried! The Reds had seen us talking to the White sentries up on the field. Our hearts beat fast. We were very frightened. In our inner hearts we prayed to God, "Please save us just this time." The Red troops came closer. They all looked at us with disdain. Nobody said a word. They didn't stop us nor did they, themselves, stop. So we rode into town. We looked back once or twice before we came to town to be sure that they were not following us.

When we arrived in town, people wondered at our stupidity. We had taken off without any thought about the dangers involved in trying to visit the White army. People were also surprised that the troop of 15 Red soldiers had let us pass so easily. Only then did we learn that they had ransacked the town while we were gone: taken food from any home they wanted, burned buildings, and threatened people with their guns and sabers.

We also discovered that Mr. Braun and his helpers had collected the food supplies. After collecting the food, they started to take the same wagon trail through the fields that we had taken, maybe to get the food to the White army. At some point, they must have felt that the wagon trail through the grain fields was too dangerous so they turned around. But while they were out of town, the troop of 15 Reds, that had ransacked the town, had missed him and the wagon of food. So the Reds did not get it. Mr. Braun and his helpers returned to the town and put the food in Mr. Boschmann's shed. They made sure that the Reds would not find the food. In spite of our stupidity and the danger from the 15 Reds, everything had turned out well. Our Lord had been a wonderful help.

All this happened in the morning. The afternoon was quiet in town but we could hear the rattle of machine guns in the distance. There were rumors in town that enemy Reds were hiding in the grain fields. That's how it was till evening. Everyone was scared.

My Near Death Experience

The sun was setting as a messenger ran into our yard. He told me to hitch horses to a wagon and get them to Mr. Braun immediately. I took my time getting out the wagon and hitching the horses. As I did, Mr. Braun and a White commanding officer raced into our yard on a wagon that belonged to Mr. Boschmann. A soldier on horseback rode up behind them. The officer jumped from the wagon and ordered me to get the best horses and the best wagon ready immediately. His voice was urgent and demanding. Mr. Braun urged me to hurry too. The horseback soldier dismounted from his horse to help me get the wagon hitched up. When I asked what the rush was, I was told that the Whites had taken the town and that I was to get a machine gun from the field for their support.

I understood that. But I noticed something very strange on the uniform of the rider who was helping me hitch the horses. I noticed he had a small red stripe on his uniform that regular White soldiers did not have. As I passed Mr. Braun during the hitching up of the horses, I whispered to him, "He is a Red. He's only faking that he is White." This was real danger because if this man really was a Red soldier, so was the commanding officer. Then we were in real trouble.

Mr. Braun said, "No, Henry, everything is OK. Just hurry up and get the horses hitched to the wagon." I trusted Mr. Braun. He had always known what was happening. So I calmed myself by telling myself that we were helping our rescuers from the Reds.

My mother came out of the house, obviously very much afraid because we were rushing around so urgently. She asked Mr. Braun, "Is there danger?" Mr. Braun said in German, "Mrs. Bartsch, you don't need to worry. Be happy that we are getting rid of the Red bandits." The officer noticed that my mother looked so frightened. He said to Mr. Braun, "What did she say?" Braun laughed and said in Russian, "Women are afraid of the Reds. I told her to just calm herself."

With horses hitched, we were ready to go. The commanding officer and Mr. Braun got into my wagon and sat on the seats behind me. I climbed to the raised seat from where I held the reins to direct the horses. I was the driver. The officer commanded the messenger boy to get on the wagon too. The soldier on horseback rode behind us. I took off with a burst of speed. I noticed that people peeked from behind their curtains. They suspected danger.

As we passed the home of the messenger boy, he jumped off the wagon. The commanding officer and Mr. Braun were in full conversation in Russian. The commander demanded answers from Mr. Braun about the events of the day in our town. When the messenger boy jumped off, he turned sharply in surprise, but recovered quickly. He let the boy go and continued to ask Mr. Braun about the "Red Terror." Mr. Braun was only too eager to help. He still believed that the commander was a White officer. He pointed to me and said to the officer, "And this guy, he was there with you folks today. He could easily have been wiped out by the Reds." I turned my head slightly to see the commander out of the corner of my eye. Mr. Braun continued by saying how I had stood by his side, had helped him, at the time of the "Red Terror" in our town.

When we arrived at New Street, the commander ordered us to stop. Another solder joined us on horseback. Another two riders came from another yard. They had stolen horses from the farmers. So now we had four soldiers on horseback: The one who had been with us when we hitched the horses and the other three that joined us here. We waited for the commander to give orders to carry on.

Suddenly the commander jumped from the wagon. He began to curse and scream at the three soldiers. He even threatened to shoot his own soldiers for robbing the farmers of their horses. I observed this and felt happy that the new White government officers would keep order. They would not let their soldiers rob people of things they wanted for themselves.

Then something strange happened. One of the soldiers stood directly in front of the Commanding Officer and said to him, "Sir, you are being very hard on us." The Commanding Officer burst out laughing. Then he caught himself. He had been putting on a show for us. He had tried to convince us that he was a White officer when really he was a Red. He had tricked us. And we had told him secrets about how we had helped to fight the Reds, his own soldiers.

I whispered to Mr. Braun, "We are in the hands of terrible bandits and murderers." He was pale with fright.

The Commanding Officer noticed that we sensed the situation, but he immediately acted again as our White friend. We wanted to believe so badly that he was our rescuer that we began to trust him again. We passed Mr. Braun's yard as his wife came running out in great fear. "Who is that?" asked the commander. "It's my wife," said Mr. Braun. "Tell her not to worry," said the commander.

We had just passed Mr. Braun's yard, when two soldiers on horseback came up beside the wagon. Till then, they had been behind us. I drove the two horses at full speed again. The commander laid his rifle down, pulled out his revolver and pressed it against my left ear. He roared at me, "I'll teach you to feed White soldiers. I'm a Red Officer and you're not getting away this time!" Two of the riders came right next to the wagon. They drew their sabers. The other two riders behind us cocked their rifles so they were ready to shoot.

We got to the end of the street. There was a "Y" in the road. The one went to one town and the other to another. Up the road to the left, was a wood that we called, "Windwehr."

The commander shrieked in my ear. He threatened to blow my brains out any minute. There was no way to escape: I felt the revolver next to my left ear; on either side and above me were sabers threatening to cut me to pieces; behind me were two soldiers that could shoot me down in case I tried to get away. I had only one way to go. That was to go to God, the Lord of life and death. If I should die at the hand of these murderers, I would be with Him.

The two horses went as fast as they could, as though they sensed my danger.

The commander shrieked again and again, "Turn right, turn right." In the back Mr. Braun pleaded, "Have pity. Have pity."

Instead of turning right, I pulled the horses to the left. I wanted to get as close to the woods as I could. I was about 120 to 150 feet away. Then, in desperation, I threw myself into the arms of the Almighty. At full gallop, I threw the reins between the horses, jumped on the tongue of the wagon, swung around the neck of the horse to the left, landed in the grass as the wagon and the riders raced by. I heard gunfire as the bullets whistled past my ears. The commander screamed, "Fire. Fire." He was the first to shoot when I started to run into the woods. The two riders with their sabers drawn turned and began to chase me on their horses. But I had a head start because they raced by when I swung around the horse on the left. My move had caught them off guard, so they raced by. But they continued to shoot. I ran for my life, as fast as my legs could carry me. Finally, I reached the safety of the woods. The horses that had chased me had stopped. Not one bullet had hit me.

I had fallen into the arms of God and not into the arms of the murderers. Although my enemies tried to exterminate me, they didn't succeed. The Lord protected me.

My Recovery: God's Loving Presence[6]

Mr. Braun tried to escape, too. When he saw that I had leaped onto the tongue of the wagon, swinging around the neck of the galloping horses, he jumped over the side of the wagon. The horseman had his saber ready. I found out later that as he jumped, the rider on horseback hacked off his arm. Mr. Braun made his way back to his own farm, not far away. While the riders pursued me, the

---

[6] *Der kleine Africa Bote*, September 1938.

commander turned the wagon around and met Mr. Braun on his yard. His wife, son and servant came out and pleaded for his life. They gave him an expensive watch, a large amount of money, and a wagon with horses, in exchange for his freedom. With that the commander was ready to leave.

But then the riders arrived. They were furious that I got away. They swore and carried on in a shameful way. They demanded that Mr. Braun stand up in front of them. Remember, he had had his arm hacked by the saber and was bleeding. He stood up and said, "Go ahead, shoot me. I am ready to die." One rider shot him in the chest and the other shot him in the head. He died. The commander said nothing, but rode off with Mr. Braun's wagon, his watch and his money.

While this was going on I sneaked out of the woods, crawled along the ditch, hid behind a hedge of bushes and got into Mr. Neufeld's barn. From there I could see the street without being seen. Then I sneaked into the field of rye grain where I sat and waited for darkness to come. My heart beat fast. My life had been saved from sure death. I thanked God for my rescue, but didn't really know what happened to Mr. Braun till later.

As I sat in the field of grain, catching my breath and slowing my heart down, I heard voices. This scared me. Then I heard that they spoke German and not Russian. I knew then that they were Mennonites. When I peeked from behind the grain, I saw that they were my two neighbors: K. Dueck and G. Harder. When they drew closer, I rose up from my hiding position in the grain.

They were shocked. "We heard a rumor that you and Mr. Braun had been shot."

I was happy to tell them that not one of the nine shots fired at me had hit. We sat in the grain field till it got dark. We talked about life and death, about eternal things. I told them about the decision I had made, that I had committed myself to offer the rest of my life to the Lord completely. Looking back, I hardly knew what this meant, but as I said it, I knew it was real. Both of them said they, too, wanted to become followers of Jesus. I was glad I could help them find faith.

I often remember that time. Darkness began to fall. They were getting ready to leave. I had survived such horrendous and traumatic events, all in one day. All my senses had opened as they do when we face really scary events.[7] Anything could have happened to me. I could have been shot the way Mr. Braun was shot. But I was rescued, and then God provided me with two neighbors, Dueck and Harder, with whom I could talk about the events and the decisions I had made. I felt a deep spiritual connection with them that I still remember vividly, hiding there in the grain field. God spoke so clearly, and was present with us so closely because He loves us so much. I've been close to death several other times, but because I had life in God, I didn't have to be afraid as I once used to be. My faith had been tested. It was real. It has sustained me to this day.

Later I came back to my mother's house. She was particularly happy to hear about God in my life. She later told me that I had almost died of illness when I was very small. She said she had taken me in her arms and dedicated me to the Lord and that I had recovered soon after that.

Some Further Ordeals and My Exit to Canada

I was a marked man. The Reds had won the war against the Whites, so they set up government offices and began to manage the country in their own way. I was on their blacklist.

Daily fighting on the streets stopped. The new Red/Communist government was trying to establish order. They still searched out those who had opposed them. I lived at home with my mother but was careful not to be seen when any Red soldier or government official showed up. Once, when they caught me, I was put into a sort of makeshift prison. It was evening and one of the mean guards promised me that they would hack me to pieces by morning. Knowing how they treated prisoners who had been helpful to the Whites, I believed he would do as he said.

---

[7] This is a traumatic event. It is a sudden, life-threatening event that would scare almost anyone and is outside the range of normal human experience.

Even when they said that to me, I can honestly say that I felt love for my persecutors. So I prayed for them. I know that it was faith in the sacrificial death of Jesus on the cross and the power of His resurrection that enabled me to do that. I am grateful that that faith kept me going, even when I faced dying.

This does not mean that I had to lie there in prison to wait for them to kill me. The "prison" was not that secure. A guard with a bayonet stood at the door. I checked him out. At one point I noticed that he stood with his back to the door and looked to the right. There was enough room for me to slide out behind him if I could do it quietly. I opened the door enough to slip out and he did not hear me. I ran as fast as my legs would carry me. I ran to my aunt's house. She was surprised. I said, "Do you have something to eat?" She did, and as I began to eat, we heard the Reds at the front door trying to get into her house. I had another bite and went out the back door as fast as I could. I escaped again.

By 1923 things had settled down a good bit although life was not the way it had been before the war and revolution. Things were not as bad as they had been. There wasn't the daily threat on our lives. During this time, I grew steadily in my Christian faith. It became clear to me that I really wanted to study at a Bible school. I considered one in Russia but then also received an entry permit from Canada. This meant that I could enter Canada if I could only get out of Russia. But that was a problem.

It was a problem because of the Red/Communist Secret Police, called the G.P.U. To leave the country of Russia, a person had to get clearance from the G.P.U. For me it meant almost sure death, because I was on their blacklist. They had a record of the times I had supported the Whites, had escaped their commanders, had been in prison and had escaped.

I took the risk of asking our village and district government office for permission to leave Russia. I was worried. The government official laughed as he filled in the paperwork. As I left his office, the senior official said sarcastically, "Greet America and travel safely." He was mocking me because he knew that I had to get permission from the G.P.U. which had my past records of opposition to the Reds. "You won't get past them."

I trusted in God, but this didn't mean I was not scared. When I walked past the military guard through the huge doors of the den of murderers, my heart pounded. When I entered the door of the building, I felt as though I had crossed the line into death. I felt hopeless and scared as I thought of my name on the blacklist. I sat in the waiting room feeling like one condemned to die, yet I needed to take the risk and get permission to leave. Every official that walked by me seemed to look at me strangely. Someone asked me what I wanted. I said, I wanted a meeting with the leader of the G.P.U. In a little while I was led into a room where a woman identified herself as the leader of the G.P.U. After she looked through my paperwork, I filled out some more papers. She told me to come back in four days.

I arrived early on the fourth day. At 10 o'clock, a short little man came and asked me for my name. He was very friendly. "When did you come to town? Why didn't you call on me at home? If you had, I would have given you your papers yesterday." I followed him to his desk. He was most friendly. He asked me to sit down. He excused himself for having made me wait so long. He filled in the necessary papers in thirty minutes, gave them to me and wished me luck in America. When I shook his hand, I asked him if could pay him for his help. I knew that it was customary to pay government officials something extra for their work. We might call it a "tip" or a "bribe." To my surprise, he didn't accept any money. Anyone who knows Russia knows that this was an even greater miracle than the miracle of the permission to leave Russia. I thanked God.

So I left Russia legally. I did not have to sneak out the way my younger brother Abraham did. He took the Trans-Siberian railroad, the long way across huge Russia, crossed the Yalu River into Korea, got into Japan and then to the USA.

I arrived in Canada shortly before the Christmas of 1923. I had just turned 27 years old.

— Chapter 2 —
Call and Response
1930-1932

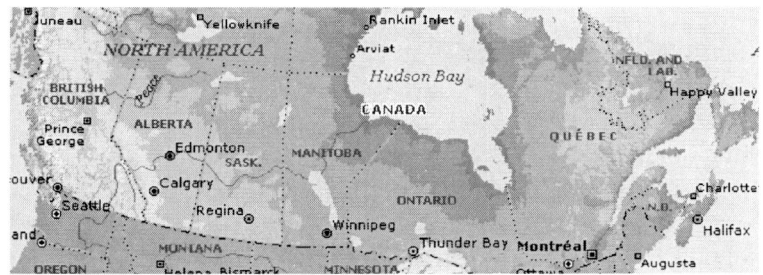

Canada, Land of Opportunity

I landed in Halifax, Nova Scotia, then took the train to Saskatchewan, Canada, where I met my uncle, H. A. Bartsch. In order to pay back the money for the tickets to cross the ocean and the train across Canada, I got a job on my uncle's farm. I worked hard and was able to pay off my travel expenses in two years. I began my new life in Canada.

You remember that when I was in Russia, I wanted to go to Bible School. I still wanted to do that, so in the winter of 1925, I went to such a school, first in Herbert, Saskatchewan, and then in Winkler, Manitoba. I loved going to school. I graduated in three years.

During this time, my uncle's son Jake died in a drowning accident. This was tragic but it also meant that I was next in line to inherit my uncle's farm. Suddenly everything opened up

Mother and Dad's wedding picture, May 20, 1928.

for me to get settled in the new land. What I needed was a wife. When I met Anna Funk in Bible School, I knew that she was the one God had set aside to be my wife. I wrote her a letter asking her to marry me. I gave it to our teacher, Abram Unruh, to give to her. In the letter I said that I believed she was the one to whom the Lord had directed me. She was to be my life partner. She said yes. We were married on May 20, 1928.

I am telling you these details because of what was to happen next. The stories I told you about my near death experiences in Russia had lead me to commit my life to God. You remember me telling you that! You also remember me telling you how, miraculously, I had been given an exit visa by the terrible G.P.U. that had me on a blacklist to kill me. I felt deeply then that God had a plan for me in rescuing me from the Russian "hellhole." But often promises made in desperate situations are not kept later. Was this going to happen to me?

I was able to pay off my debts quickly. I was proud of the fact that I could pay them off in two years. Then my uncle gave me a farm. I inherited it, because my cousin, his son, had drowned. I was able to go to a Bible School. And I found a wife. Things were looking good for me. I could be a successful Canadian farmer.

You would think that, after God had rescued me so dramatically, and after studying the Bible for three years, I would want to become a preacher or missionary. But that was not so. I couldn't see myself as a minister. It was too much responsibility. I also had little interest in missionary work. In fact I didn't take any mission courses in Bible School. God had saved me from Russia and I wanted to serve him, but when my uncle offered me land and tools to become a successful farmer, I took it. I felt settled in May 1928, after I married Anna Funk, who also came from a Mennonite village in Russia. We had an excellent crop that summer. Life was good. I was now 32 years old.

God's Surprising Call

All our plans changed in late fall that year. It began on a Sunday night when Mr. A. A. Janzen and his wife came to visit one of our churches in Saskatchewan. The Janzens were missionaries in Africa, and showed us slides and told us about the needs of the African people. Half-way through the slide show and talk, I heard another voice, other than A. A. Janzen's voice. It was very clear and pleading. It was not a voice anyone else could hear. Only I could hear it. It came from deep inside me saying, "You are enjoying your life of comfort here, and out there people are crying for light and truth."

I was totally stunned. I could hear nothing else in the church service. I don't know what else the Janzens said since I was totally focused on that voice inside me. I drove home in our car with Anna, my wife. I casually commented to her on the good presentation that the Janzens had made. Before we went to bed, we prayed for the people of Africa but I did not talk to her about the other voice I had heard inside me. I thought it might be gone when I went to work in the morning.

Farmers in Saskatchewan, Canada.

Next day, I got up early to plow the field. I was out there for about an hour when I couldn't stand it anymore. The voice in me became so loud, it came with such force, I just couldn't stand it. I stopped the tractor in the field, ran into our house and confessed to Anna, my wife, what God, through that voice, demanded of me.

"If I resist this call of God in my life, I will endanger my salvation," I said almost in tears. She was stunned. To my surprise and joy, she confessed that she felt the same way. We were scared. In fact we trembled. What would God lead us to do? Was this a turning point in our lives? It would certainly be a change for us. We knelt down together and prayed. "Use us, Lord," we prayed. "We give you our whole selves. If you want to use us, provide for us what we need to serve you among the African people." We calmed down. Our spirits quieted.

We decided to tell no one about our decision. We couldn't expect others to comprehend what we felt when we could hardly do so ourselves. But that changed several months later when a dear friend came to visit. We told him what we had experienced and what we had decided. He listened intently and then turned to Exodus 3:14 in the Bible. In this story God calls Moses to lead his people out of Egyptian captivity. Moses sees the burning bush and hears God's voice to him and so he asks, "What is your name?"

"I am who I am," is God's answer.
This means, "I am present. I will be there for you."

When our friend read us the story we knew again that God was calling us, but we agreed with each other not to talk to anyone else about our decision to become missionaries. In fact, we didn't speak to anyone about that decision for a whole year after that.

During the next year we often questioned ourselves about the "call." Had we heard correctly? Maybe in time this would wear off! Maybe it was simply something we had made up! We tried to find reasons why it was unreasonable for us to become missionaries. We even tried to find passages in the Bible to support how unreasonable it was. But always the Spirit, within us, reminded us of our call to surrender everything.

On July 4, 1929, our first daughter, Erna, was born.

We had a good crop of wheat in 1929. We took it to the Saskatchewan Wheat Pool and counted on a good income, but then the Pool went bankrupt. The Depression came in October 1929. They could not pay us because of the economic depression.

First Steps in Response

When autumn came in 1929 it was one year since the Lord had called us. We knew we had to do something. Besides, I had lost all interest in farming. We agreed to sell the farm, the cows and farm machinery. So we had an auction. But, because of the depression, many people could not pay us in cash. So although they bought things, we did not receive all the money from the sale.

We moved off the farm to a little apartment with our little baby.

Faith and Doubt and Faith for a Year-and-a-Half

When people asked what we were planning to do, we hardly knew how to answer them. When we told them about God's call and our commitment to become missionaries to people in Africa, in a time of depression, we felt scared. We did not know how we would get there. Then we continued to question whether God had really called us. I prayed earnestly. Often I prayed without words, to somehow break through the dark barriers inside myself to God's presence and assurance. I had to! I just had to make contact with God. Once, during this time, when we were particularly discouraged, and when we were almost out of money, someone asked me where we were heading, I said, "Africa." His enthusiasm was immediate. He made several suggestions about how we could get the money to go. I found this very encouraging.

During the next year-and-a-half, that is, till Christmas 1930, we often felt desperate about our need for financial support. We needed money to pay for the tickets to go to Africa. We questioned God's call again and again. It seemed

Mother, Erna, Dad, and mother's brother Corney.

so crazy. Then a lady sent us $.50 for the trip. Of course that half-dollar could hardly buy us anything. It was ludicrous. But she sent it to us with good wishes for the trip to Africa. I burst into tears. I was so moved. Someone had actually given her last little bit to send us to Africa. Within a week more letters arrived. Many people sent small amounts of money for the trip. One letter had $500 from an anonymous donor. This was a lot of money in those days, especially because there was a severe economic depression. Within a month, we had enough that we could actually consider paying for the trip. I went to the ticket office to find out how much the ticket would be to catch a train to New York and from there a ship to Europe. We had to go to Europe to get our visa to the Belgian Congo. The ticket agent gave the cost of the trip. We had exactly enough money.

Preparations to Go

The Mennonite Churches in Winnipeg had a farewell for us. They also collected more funds. When I went to the ticket office the next day to actually buy the tickets, I was told that I had been quoted the wrong price the first time. The price of the tickets was more than the price quoted before. In fact, the amount of money collected by the church the night before was just enough to pay for the additional amount we needed. We wondered if God was trying to tell us something! Maybe we weren't supposed to lose our trust that God would provide.

We left our friends and supporters in Winnipeg, Manitoba, on March 13, 1931. We visited a number of churches and made many friends in Kitchener, Ontario. We took the train to New York, where we boarded a ship, the *General von Steuben*, to Germany. Our daughter, Erna, age one-and-a-half, managed the ten-day trip very well. My wife and I got very seasick. There were times when I could barely stand straight. We arrived in Germany on March 31, 1931.

The Visa Ordeal

We planned to be in Germany for only a few days–seven at the most.[8] We had come only to get a visa from the Belgian government. I went to the Belgian Consulate in Hamburg to ask for a visa to go to Belgian Congo. I thought it would be a simple matter. It turned out to be much more complicated than I had anticipated. Rather than seven days, it took us seven months.

When I went to the Belgian Consulate in Hamburg to ask for a visa to the Congo, the officer screamed at me. "You can't go there. They have enough missionaries. Why didn't you get it in Canada?"

I argued back, "I was told in Canada to come here to get my visa. I have their instructions in writing."

"You want to put your head through the wall. You can't do it," he said. He really was mean! I was reminded of my experience with government officers in Communist Russia.

I thought to myself, "These walls are pretty hard. I would hurt my head if I tried that. But King David says in the Psalms: "With my God I can jump over the wall. That's what I want to do."

He gave me papers to fill out.

A song played itself in my head:

Keiner wird zuschanden, welcher Gottes harrd.
Sollt ich sein der erste der zuschanden ward.
Nein das ist unmoeglich, du getreuer Hort,
Eher faellt der Himmel, denn mich taeuscht dein Wort.

(No one will be put to shame, who trusts in God.
Is it possible that I would be the first to be put to shame?
No that is impossible, you, faithful shepherd.
Heaven will fall before your Word proves me false.)

I shared my terrible experience at the Consulate with my wife. Both of us felt depressed and hopeless. We prayed together. We called to God for help. "God, you brought us this far. Do we

---

[8] *Der kleine Africa Bote*, December 1938, pp. 8-11.

need to go back now?" Even if we had to turn back, could we ever have faith in God again? Could we still thank him then, even though our plans had not worked out? Weren't they God's plans for us? Had we heard incorrectly? It was as if heavy clouds had rolled in. Our vision got darker and darker. I felt as though we were walking in the shadow of death. What would our friends say? Those who had given us money, those who prayed for us, what would they say now? What would they say?

To make matters worse, the shipping company, being responsible for bringing us to Germany, began inquiring about our financial support in Canada. Since we had not been sent out by the Canadian Mennonite Brethren Conference, but rather by an informal association of supporters, the M.B. Conference could not guarantee our support in Africa. While this is understandable in retrospect, we felt discouraged by this turn of events.

An Angel Arrives[9]

Sitting in our fifth floor apartment room in Hamburg, Germany, we heard a knock at the door. An upper-class lady arrived with a basket of goodies and cheerful demeanor. She encouraged us. "Don't give up. Keep the faith in the one who has called you." We knelt to pray together.

In retrospect, I am amazed how a brief visit by someone we did not know, a few cookies and a cup of coffee could transform our inner spirit. I felt as though I emerged from that visit as one who has bathed in clean water. I learned again how little acts of kindness and encouragement dispel the dark of night.

On the thirty-second day of our stay in Germany, major demonstrations began to take place in Hamburg. The economic depression had hit Germany very hard. Unemployment was high. People were desperate for answers. So the Communist Party of Germany seized the opportunity to make political gains. Remember this was April and May of 1931, two years before Hitler got control of the government. I went to some of the

---

[9] *Der kleine Africa Bote*, January 1939, pp. 8-11.

communist demonstrations, listened to the speeches praising Lenin, the founder of Communism in Russia, and shuddered at the prospect that the Communists would take over in Germany.

On May 2, 1931, our second daughter, Lydia, was born in Hamburg, Germany. While my wife rested and recovered in the hospital I was able to find better living quarters at a seminary. Our little Erna, now approaching two years of age, may have distracted some of the students, but she certainly provided them with a lot of enjoyable entertainment as I attended some of the classes.

Henry and Anna Bartsch, with daughters Erna and Lydia in Moeln, Germany, 1931.

One day I received an invitation from a Baptist minister to join him on a visit to Moeln. Moeln was a refugee camp for Mennonite escapees from Russia. I knew many of them. Some of them were related to me. They had escaped Russia in the 1920s but neither Canada nor the United States would give them entry visas. They had no place to go, so Germany kept them in this refugee camp. They invited us to move in with them, so we did.

Two Lessons I Learned

I learned two lessons during this time. The first concerned humility. Someone had told me years before that I was somewhat arrogant and proud. I didn't think of myself as arrogant. I never thought of myself as proud since I often felt inadequate to the tasks before me. (The remark stung, but I forgave him.) In any case, I mixed with my kinfolk from Russia and tried hard to be and speak at their level. Nevertheless, people noticed that I had been in Canada for several years, had a Canadian resident status, while they did not. They were "stateless refugees." I was secretly proud and the Lord showed me that fact about myself.

This led to my second lesson: patience. Instead of staying at this refugee camp for a week, as we had thought, we had to stay there for five-and-a-half months. This was not our plan, though

I believe it was in God's. My impatience, my pace to get things done, would have made me unsuitable to work among the people of Africa. I now know that a European temperament along with a North American pace is the greatest barrier to mission work among African people. I had to learn to become quiet, to watch and wait among our kinfolk from Russia.

Many of the Mennonite refugees helped us overcome our own impatience and spiritual battles. They had faced near death experiences and knew from personal experience how the Lord had rescued them. Maybe that kind of experience is necessary for one person to assist another.

Visa Resolution and Deposit Concerns

After two months in the refugee center, we finally received notice from the Belgian Consulate that we could get a visa to go to the Congo, on one condition. The condition was that we would leave a deposit of 20,000 Belgian francs with the Belgian Consulate. We barely had enough to live and the refugees certainly could be of no financial support. They certainly could not give us anything. I considered borrowing the 20,000 francs. But who would lend me such an amount? A top government official tried to get the required deposit waived. He was not successful.

Then one of the refugees came to tell me that he knew of someone who might be able to provide that deposit. He believed that this woman would provide the deposit if she heard about us and the purpose for a deposit, to go to Africa as missionaries. To our surprise, the money arrived a few days later.

The woman was a medical doctor. In the note she said that we could have money at a very low interest rate. I wrote back that we did not expect to earn enough in Africa to pay the interest. She wrote back that we could have the money and pay her back when we came back. I wrote back that we did not expect to return to a job with which we could pay back even the principle. She wrote back that she could not sleep. We should just take the money and follow God's call to us to go to Africa.

The visa arrived and the date of our departure from Germany to the Belgian Congo was set for November 7, 1931. The name of our ship was a German freighter called the *Tuebingen*. As the ship set sail, we told ourselves, "We did not have to put our head through the wall," as the Belgian consul said to us. "But with our God we did jump over it."

The morning sun[10] broke out beautifully over the ocean waters. We had breakfast with the captain of the ship, Mr. Gugath, the ship doctor, our two daughters, Erna, 2, and Lydia, 7 months. Mr. Gugath was a most hospitable man. He loved to baby-sit our two children. He said he missed baby-sitting his own daughter. That enabled my wife and me to go ashore when we off-loaded or took on supplies on our way to the Congo.

Storm conditions threatened when we passed the Bay of Biscay. The storm got worse. Our trunks slid from side to side and the children were upset that they were constantly tossed from side to side in their beds. Finally, after the fourth day, calm conditions returned as we approached the Canary Islands. We docked to take on supplies in Tenerife (spelled Tenerifel today). My wife, who gets very seasick, was most relieved to set foot on solid ground. The town was crowded. You could not walk on the sidewalk without being bumped from side to side by people. It was very hot and humid. Cars honked constantly. Animals mingled with people and automobiles.

It was a relief to get back on the ship. Dolphins led the way as we sailed on. We anchored at another island, some distance from shore. My wife stayed aboard while I went ashore for a load of supplies. A German-speaking guide showed me some very ancient artifacts in the Catholic Church: old bones, a first century Bible, relics that supposedly St. Paul had used. They were holy relics to this man. He said these came from first century Christianity and I was careful not to disturb his simple faith. To shake a person's simple faith creates more damage than blessing. Later, after we left the church, I talked to this deeply pious man about genuine faith.

---

[10] *Der kleine Africa Bote*, February 1939, pp. 6-9.

As we set sail again, we stopped at another island to get salt for the Belgian Congo. I went ashore again. I expected to see some trees and vegetation, but there was none. Everything looked dead. A French businessman and about 100 natives were in the salt business. About a mile from shore huge machines pumped salt and water into large vats. The water evaporated in the hot sun so the salt remained. The blacks shoveled the salt into sacks and brought it to the ship.

We stopped at thirty ports on the way to the Congo. We got very tired of this. One port looked like another. We prayed for patience. We arrived at Lobito, one stop before our destination port, Matadi, excited that we were finally getting to our destination. The ocean was noticeably green, evidence that we were in the estuary of the Congo River.

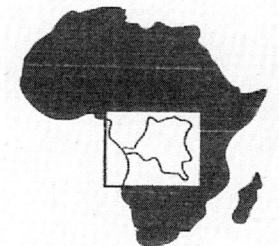

It was then that we got terrible news. At Lobito, the captain received a telegram from the ship's home office ordering the ship go to South Africa before going up the Congo River to Matadi. This would mean we would have to travel another two months before we could go up the Congo River to our destination. We were heartbroken. What is the Lord trying to do to us?

After some time we again accepted what we could not change.

"Was ich nicht aendern kann, nehme ich geduldig an."
"What I cannot change, I accept patiently."

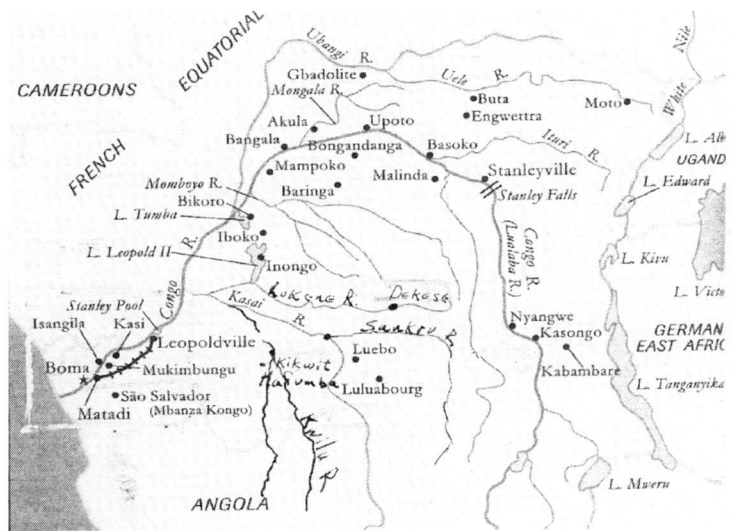

Congo River and cities/towns.

We had said this to each other many times, but now we really had to relinquish control.

The captain saw our disappointment and advised us to get off at Lobito to catch a Belgian passenger ship going up the river to Matadi. We would only have an hour to off-load our baggage and ourselves and children and board the *Albertine*, the Belgian ship. Besides it would cost us an additional $30.00 which we did not have. The captain said he would give us the money but I was hesitant to receive it. I was eager to get on the *Albertine*, but we didn't have very much time since we were anchored several miles from shore. The *Albertine* passed us on the way to the dock. I couldn't stand it any longer. I accepted the captain's offer of $30. My wife got the children ready. She, too, believed we could make it. I arranged to get the baggage out of the ship's hold and scrambled onto a small motorboat to get to the *Albertine*. The captain helped.

To board the Belgian ship we needed "transfer passes" for permission to go from one ship to the other. We raced from office to office to get the appropriate approvals.

Someone said, "You'll never make it. The ship leaves in a few minutes and you still have to get your baggage aboard." I only hurried more. We were 15 minutes late.

The *Albertine* had not moved. As we approached the ship, we thought that perhaps the ship was waiting for us. But why would it do that? There were 500 passengers on the *Albertine*, going up the Congo River to Matadi. The agent admitted us and had our baggage brought aboard. We were happy and relieved to have made it.

Then, leaning over the guard rails, we saw why the *Albertine* had been delayed. The train pulled into the station and about 50 people rushed toward the *Albertine*. It had delayed for those 50 passengers. The Lord had worked things out for us, too. It was December 24, 1931, Christmas Eve day.

We arrived at Matadi at 5 PM on the 26th. The heat of the day continued through the night. The surrounding cliffs made it feel like a heated cauldron. We settled our visa questions quickly and arranged to catch the train to Leopoldville (present-day Kinshasa) early the next day. We stayed at a cheap hotel for the night. Mosquitoes plagued us all night. The children slept well.

We arrived at the train station at 5 AM, happy to get out of the mosquito infested hotel. The train ride through the mountains was totally absorbing for me. The scenery was spectacular. My wife was terrified. The hills were steep, the bridges over the ravines perilous. Someone told us how many people had died constructing the railroad from Matadi to

Leopoldville:[11] Every meter of track had cost one black man's life; every kilometer, a white man's. I learned that black lives were cheap. Many blacks had been abused by the colonial system. We arrived late that night and made our way to the Mission Guest House where we stayed for several days.

On January third we took the riverboat up the Congo River, then the Kasai, and then the Kwilu, till we got to Kikwit. It took us 12 days. I was totally fascinated with the trip through the Congo. The mosquitoes were bad but the children handled it well. They continued to bring us much joy. Everything was so new. Our preconceptions of the Congo, whatever they had been, had to change.

We had a pleasant surprise at one of the stops along the way. At Liverville, Eva and Lydia Jantz, two missionaries who worked at Kafumba, had come to see the doctor.

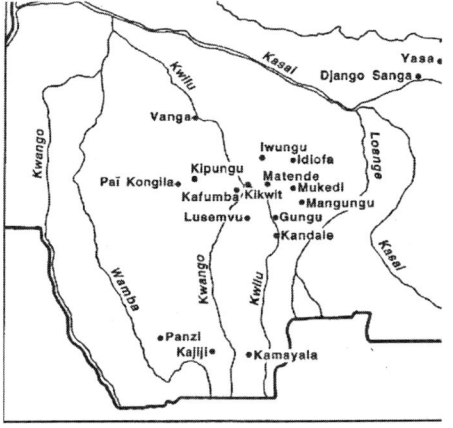

Kikwit on the Kwilu and its surrounding stations.

They were ready to return when we arrived and so traveled with us with on the riverboat to Kikwit. A. A. Janzen met us at Kikwit. We loaded our baggage and ourselves on a truck and drove to the end of the road. We had another 5 miles to go, so we walked from there to Kafumba.

Those who could not walk had to be carried on a kipoy. A kipoy is a seat in the middle of two poles. The person who could

---

[11]Adam Hochschild (*King Leopold's Ghost*. Boston: Houghton Mifflin Co., 1998) provides a well-documented account of Belgian King Leopold II's seizure for himself of the vast and mostly unexplored territory surrounding the Congo River. Carrying out a genocidal plundering of the Congo, he looted its rubber, brutalized its people, and ultimately slashed its population by ten million. Hochschild describes the heroic efforts to expose these crimes which evenutually led to the first great human rights movement of the 20th century.

not walk, or who had children to carry, would be carried by two men, one on either end of the poles. Baggage was also carried in this way. We learned to know about tropical rain on that 5 mile trek. It came down in torrents. Umbrellas were useless.

The Janzens welcomed us to their mission station at Kafumba. We were happy to be there and to unpack. We had arrived safely with our two children and our baggage. We were healthy and grateful. The blacks at the mission were delighted at our arrival. They particularly liked our little children.

Men carrying fruit on a kipoy.

Kafumba Mission

Kafumba was a self-supporting mission. It consisted of a large plantation of manioc, bananas, and 2000 coffee trees. Palm oil was very remunerative as well. A. A. Janzen put me in charge of this production.

We participated in the mission as much as we could. We sought to understand the blacks and began to do so better and better. We loved them. The Janzens treated us well. They taught us about their work, how to travel and how to learn the language. They cared for us when we were sick. We stayed at Kafumba for a year and a day till the Lord led us, as we continue to believe to this day, to go to the wild Dengese people.[12]

---

[12] My father does not give any further description of the Kafumba mission. Nor does he describe his activities there, nor why, he, my mother and three single nurses, Eva and Lydia Jantz and Katherine Harder, Willy Jantz and his wife and child, decided

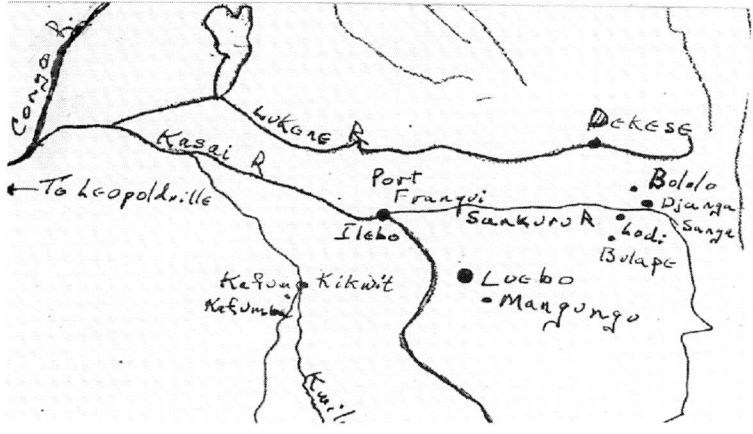

to leave. They only stayed at Kafumba a year and a day. Neither does Mother say, in *The Hidden Hand*, why they felt the Lord led them to leave for another, unknown place to do missionary work. They were very careful not to say negative things about Kafumba or the Janzens. In fact they wrote only positive things about them. But it's my impression, based on comments or references here and there that the "plantation" approach to doing missionary work was not what they had in mind when they signed up. To run a plantation along with a mission was to mix the preaching of a God of love and salvation with economic exploitation. Note, too, that old-style colonialism was still in full swing in Africa in the 1930s. Commentaries on this phase of their mission say, euphemistically, that there were personnel and organizational disagreements (J. B. Toews, *Mennonite Brethren Church in Zaire*, 1978). There was also tension over the charismatic emphasis in Kafumba and also personal incompatibility with the leadership. I see their departure from Kafumba, after a year and a day, as their way of differentiating themselves from colonial practices. They had surrendered too much, had known too clearly that God was calling them to bring good news, to spend their lives mixing the free gospel of love with economic exploitation.

— Chapter 3 —
Adversity and Faith
1933-1935[13]

Leaving Kafumba

We left Kafumba on a dull gray day on January 13, 1933 a year and a day after arriving. We were a group of seven adults: Willy Jantz and his wife and child, his two sisters, (Eva and Lydia Jantz), Katherine Harder, my wife Anna, myself and our two children, (Erna, three-and-a-half, and Lydia, one-and-a-half). Several of the women in the group were not physically well. We were short of money.

Initially we didn't know where the Lord would lead us. So we walked the five miles to Kikanj, from where we took an automobile to Simona. Simona was a large village where the A. A. Janzens had erected several buildings on a hill. The single women settled in the school house, which included living quarters and a kitchen. My wife and I took the two room clay hut with a thatched roof. We set up our cots. We intended to rest here, to pray and get clarity about the direction God would have us take next.

Finding Direction

We prayed and talked. We talked and prayed till the Lord directed us to a tribe of people north of the Sankuru River. We received direction in this way. Katherine Harder and Eva Jantz had taken a trip through a number of villages six months earlier. On their travels they had met a Belgian official who had told them about the tribe of people, north of the Sankuru River, known as the Basongo-Mene (tooth-filers). They were called this for their habit of filing their teeth

---

[13] *Der kleine Africa Bote*, April 1939, pp. 9-11.

to make them sharp in order to tear meat. We talked about this a lot and prayed about it. But how could we get there?

Willy Jantz and I made several trips through the villages near Simona. One day we came through a village called Kokobula, where the Lord arranged for Willy Jantz and me to meet the same Belgian official that had talked to Katherine and Eva six months earlier. This official gave us detailed information about the people north of the Sankuru River. He noted that no missionary had entered that territory and encouraged us to take the risk to establish a mission among the Dengese people.

The whole group of us met to decide about our plans. We agreed that Willy Jantz and his wife, their baby, Willy's sister Eva, and I would scout out the territory of the Dengese people with the aim of establishing a mission there. In the meantime, my wife Anna, Katherine Harder, Lydia Jantz and our two daughters would wait at Simona till we could come to get them or send for them.

Our Trip from Kafumba to Bololo, by Anna Bartsch[14]

It was a dull and great day. A group of missionaries with their children got into the mission vehicle that was to take them to Simona. We had been at the mission station at Kafumba for a year and a day and were following the call to go further, to a land that the Lord would show us. We didn't know where the Lord would lead us. The road was difficult. We had to get out of the vehicle and walk in the deep sand in the hot and tropical sun. We had to overcome our fears when we crossed bridges and wondered if they would hold us. When we got into swamps, we had to unload the vehicle so that it would get through the swampy area. We were very happy when we arrived in Simona.

Simona is a large African village, where the mission station had built a school with some rooms available for us. There was another building that was newly built with a cement wall and a roof. We moved into one of the rooms of this large new house. Since it was late, we set up some of the camp beds and

---
[14] Anna Bartsch, *The Hidden Hand*, pp. 91-103.

put the children to bed. They were too tired to eat. We hurried through supper and asked the Lord's evening blessing and went to bed. It was calming to rest after the strenuous day's travel. We had arrived here, but what should we do next?

We discussed together, we prayed together and we waited to see what the Lord would teach us about the next step. After two weeks, we came to a conclusion. Through a government official we learned about a tribe of people in the north that had not yet been touched by missions. These people, we were told, lived in primitive ways. We were told it was a very warlike people, with whom the Belgian government officials could do little. That's why they wanted a mission program there. In the year previously, there were reports that a white man had been captured, killed and eaten. It was very difficult to bring merchandise there for the whites. The government official told us that this was not a place for women and children, only for very strong men. None of this was very appealing. But we checked it out and discussed and came to the conclusion that it was these kinds of people that need the Lord as well. This is where our gospel applied. The gospel can make changes in people. The Lord was with us and the Lord of the mission had promised to be with us. So we did not want to hold back, but say with Paul, "I can do anything through him who strengthens me, Jesus Christ." In the meantime, another missionary couple had arrived. We decided that a few of us would go on ahead to explore what was possible, before we would settle down there. What we said, we did. Two of the nurses who were with us, I and the children stayed behind as the other ones made their way on ahead. We watched them leave with a certain amount of trepidation. This parting was very difficult for me. Everything was uncertain, and we couldn't even write each other, because there is no communication in that region. I've had to say many goodbyes in my life.

We sought to make our own life here at Simona. We had so much to do to take care of ourselves. Everything was so primitive[15] and took so long that it took all of our energy. For example,

---

[15] This was in comparison to life on the plantation-like Kafumba.

we had to bake bread outside in the yard. We had to make a large fire. Then we had to insert the bread in the hot coal. To cook the water, we put the pot in a hot coal fire and pressed the hot coal around the pot. This was not so easy. I must admit that I seldom left the fire without a skin burn. Just consider how this can happen. One day when the bread was aptly placed in the oven, the sky suddenly darkened with clouds, and it suddenly began to pour buckets mercilessly on my cooking. We quickly built a little frame with bamboo mats over the fire. The wind blew it all away. What could be done? We had to bake bread. So then I stood with an umbrella and held the edges until the bread was done. And then I thought to myself, "Is this how you have to do it here?"

The boys brought us water when we paid them with a little salt or some trinkets. On one location, they got a pair of ladies' shoes with high heels. They were very happy for them, and immediately parceled out the work. Since they shared the work they also shared the prize. Everyone took one shoe, put it on and walked into the village. The whole scene turned into a lot of laughter for us. Meanwhile, they enjoyed their experience quite naturally.

We lived in what looked like the robbers' stand. By nature, I am quite fearful. Here I had the opportunity to unlearn that trait. The walls had great big holes to serve as doorways. "Fear lives in big dark holes." That was my experience. Every morning, I would get up and see animal tracks on the dirt floor. I wanted to know what kind of creatures crawled around and made noises at night. Everything was so strange. Around the house the grass was as high as a human being, in which anyone or anything could hide. I had two little black girls with me and we tied the door shut, as well as we could. But surely that didn't help very much! When I came home with a lantern in the evening I didn't dare look around too much. Nor did I have much urgency to stay awake very long. I committed myself to the protection of the Almighty, pressed my head into my pillow so I would not hear or see anything else and fell asleep. And nothing terrible has ever happened to us. We're thankful to God for that. There was real trouble when it rained heavily. We hung blankets across the windows. If there was a strong wind with rain we had to hold the blankets tight; otherwise the wind drove the rain into all corners of a dwelling. This was most uncomfortable when it was late at night or when this happened in the middle of the night.

I had a small, hand-sewing machine, and actually wanted to sew a lot and mend our children's clothing. I was pregnant with our son, Arthur.

One day I was sitting in front of an open window and sewing. My heart began to beat heavily. I felt very scared. As I looked up I saw a frog making huge jumps and behind him a snake. I screamed and ran outside. The snake disappeared. Only the frog remained and gasped for breath. Slowly and methodically, he disappeared. I was happy all day that I had saved the life of a poor little animal. How much more happiness does it give one to save a soul. After that I carried the desire to be of help to others and had to realize what the whole matter of fear was inside me.

One day, while taking my afternoon nap, I heard some crackling. I rushed to the door and saw a huge grass fire coming toward the house. Somebody had lit the grass. The straw roof of the house could easily light. I ran inside. The children were in a deep sleep inside. I wanted to get them out quickly. What should I do? I cried to God for help. I looked outside and saw that the wind came from the other side and the danger had passed. We saw many dangers—how many didn't we see? We don't know, but the Lord has saved us from all dangers and has never come too late.

But we did not only experience fears and turmoil in Simona. We also experienced many blessings. When the natives noticed that we were staying there for a while, they came to us and asked us to teach them. We did that very eagerly. One of our sisters began with the morning service at six o'clock. At nine o'clock till 12 o'clock they received instruction in singing, biblical stories, writing, and reading. We were in a groove with them very quickly. And we enjoyed it. Although they didn't speak Kikongo, they understood it fairly well. I remember the comment of a business person on the ship as we first came to the Congo. He said, "Don't expect natives to express tears of regret. They *have no conscience." In general, this businessman was right. And we needed to learn from experience not to trust too quickly. But I have seen genuine tears of regret, such as Peter experienced after denying our Lord. And this was our experience in Simona. In discussing the story of the prodigal son, I saw a young man sitting at the back of the room crying. Later I learned that he had run away from a mission program. No doubt, the seed of God was planted in his heart. Maybe he was then able to hear the inner voice of love, in spite of the noise of the world around him. Now, by hearing God's Word he heard familiar tunes in his inner ear and his soul cried to God. I think of the many young voices that've come through the school in Bololo, who paid such attention to godly truths and later seemed to lose themselves in their own world again. The Lord can bring them back to His truth.*

Often, we also went to the village. When possible, we held worship services. One time when we had a large gathering, we saw several Catholic teachers who tried to disrupt our work by making jokes about everything. What should we do? We announced that we did not know the people's language. We asked whether there might be someone who could understand Kikongo and could help us in the translation. Some boys immediately offered to do that. They were cleanly washed and made a good impression. They were proud that they understood the language and did their best. We saw the attention that people paid them and how seriously the people listened to them. We experienced blessing and not cursing. Instead of being an obstacle to us, they were a help. May the Lord be praised!

We still had no word from our loved ones who had gone away to the new territory.

"Rejoice my heart, for it is March." This rhyme came to me when I woke up in the morning. I began to realize that it was March already. The weather was much like I felt on the inside. I was worried about my loved ones. This is anything but happiness. I told myself that everything has an end and that this too would end. This is what I told myself. This sense of waiting also had a good ending. It is written in the Bible that the waiting of the righteous will be their peace.

The change occurred that evening. A large number of men, about 30, came onto the yard. They brought me a letter from our loved ones. They arrived at the new regions safely, and we were to come and follow them. Brother Haller of Mangungu mission brought them with his automobile and was prepared to take us there too. He sent the men to us to get us. It's a three-day trip to Mangungu.

We packed feverishly for the trip. We had to include provisions for three days because there is nothing to buy on the trip. We packed things up, tied things up so that with all the movement nothing would get lost. We included beds and mosquito netting, tables and chairs, buckets and lanterns, tin buckets and little buckets. Everything was piled together: Everything had its worth. In spite of all our concern, we left our tripod that had been so helpful to us when we wanted to cook some food over the fire. We examined our kipoys to make sure that they were sturdy. It certainly would be uncomfortable for us if something was to happen on the trip and some of us were to remain behind.

The kipoy is a chair without feet and without legs. It is tied together, that is, tied to two long poles, which are carried on men's shoulders. Behind the chair is a container attached for necessities on the trip. The kipoy is carried by four men, two in front and two behind. If you go on a longer trip, you take extra supplies as a reserve. This appears to be a wonderful thing, to be carried this way through the world. But the reality of it is that it's not very comfortable. The ride can become very unpleasant. The men carrying the kipoy see that they have a long way ahead of them and break into a dizzying trot and we are jolted in such a way that our necks nearly break off. The eternal swing and sway of the

Katherine Harder on kipoy.

kipoy has quite a nauseating effect. This often results in headaches and unsettled stomach and vomiting.

I once had such a frightful experience! We traveled for three days and I just couldn't take it anymore. There I lay in the forest beneath giant trees, on the soft underlay of leaves, a helpless creature, writhing in agony, not knowing where to turn. My husband who normally was nearby, was far ahead somewhere with his bicycle and couldn't be contacted. I saw the anxiety of the kipoy carriers, who knew they couldn't proceed at the pace they had taken. After a while, I crawled back into the chair again, and the train moved ahead carefully. Luckily, there was a place ahead where we could stop and take a short rest. My husband met me there and things went more smoothly after that. That is what is meant by traveling in Africa. My neck had been so badly twisted that I couldn't move it for a week.

Well, comfortable or not, we were happy to have at least this means of transportation. Our kipoys were ready. What about the children? It was dangerous for them to travel in a kipoy by themselves, since they could fall asleep and fall out. Or they could forget to keep their hats on and suffer sunstroke. The ultraviolet rays cannot be endured by the white man here. Just before we were to go, Miss Harder had a solution. She advised that a kipoy be built for the children. The boys cut branches and leaves which were tied on the kipoy in an arch. The whole thing looked kind of like a gypsy caravan without wheels! We were ready to move on.

Our plan was to leave early in the morning. Sadly, we had to say goodbye to our friends. We had learned to love them, but we had to leave them behind. Kangi was one of them and I was brokenhearted. She had been with me from the start and would never leave me. She was 12 years old, honest and faithful; I could see that in her dark eyes. I was always at ease when she took care of the children. Everything was ready. We boarded. "Bika mbote" (keep well), we called out. "Kenda mbote" (travel well), they answered back, and off we went. The long caravan snaked its way through the forest. First there were the baggage carriers, in pairs, each carrying a large box slung around a bamboo pole on their shoulders. After them were the passengers, first the children in their covered "arks," then the three kipoys, for myself, Lydia Jantz and Katherine Harder. We had warned the carriers that the arcs with the children had to be up front where I could see them at all times. The children were calm, chatting with their bearers. We were surprised to see how much attention they got. The natives generally paid a lot of attention to the children.

The entire train was moving at a gentle trot along the narrow trail. It was morning. The air was fresh. We were all excited and I felt like singing. Often I sang on my journeys. The carriers enjoyed it when I sang. Sometimes they themselves sing in their own fashion. One of them takes the lead. He suddenly breaks into song to express his feelings and thoughts in tones high and soft. He composes his own song. He becomes a poet and a conductor at the same time. As soon as he expresses an idea, he is joined by the others in the accompanying harmony and rhythm, echoing the original idea in brief. This is how they compose seemingly endless verses about the people they are carrying, until they are tired which sometimes takes a long time. The load seems easier when they sing. I like that. Unity in song gives strength.

Sometimes they can be silent for hours; they trot along and do not say a word for a long time. The burden seems to be getting heavier; the pace slows down. How refreshing it is for them when they discover a small stream in the forest, and can stop to drink. Then they continue again under the blazing African sun, through the grasslands and barren stretches, over rickety bridges and shallow streams. How dangerously close we come to an unwelcome bath! Once one foot of a carrier slipped as we emerged from a creek, and we nearly toppled. We breathed easier when we passed such obstacles. Luckily we were spared any disaster. That was our first day with the kipoy!

It was getting dark, as we entered the village. We spotted the shelter they called "symbolo" where we could rest for the night. These shelters could be found throughout the country. They were earth huts which the Belgian state officials had erected for white travelers in the area. The native chieftain was responsible for seeing that they were kept neat and clean, and that the dusty sand area around the hut had been wetted down. Often, however, *it was found that goats had made themselves comfortable here, and the place first had to be swept out. The chief also had to provide food for the carriers as well as wood and water for us, naturally at a price. Very soon the chieftain arrived. He asked if we needed anything.*

Bedding down for the night was quite a procedure. Cots, table and chairs and other things had to be untied and set up. The water had to be boiled and allowed to cool overnight for drinking purposes. After we had eaten and said our evening prayers, the lanterns were extinguished, and we committed our cares and fears to the Guardian of the night. How benevolent were these nights. How brave our two little girls were! Erna was nearly 4 years old; Lydia not yet 2. They didn't cry; they were so peaceful and quiet and loved by everyone.

As I look back now, this entire three-day journey with my little children and with me in the fifth month of pregnancy was impossible without the angels who watched over us. We had to go again early next morning. After refreshing our bodies and spirits we had to pack everything again, pots, dishes, pans and kettles, and everything had to be tied up; nothing could be forgotten. Medicine had to be available for an emergency, salve for wounds, Epsom salt for upset stomach, castor oil for a cough–marvelous how effective they were. Again, we began the long, tedious trek through the jungle with quick short steps. The carriers were careful. We also made great headway on the second day. Again, we made the same preparations for the night; again the same resolution for the day's journey. The day ahead would be a difficult day, but we didn't know that.

After a good night's rest, we embarked on our journey anxiously awaiting the end. Soon, however, our path led to the desert. The dryness and desolation of the area became more evident as time went on. There were no villages, no forest, and no refreshing stream to stop at. Instead we had heat. Loose sand appeared under our feet and the scorching sun was overhead. The carriers were quiet now, languishing, thirsting for drink. We stepped down and struggled on foot through the deep sand with very little progress. There was still some water for the children, but when that was gone, what would we do? The carriers walked behind us, slowly and quietly. The baggage carriers had long since disappeared ahead of us. How infinitely large the world was for a time. We walked. We could talk about a few things, but then, nothing seemed to be important anymore. We tried to encourage one another: We couldn't give up now. "To endure" was the watchword. Even this day finally came to an end!

Towards evening, the carriers pointed to a dark spot on the horizon. It was Mangungu. We were asked to crawl back into our kipoys and, with the last burst of energy accomplish the final stretch. Here Missionary Holler and Miss Forel received us with great joy. How good we felt after a refreshing bath and a tasty dinner!

We intended to stay this Sunday, and on Monday Mr. Holler was to take us to Bololo in his vehicle. Man plans, but God directs. The stress of the previous day had taken its toll. I became feverishly sick and couldn't move. However, with quinine and the needed rest, things were under control again. We got mail from Kafumba. There was a letter from my mother in a concentration camp in Siberia, dated November 1932. She wrote that my father had died. I saw my parents for the last time in 1927, when, on their advice, my sister Lena and I had left them to go to Canada. They had planned to join us, but things didn't work out that way. They, too, had come to the gates of Moscow, but instead of going to Canada, father was sent to a prison camp in Siberia and mother joined him voluntarily. He was 70 years old. There they worked for three hard years in slave labor camps. Finally even father's strong body gave way and he succumbed.

News of this shattered me. My fever returned and rose to 104°F. It was so severe that Dr. Eicher of the Mission was called, and he stayed with me until the crisis had passed. Quinine could not be used effectively in my late stage of pregnancy. Thanks to the prayers of the missionaries, the feared outbreak of Blackwater fever was prevented. In the meantime, Henry was returning from Bololo to meet us and was waiting for us at Lodi. He was waiting for Mr. Holler to bring us slowpokes. He had been there for several weeks and was anxiously waiting for us, hour after hour. In his diary, I now read that he had been very sick during this time, that he had run out of food, and that the Lord had raised him up in the midst of his troubles. He wrote that, one evening when he had gone to bed hungry, someone had come to his hut late at night and brought him some food. "Bekelenge" (White Man), he said, "I know you are a child of God, and the voice has told me that you are hungry."

After several weeks of waiting, as it turned out, he finally heard the sound of a motor vehicle. It was Mr. Holler who arrived alone and reported on recent events. He had brought only Mrs. Willy Jantz and Lydia Jantz. The women then continued their way to Bololo, while Henry and Mr. Holler returned to Mangungu, where I remained because of my illness.

Travel to the Sankuru River: Dad's Report

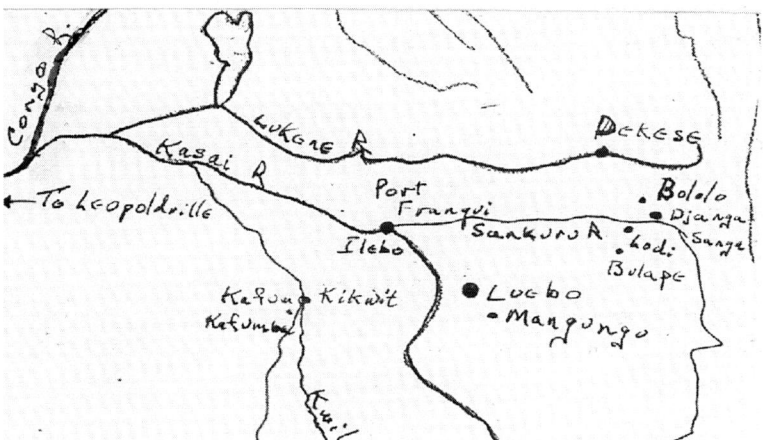

We didn't realize at the time that we would have to travel about 500 miles to get to the Dengese territory. We had to walk, or ride kipoys. We had only a few men to carry the kipoys. With the sun as hot as it was, the men withered quickly and threatened to quit. After two-and-a-half days of tough travel we passed through Mangungu, a mission led by George Holler. We also agreed that Mrs. Willy Jantz would stay at Mangungu with the baby till we would come back to get her and the others. The people were glad to have them.[16] The Hollers' hospitality was an answer to our prayers.

George Holler offered to drive us to Lodi, a village on the Sankuru River. This was a lot easier than walking or riding the kipoy. It would take us four days in a vehicle. We left with the barest necessities on Monday, February 6: Mr. Holler, Willy Jantz, his sister Eva and myself. We made our way from one mission station to another. After the Holler Mission Station we passed through The Congo Inland Mission and the American Presbyterian Mission. At each of these we listened eagerly to the experiences of other mission pioneers for things that would help us in the mission we wanted to establish in the Dengese tribe.

The last mission station before reaching Lodi and the Sankuru River was Bulape. The leader of this mission, Mr. Washburn, was hospitable, providing us fresh provisions, gasoline and oil. Being close to the Dengese region, he knew about the Dengese people. He recommended that Eva Jantz not go with us into the Dengese region, so she remained at the Bulape mission. That left Willy Jantz, Mr. Haller and myself.

First Contact with the Dengese People

Before we left we were surprised and extremely pleased with some good news: Two native teachers of the Bulape mission announced to us that the indigenous Black Church from the area was sending them with us for two months to help us get started among the Dengese. This was most welcome news from the Black Church. When we discovered that these two teachers also spoke the language, Bosongo-Mene, and knew the lifestyle of the Dengese, we were even more thrilled. The five of us were set to leave for Lodi and the Sankuru River the next day.

That evening, sitting around a fire, one of the teachers, Katschunga, told us about the Dengese people. We listened with fascination. He told us how fearsome they were. We became

---

[16] Anna Bartsch, *The Hidden Hand*, p. 105 (Henry's Diary) translated by Arthur Bartsch.

afraid and gloomy. In fact we felt like turning back when Katschunga suddenly dropped his head between his knees and whispered something that we could not understand. When we asked Mr. Washburn what Katschunga had said, he translated for us: "That must be a strong Jesus who sends these white people to the Dengeses."

On February 11, we arrived at Lodi at 9 PM. We asked a Portuguese businessman about the road conditions on the other side of the Sankuru River. He said there were no roads on the other side, so he gave us his kipoys.

To get to the territory of the Dengese region we had to go downstream by boat. We expected the trip to take about four hours. We loaded our things in a dugout boat and took off downstream to Djongo Beach. As we arrived, the Dengese people fled into the forest. They were afraid of us white folk. Their fear and flight saddened us. After all, we had come to tell them good news, news  about a divine healer and redeemer. We were also saddened that they had all run away and so were not there to help us carry our things. We haggled for a long time. We begged and promised good pay till, finally, the people of Lodi were willing to carry our things and us to Bololo.[17]

The path through the forest was almost impassable. We arrived at Djongo as the sun was setting. We wanted to get to Bololo, but the blacks said it would take a long time to get there, so we stayed in Djongo for the night.

The people in the town were terrified. The old men and women looked at us suspiciously. The younger folk stayed in the dense forest out of fear. The little children hid behind stacks

---

[17] The Belgian colonialists had severely exploited the black population. They extracted taxes and abused women and took raw materials at will. So the blacks were naturally suspicious of white people.

of leaves. They screamed as if we had come to slaughter them. Wherever we went, we saw this tremendous fear.

Arrival in Bololo

We woke early and prepared to go to Bololo. We planned to travel for a day but were surprised to arrive there in an hour. Bololo is a large village, perhaps the largest in the Dengese region. Actually it consists of three villages with the same name. There are approximately 1,200 inhabitants. The leaders of the town seem to be friendly. The older folk are as suspicious as they were in Djongo. The government official has had a hut built for European travelers. The village chief was responsible for taking care of the hut. We were the first guests in this earthen hut. As evening approached, some young people brought us an antelope, rather smelly and rancid. Perhaps they meant to test our comfort level.

We arrived on Saturday and stayed through Sunday. The teachers that had joined us at Bulape explained to people the difference between missionaries, government officials and businessmen. After that people seemed to accept us well. After that the King, Ikongo-Samu, came to visit and warmheartedly discussed things with us. We began to feel comfortable with the Dengese people. We became eager to settle in Bololo. The many children in the village could attend a school that we hoped to begin. The King pointed to a hill where we could set up our mission station but said that permission to build would depend on the Belgian government official. Since the Belgian government was the colonial power in control of the Congo, we needed to get the permission of the Belgian government official before we could begin any

King Ikongo-Samu.

project, such as a mission. So George Holler, Willy Jantz and I had to meet with the government official at his home in Dekese.

To get to Dekese, we needed thirty carriers to convey us. We gave the King a pocket watch; he promised to get us thirty carriers the next day. After we got everything ready the next morning, the King let us know that he needed the thirty men himself. That was our first confrontation with him. He eventually gave in and we got on our way.

Travel to Dekese

There were two ways to get to Dekese. The one went through Busangu, the King's residence, the other through Yasa. We expected the trip to take about two-and-a-half days on a road through a dense forest. The King suggested we take the Yasa route. We had to spend the night in the forest. The spot where we bedded down was rather uncomfortable because there was no water. The blacks didn't seem to worry though. When they noticed that we were concerned about water, they brought us sticks, about as thick as our arms, held them up and water ran out of them. We had excellent water to drink.

To get to Dekese[18] we had to cross the Lukene River, a narrow, rushing river. We found only two canoes, each made of a single, hollowed tree. But they lay on the other river bank so we had to whistle and shout till the boatmen finally came. The two black teachers from Bulape thought we should take the boats to Dekese, since the Belgian officer had office hours only till 12 noon. If we would walk to his place, on

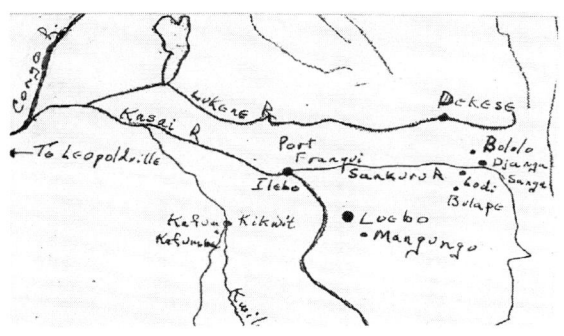

---

[18] *Der kleine Africa Bote,* May 1939, pp. 6-9.

the other side of the river, we would likely not get there in time to meet him at his office. The boatmen did not want to take the river all the way downstream. They only wanted to ferry us across and have us walk through the marshes to get to Dekese. Finally the one boatman gave in to our requests and gave us his boat. But only three persons could sit in this boat, and that without baggage. We agreed that George Holler and Willy Jantz should go on the boat because they spoke at least some French. They could negotiate with the Belgian officer in French better than I could, because we assumed that he did not speak German or Flemish. So these two brothers got into the boat and traveled along the right bank of the Lukene River while I made my way on land to the village of Dekese.

I estimated my trip across land to take about three hours; our brothers over water about an hour-and-a-half. The carriers of our baggage were delayed, since only one person could join the boatman at a time. I felt lonely as I walked alone. I prayed to the Lord often and extensively for help. I prayed that the Belgian official and I would understand each other. I arrived at Dekese at 2:30 PM. Our brothers had not yet arrived. Trusting the Lord, I approached the home of the official. To my surprise he spoke German as well as I did and spoke Flemish, as well as some English. I was immensely thankful. He was very friendly, invited me for lunch, and soon we were into a lively discussion.

When I finished my lunch, the other brothers arrived, soaking wet. The dugout had leaked badly so they had to sit on the bottom and bail water throughout the ride. All three of us sat there, telling the official (his name was Schaefer) about our trip.

Around 3 PM we went to his office where he introduced us to his assistant, who was a German. We now negotiated the arrangements for beginning our mission. What was so encouraging to me was how well the official understood our whole missionary enterprise. He told us how he had invited other missionaries to work among the Dengese people, but none had come, except two Catholic priests. These two priests had settled near Dekese, but he said they had done very little. We saw more clearly the leading of God in our efforts to establish a Protestant mission.

He suggested we go further north to Djia, about three days travel north, deeper into the wilderness. The villages were not so far apart there, he said, so we could do better work. However, I could not see how I could bring the women and children to such an isolated place such as Djia. The Bololo region was remote enough. So I suggested to Willy Jantz that we settle in Bololo. He agreed. The official shrugged his shoulders. He agreed, too. He sent the necessary documents to higher authorities; we directed our attention to Bololo.

From my diary:

[19]Sunday night I had a fever. I rested in bed all day. The fever left me but I feel very weak. We are still thinking of going north. It appears there are many villages there and the region is beautiful. But it may be a bit too far for us to get there.

Have thought very much about Anna and the dear children in the last little while. How I yearn for a home! Will it ever be granted to me on this earth? Yet we are the Lord's and want to remain His children. The way He leads us will be good for us: Even if He should call any of us to Him, I shall be quiet and accept it for we are in His hand. Oh Lord, give me fellowship with your people!

The ways of the Lord are utter goodness and truth.
Commit thy way unto him and he will bring it to pass.

Tomorrow morning we all hope to go north. Mr. Holler will come with us.

February 25. Mr. Holler drove back to Mangungu on the 24th in order to get the others. They could all be here on the 10th of March. Mr. Jantz and I are sitting on the symbolo in Lodi and are waiting for Eva Jantz

---

[19] Anna Bartsch, *The Hidden Hand*, p. 105, (Henry's Diary), translated by Arthur Bartsch.

(who had remained in Bulape, the previous station), and then we will go to Bololo and begin to build.... We are waiting for the carriers of our people but it does not appear that they are coming.

On February 28 we left Lodi at 3:30 PM and had to stay overnight in the next village. Then we headed for Bololo. We arrived here on March 1.

We went to look at the place twice. Once, the Chief came along. He had been waiting for us a long time. He desperately needs some medicine for his worms. Was most disappointed when we didn't have any. In the evening we read Psalm 49 and prayed.

March 3. We are in Bololo and have begun to build. The people are not interested, however. Settling our accounts with the carriers was very difficult. They did not even accept our offer of the money. The prospects are bleak. How can we continue? But the Lord who has called us can help. We shall trust in him. On the 10th the others will arrive. How slowly time passes! Felt so down-hearted all day yesterday. We must go ahead with determination. Sometimes we want to build on the hill above; at other times down below. We have to have courage and determination.

Building the Mission

With the help of the government official and the king's help, we got workers to help us build the mission. The first building was the church, where we would proclaim the name of God and salvation in Jesus Christ. The building was to be 10 by 30 meters, with the verandah. At one end we planned to build a room for my family. We planned other separate houses for the other missionaries. Brother Jantz and the teachers that came to help, along with his sister Eva, who had joined us, continued with the construction.

From my diary:

[20]March 6. The workers we had hired to build the house have gone home. They were to be here today but no one has come. We sent men to the government official in Dekese to inquire about land. The Lord has to help us—we are completely dependent upon him. If the government permits us to build we shall continue. The people are kind to us and bring us all kinds of vegetables to eat. The language is difficult. Much is depressing for us but we shall go forward in faith. The Lord will not forsake us. Stayed up a long time last night and enjoyed seeing the beautiful moon in the sky. My thoughts were carried back to my former homeland and to America.

March 7 . . . . Worked on the bed and the benches. Later workers came. In the morning some old men came to ask us what we actually wanted to do here. When we told them, they were happy and said goodbye.

March 9. The people do not want to work. It is hard to win their confidence and require them to work at the same time. Tomorrow I shall go back to Lodi. I wonder if they (my family) will come? I can't help thinking about the story of Jacob.

Waiting for My family

I went to Lodi to pick up my family. They were to arrive on March 12.

March 12. Yesterday noon I arrived here in Lodi. There were two officials in the government building. Neither of them could speak English or German. I stayed at the Chieftain's place for the night. The reception was great. Late that night when I was already in bed a man came and asked if I could bring him something to eat. He was convinced that this was

---

[20] Anna Bartsch, *The Hidden Hand*, p. 106, (Henry's Diary), translated by Arthur Bartsch.

God's will and if I were God's messenger, I would do it. After all, he claimed he was a Christian.

I am sitting and waiting for Anna and the children.

March 14. I am still sitting in Lodi and waiting for our people. I often feel very lonely. The Word of God strengthens me again and again. At breakfast today I read Psalm 73. How secure one can become in the arms of God! This is the grace of God for a sinner like me. Yesterday at 5:30 PM I went to a Bakuba village to look for a milk goat, without success. The Lord will provide! Two boys went back to Bololo. Two remain. Want to write a report to the *Rundschau* (Mennonite Observer). "Lord give me the right words so that I can be a blessing to all."

March 15. Am still sitting in Lodi and waiting. It's quite unbearable, this long wait. What shall I do if they don't come this week? My situation is critical. Or has there been an accident on the way? Daily I pray that the Lord will bring them safely to me. His way has always been the best and will continue to be so. As a result I assert my confidence in Him more fully. In Russia, too, everything is in God's hands. Therefore one can be at peace.

March 16. Stayed in bed until 8 AM. Have thought much on the developments of the past. My food is nearly gone. Haven't got much money. How long can I wait for our people? Will they arrive today?

If not I will go out to meet them, or I shall have to go back to Bololo. Oh, that the Lord would send them to me! I shall write as many letters as I can.

March 18. Still no response from our people. How long must I wait here? God give me patience! My food is gone now. I shall wait till Tuesday and then go back. Has there been an accident or some disaster? The Lord knows.

I had a very hard time in Lodi. Hunger, heat, mosquitoes, and impatience tore at my courage and confidence. I took up residence in a native hut. In spite of all of this, I could preach God's word in the Kikongo language. But it all appeared to be accepted so superficially. I said to myself, "If these people are so cold, how will we fair with the people on the other side of the river, where people have fallen, in some respects, to levels below that of animals?" Despair gripped my soul. I was hungry. I argued with God. I went to bed without food. I lay awake. I could not sleep. I sensed something terrible. Finally I fell into a half-sleep when I heard someone at the door. I called out, "Who's there?" A woman's voice answered and said, "I brought you food, Lusanganye (teacher). Don't you want to eat? We know that you are a man of God and we cannot sleep if you are hungry." Then she begged me to take the food and to eat. I ate the food and had a late but simple dinner. Then I begged God to forgive me for my discouragement and despair. Later I found many children of God in Lodi. I will never forget this experience. We have experienced many similar events where the Lord taught us that the work was not useless, if we do the work among the heathen according to His will. The remaining days were easier and I had genuine joy in preaching.

> Sunday, March 19. Still no trace of our people. Have gotten very impatient. Have seen the godless behavior of the government official today. The people are forced to produce food for small payment. How can one still have faith in the white man?
>
> Monday, March 20. The despicable government official finally left early this morning. I chanced to meet him again at the market place. He was very nice to me, but we had very little in common.

On the evening of March 21 a vehicle arrived from the direction of the Kasai River. It could be none other than that which I expected. And that's what it was. Mr. Holler came to Lodi. He stopped the car and ran towards me. I suspected no good. He greeted me and then told me about the bad news, the reason why my wife, Anna, the two girls, and Katherine Harder had not come along. Anna had been very sick, in fact she almost died. He told me all about this in great detail and that he planned to take me back to Mangungu immediately. Willy Jantz's wife, child and sister Lydia, who had come along, left for Bololo the next morning while Holler and I went to Mangungu.

When we arrived at Mangungu, we found that Anna was on the way to recovery. Dr. Eicher had saved her life with the help of God. She was to rest for another month before she attempted any more risky ventures. At the end of April, Dr. Eicher came with his truck to take us to Lodi. Katherine Harder, who had remained with us so faithfully, Anna, our two children, and I were on our way to Lodi and then to Bololo. As Dr. Eicher said goodbye to us, he handed us 1000 Belgian franks. Instead of taking payment for his services, he gave us money. We could use it very well as we began our work among the Dengese. We arrived in Bololo safely and were welcomed by our brothers and sisters. How very kindly the Lord leads us.

Unexpected Help in Our Adversity

The building construction at the mission proceeded slowly. Our confidence often wavered. The two teachers from Bulape became discouraged and were glad that their two month commitment was complete. They wanted to leave and not return. Willy Jantz was discouraged, too. He wanted to go back to Kafumba and from there, if possible back to America. That's what he did. It seemed too much for us to bear. Our money supply had dried up. The leaving of the Willy Jantz family was a particularly heavy blow to me because I remained the only male missionary person and I had so little experience in working with Africans.

But the Lord cared for us. Even before the Willy Jantz family left, a businessman, Mr. Henri Gustav Van de Velde, came to visit us.

Mother notes[21] that he was a Belgian from Flanders and spoke German, English and French plus a number of native dialects. He had heard about the mission and had taken a detour to come to see it for himself. My parents invited him for a noon meal at which mother sang a song with guitar and Dad read Luke 15, the story of the prodigal son's return and the father's warm welcome of the son.

"Then the big, burly man broke into tears and wept bitterly like a child. 'That's me!' he cried. 'That's exactly me. I'm the prodigal son. I've ended up here with the husks.' We were all quiet and shocked. 'I have found what I have been looking for 40 years.' We women withdrew and left Van de Velde with the men. Mercilessly he peeled back the dark pages of his sinful past; the religions he had tried to follow in his search for peace. He had been a Catholic, had tried the eastern religions, had joined a lodge, had practiced native cults, and had even been baptized by sorcerers in the jungle. Henry and W. Jantz told him about the great mercy of God: 'Though your sins be as scarlet they shall be as white as snow.' He accepted it in faith and found forgiveness and peace and went to bed late that night as a new creation. Now, like Zacchaeus, he had much to amend since Jesus had come into his heart. He sent his native women home with a letter and a payment to their parents, explaining what had happened to him. Alcohol and tobacco, which he had used to drown his conscience, were no longer a necessity. Next morning when Henry visited him, he had already laid them aside, and as far as we know he no longer made use of them. . . . He asked Henry to baptize him. . . . This marvelous experience was as refreshing as an oasis in our spiritual desert."

He not only gave us material things to survive but he taught us a lot about ways to interact with blacks and whites.

---

[21] Anna Bartsch, *The Hidden Hand*, pp. 115-116, translated by Arthur Bartsch.

The difficulties in getting the mission started continued. We whites could not meet the high expectations of the Africans. With our presence, they hoped that the Belgian government official would have no more power over them, such as levying a head-tax. When their high expectations were not met, they withdrew. We could get no students, no workers, and not even help in the house.[22] They didn't bring us wood, nor produce. Things were desperate.

---

[22] *Der kleine Africa Bote*, May 1939, pp. 7-9.

Chapter 4

Beginnings and Hope
1933-1935

A Child is Born: God Lives Here[23]

The Lord spoke to the people through the birth of our son, little Arthur, on July 5, 1933. The birth of a white child on Dengese territory had a significance we could not have imagined. This event completely transformed people's attitudes towards us. The women became very friendly. They assured us that they had washed their hands. They came repeatedly to see the little white child born on their soil. They hardly knew how to express their happiness. They provided help to run the household and workers to assist with the building projects.

Mother writes:[24] *"That morning I had been in the garden with the women. Miss Harder was a registered nurse. She came immediately and within an hour he was there, a healthy boy—after all those difficulties and trials, not a fault in him. How thankful and happy we were! I can still hear Henry's buoyant attitude in the other room with the ladies at the dinner table. ..."*

The King came to express his happiness. On one occasion he sat at the table across from me, slammed his hand on the table and said: "The loving God lives here in Bololo. Lusanganye (their name for me), don't contradict me. I know this. All the people in the villages say this. Because where children are born, there is God."

---
[23] *Der kleine Africa Bote*, June 1939, pp. 7-8.
[24] Anna Bartsch, *The Hidden Hand*, pp. 116-117, translated by Arthur Bartsch.

Ikongo-Samu wanted to prove to me in many other ways that God was with us.

I had never doubted God's presence. But I had not anticipated that these people, in this remotest of regions, would come to this understanding. It surprised me.

To prove his sincerity, King Ikongo-Samu gave our son his honorary name and sent him a milk goat.

King Ikongo-Samu and deputy.

He sent servants to get meat (antelope) from the forest. The King's influence on his people was very noticeable. Attendance at our meetings grew. When Lydia and Eva Jantz invited students, they came. I could preach in the villages without disruption, even though I used a translator. Katherine Harder had some success with injured patients who were brought to her. People's trust in us grew steadily. We even developed a good reputation with the Belgian government official. We could interact with him as a friend. On one occasion the Commissioner of the district came and gave us helpful advice and help. They built a four-room hospital unit and a large six-room residence for nurses.

Eva Jantz had the assignment to study the Dengese language thoroughly. This was not easy, since the language had not been put in writing and so had no literature and no help to get started. A teacher, Joseph Jomba, from the Batatell tribe came to visit us and volunteered to teach us the language. He helped Eva Jantz for a while, but he proved to be unreliable. Early in 1934, Eva became ill and had to go back to the USA.

Katherine Harder went to Bulape to study different tropical sicknesses. I had to do some business in Fort Francqui. While I was gone we had a beloved visitor, Brother Althorp, from Lobo. Lobo is a station about 10 days travel. He gave us good advice and invited me to visit him in Lobo. In February 1934, I traveled diagonally through the Dengese district to get to Lobo. On this trip I decided how necessary it is to give the people the gospel. In Lobo I could see a mission among people that are similar to the Dengeses. I returned home with a lot of enthusiasm and clarity of vision.

When I preached on the trip, I noticed how difficult it was for people to accept the Word. I became convinced that we had to establish a school. We needed to lay a foundation. If we wanted to establish continuing communities of faith we had to teach students in a systematic way. The mission, I concluded, would have three components: Medical work, education and evangelism. These three would form the basis of an effective missionary work. So my first concern in March 1934, was to get students. We prayed about it a lot and the Lord heard our prayers. In time, he sent us 200 students. These are the three arms of the mission we founded. We called it "Peniel,"[25] because we were convinced that "the Lord had done this and it was a wonder before our eyes."

The Sorcerer's Magic Is Overcome

By the second year of our work among the Dengese people, we had seven teachers. They and their wives and children had separated themselves, to some extent, from the events in the village and had settled in huts around the mission on the hill. They fit into the structure of the mission life, removing themselves from the duties in the village. The 100 or so students had their huts in a row next to these workers.

The students seemed to adapt more quickly to the structures of the mission than the older workers with their

---

[25] The name, "Peniel" comes from the story in Genesis 32: 22-32, in which Jacob wrestles with a man sent from God, perhaps an angel. "I have seen God face to face, yet my life is preserved," he says. So the name given to the mission, "Peniel" refers to a place of wrestling until a blessing is received and a place in which transformation takes place. The qualities of character required are courage and tenacity, both of which Henry exhibited in setting up the mission.

families. In the classroom and at work, such as building new huts or classrooms, old heathen superstitions seemed to be on the decrease. Their cooperation with the mission indicated that we were having an influence on them. This disturbed the heads of the village and especially the medicine man. They realized that they were losing their influence on their best people.

An unexpected event occurred early one Monday morning. Someone from the village had placed sorcery potion under the door of Djema Payula, our work foreman. To his horror, Djema discovered it, as he got up in the morning. He had stepped over the sorcery potion, and so was exposed to death. Djema cursed and raged outside his hut. He cursed his wife and the sorcerer in the village down below. Although it was time for classes and work projects to begin, everyone gathered around Djema's hut, as though thunderstruck. Everyone expected the worst. This was terribly frightening for these poor people. It was also a critical event for the beginning of our mission.

Two little boys ran up to our hut to tell me what happened. They also explained the power of the potion. It was clear to me that unless God would do a miracle, the entire work of the mission was in jeopardy. It was traumatic for me to imagine that: All the work we had done inviting people to the mission and winning their trust would be wiped out by one sorcerer's plot. I cried out to the Lord for wisdom as I raced to the scene. There was no time for a sit-down prayer. I needed to act immediately. I found everyone in an uproar. The wives of the workers were ready to move back into the village. I called out to get their attention. They listened. Everyone was stunned. They wondered what I would do.

I called out with as loud a voice as possible to my students and workers, "Whose land is this on which your huts are built?" Everyone said, "It's yours, Lusanganye (my name among the people)."

I called out again, "Whose houses are these–the houses in which you live?" In chorus they shouted, "Yours."

"Whose are you?" I called. "We are also yours," said everyone.

"Well," I said. "If all this is mine, all that's in this yard, then the sorcerer's potion is intended for me and not you. If someone is supposed to die of this potion, as you say, then I am the first that the evil Spirit will kill. I am ready to challenge that Spirit!"

Everyone looked at me in amazement. Some started to trust me. Others doubted my capacity to survive.

Then in full view of everyone, I walked to the door of the hut, where the sorcerer's potion lay partially hidden under the lentel board. I picked up the board, and pulled out the little container, about the size of an egg. I opened it, and poured the "little devils" onto the ground and stepped over them several times.

I had everyone's attention. Not an eye turned away. When nothing happened to me, the evidence was there: I was stronger and the medicine man of the village was weaker. The people screamed with deafening delight. The students went to school. The workers went to their assignments. No one needed to die, something which had always happened before. The mission station was saved.

Although the "snake" of superstition came around again later, the hand of the Almighty didn't allow anything evil to come upon us. I give Him the honor and glory. Psalm 91:10 and 11 were wonderfully realized in our lives. We are thankful to Him for that.

He who dwells in the shelter of the Most High,
Who abides in the shadow of the Almighty,
will say to the Lord,
"My refuge and my fortress;
my God in whom I trust."
For he will deliver you
from the snare of the fowler and
And from the deadly pestilence;
He will cover you with his pinions, and under his
wings you will find refuge;
His faithfulness is a shield and buckler.
Psalm 91:1-4 RSV

A Summary Report of the Mission Work[26]

Before giving you a summary report of the work we are doing, I direct your attention to a Word of God, which has been the foundation for us this year. II Corinthians 9:8 reads,

"And God is able to provide you with every blessing in abundance, so that you may always have enough of everything and may provide in abundance for every good work."

It is our experience that God is able to provide, even when human energy gives out. God's grace has been poured out on us when we place our work in a godly light. And we have received plenty of good, with respect to spiritual and material things. God has not failed us but has enriched us to do good for others. We give Him the thanks for that.

Evangelism

I begin this summary report with the most important aspect of our work here: The sharing of the good news about the death and resurrection of our Lord and Savior.

We have general meetings twice a week. We have special meetings with believers twice a week as well. In addition, on Friday evening, we have prayer meeting and on Saturday we have conflict resolution meetings for all mission-related people.

Since our church building is only a half-kilometer from the village, we hold the general meetings in the church. Too

---

[26] *Der kleine Africa Bote*, September 1936, pp. 2-6.

The main building: one half is the church/school and the other half is the home of the Bartsch family.

The residence of Katherine Harder and Eva Jantz. (The home and yard are enclosed by a five foot fence.)

Arthur in the yard of our house.

The front entrance to our house.

many things interrupt us if we have our meetings in the village. Actually, the people come to the church rather willingly, that is, those who are willing to hear what is being said. Most of the seats are filled with young people.

The following is the order of service: First, several songs are played on the gramophone. Then we sing one or two hymns as a congregation. Then we read a Psalm or a group of students recites a Psalm. This is followed by prayer, after which we sing another song. Then we tell students one or two Bible stories. After this, a white missionary talks about some applications of the stories, we pray, take an offering, sing a song and depart.

School boys singing from the printed page.

The School

The next aspect of the mission is the work done in the school. My wife, Anna, has the leadership in this aspect of the mission. With only a few exceptions, 120 students were provided instruction on a regular basis. We divided the whole group into seven classes. In each class we appointed the leading student as teacher. This lightened our load even though we could not make too many demands on these young teachers.

During vacation periods, we sent the teachers out to the villages to instruct children who had not come to school. In the evenings they had meetings to spread the Word of God. The results were beyond our wildest expectations in most of the villages. On one of my travels to Port Francqui, I had the opportunity to visit one of these schools. My, how pleased I was with these little kids! We have never seen the local people as happy as when they returned from their vacation teaching experiences, and told us about the results they saw in their teaching. It wasn't as though these young disciples of Jesus could drive out devils, as in the time of Jesus. But, some of these young teachers reported that they prayed with, or rather for, very disturbed people and they had them calmed down.

In the school we teach the following subjects: Bible stories, reading, writing and basic adding and subtracting. Everything must be translated into their language. This made it difficult in the school. We are always short of supplies for teaching. We expect to teach in the Lingala language and hope that books written in Lingala will be available.

A new group of students.

The first teachers.

Anna Bartsch translating into Dengese.

1934–Mrs. Anna Bartsch and Erna with the students at Bololo.

First girls class with L. Jantz.

Boys doing morning excercises under the direction of Mr. Van de Velde.

Medical Services

The medical work (and worries) became my responsibility after Katherine Harder left. The Belgian area doctor commented about life in the villages: "It's a living cemetery and death candidates are running around at large."

I knew little about medicine. I had served in the medical corps in Russia but knew little of the medical needs of people in tropical settings. Often I stood dumbfounded, not knowing which medicine I should give or what I should do. To the honor of God, I can say

Mother carries son to our clinic.

that I have been prevented from making huge mistakes. In 1935, we heard that a doctor, sent by the government, had come to the Dengese region. I felt so relieved that he would take this burden from me. In part, this happened, but in this region people will not go to western doctors because they distrust them. They say that an itinerant government doctor gave a large number of people shots of Demerol a few years back and that half of them died of complications. We used the same medicine for frambesia, tropical sores and syphilis, and the Lord has given us much success with this inexpensive but dangerous medicine. Now these poor sheep come to us instead of to the doctor. If we send them away to Dekese or Bulape, they leave,

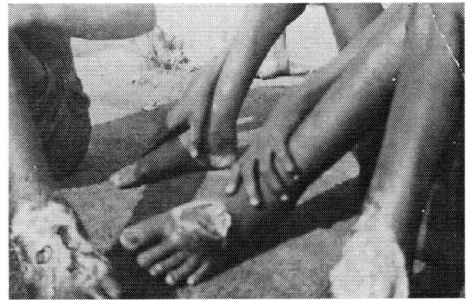

but will not go to a white doctor. Rather they go to any medicine man. Sensitive whites know that our effort to save a human life is done in the face of so much death. So we accept whoever comes to us and do what we can, with God's help. We can rely on local people's assistance in only the rarest occasion.

Assistants from the local population tend to over-prescribe medicine. Many a person here has died of overdoses. So it becomes very important that the white man oversee the use of medicine here. Even a harmless medicine, such as quinine, can lead to death if the exact dose is not followed.

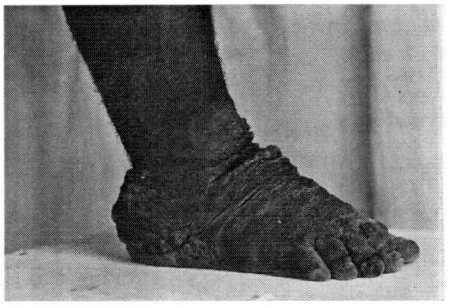

The hospital that we built soon after arriving in Bololo was designed as follows: One section was intended as a pharmacy and reception room. The second was intended for those who need to stay for a while, the third, for patients with infectious diseases, and the fourth for various other illnesses. But the practice is often different than the intention. Women come to the hospital only when they are critically ill and then they do not stay overnight. They are so afraid that the evil spirits of their relatives will drag them back into the village. Of course, we cannot oversee their care then. Conditions are filthy; treatment by townspeople, inhuman. We are not surprised, then, when the health of these poor invalids deteriorates. The outcome is that some people blame us and, worse, some withdraw from the help we can give them at the mission.

A woman was brought to us in February. She had been in labor for four days before coming to us. People from the village carried her with a kipoy for 8 hours. The grandmothers of her village had done everything they knew in the previous four days. The child was still-born in our hospital but we hoped to save the mother. Two days after the birth, the woman got a high fever and died on the third day.

Another woman took my wife Anna's hand and held on during contractions. Because it was too late for us to do anything, she died a pitiful death while giving birth. It is so difficult to win the confidence of the women, when they only come with abnormal or complicated births. It is hard to explain to people that even a specialist would have difficulty in such cases.

My intention of telling you about the medical problems is not to communicate hopelessness about the situation. Rather it is to point out how poor the medical services are here. If someone should make a legal claim against the mission because of a death at the mission, our work could be severely crippled. This is certainly one of my concerns. We invite brothers and sisters in America to prayerfully remember us regarding this.

A very sick man brought to the clinic.

From January to July, we attended 450 sick people here. Only three died during these six months.

Our Plans and the Turn of Events[27]

After we closed the school on March 1, we tried to find time for ourselves in order to prepare material for instruction, to translate the Gospel of John into Dengese, and if possible to mimeograph the material for students. But the Lord had other plans for the mission. At the end of February we informed students that it would soon be their vacation. On vacation they could do what they wanted, could construct new huts for themselves or could till their gardens. To our surprise most of the students did not seem to be happy about this. This seemed strange to us since we had expected gratitude for the release from school.

---

[27] *Der kleine Africa Bote*, June 1936, pp. 3-5.

When some of the believers asked me if I would no longer call them for morning worship services, I said, "No, I won't. Now you are free. If anyone wishes to be released from the school regulations, he can be released. I only ask that he cross his name off the list." After I told them that, a group of 20 believers came to me and said it would really be a shame if their classmates went back to the villages and got themselves lost in the sins of their old ways. So we consulted with each other about the situation. We decided to keep the students here and to give them a weekly ration, even if there were no formal classes. Everyone was relieved. There seemed to be a genuine sense of unity and satisfaction.

At one of our evening meetings we agreed to send our best teachers along with a fellow believer to the villages to conduct school and to preach God's Word. The teachers along with their assistants went to five villages. According to the reports that we received, town chiefs were willing to receive the teachers and sent many children to their classes.

Here in Bololo, many people reported that they wanted to turn to God and wanted to break with their old heathen customs. At first only one person came. Then several came in pairs. Then they came in threes and fours and more at one time. We all prayed earnestly in the prayer meetings that many who had heard the Word would turn from evil and come to Jesus. Before we knew it, we were in the middle of a revival. We didn't have to do anything but to show people even more clearly how they could find peace through salvation. Dozens of strong young men, with tears in their eyes

Henry Bartsch discussing an issue with a group of students.

and beaming faces, said they wanted to stop fighting against God and wanted to commit themselves to Him forever, yes even till He should come again. We eagerly sat late into the night with them and rejoiced with the angels in heaven that sinners repented of their ways. We counted 69 believers.

Canadian Citizenship Problems

By mid-1934, the mission was in full swing. The sick were being treated in the hospital, workers could be hired and children brought fruit from the forest. The school was organized and functioning in an orderly way. In the church and in the villages, services were held regularly. People received the Word with joy and were converted. People became children of God despite Henry and Anna's difficulty with the language.

However a problem arose about the citizenship status of the Bartsch family. In 1929 Henry and Anna had become Canadian citizens. An official notice arrived from Ottawa indicating that their citizenship had to be renewed after five years. They had three choices. They could continue to work and ignore the Canadian Government and so become stateless, they could return as a whole family leaving the work to suffer and likely not return for lack of funds, or Henry could go alone, leaving his wife Anna, 4-year-old Erna, 3-year-old Lydia, and 14-month-year-old Arthur in Bololo.

They talked about it for some time, knowing they had to make a decision. Finally Henry said to Anna, "Today, I must have an answer from you." Mother said she went aside and cried desperately, and then turned her life over to the Lord again and said, "Lord, as you will." They decided that Henry would go alone.

Katherine Harder, Lydia Jantz and Mr. Van de Velde offered to stay.

Mother writes,[28] *"Toward evening we as a family took a short walk. Henry took little Arthur in his arms. He was 14 months. The girls jumped around, quite happy that we were together as a*

---

[28]Anna Bartsch, *The Hidden Hand,* p. 130, translated by Arthur Bartsch.

family, unaware that we would soon be parted for a long time. We saw the beautiful sunset and actually had very little to say to each other. This was the path that Abraham took when he was sent with his son Isaac to Moriah. Here we, too, had been laid on the altar of sacrifice!"

The Mission in Henry's Absence

The next morning I, our two girls, Katherine Harder and Mr. Van de Velde accompanied Henry to the Sankuru River, a distance of about three hours' walk. At the water's edge we sat a few hours and ate our lunch. Henry finally tore himself away, stepped into the dugout with two black oarsmen and pushed off into the river. We stood and watched as he disappeared from our sight. Now we needed courage! It was September 23, 1934.

September 30, 1934. Today school started again. Four new classes were added ...

October 2, 1934. Van de Velde is back at his job and rings the bell at 6 AM. Mr. Van de Velde was able to organize the boys for morning exercises.

November, 1934. Just received news from my mother, Lena Funk, who has returned to southern Russia again after spending three years in a Siberian prison camp with my father.

Erna wakes up at night and asks: "Mama, are you absolutely sure Daddy should have gone away? Was that written in the book?" When I assured her that it was, she put her head back into the pillow and fell asleep again.

January 1, 1935. The echo of Christmas is gone now and we are again immersed into a sea of troubles. We had to learn the hard way that we had to trust the Lord and that we could not depend on people. Mr. Van de Velde wanted to leave us. We are dismayed–what would we do without him! Fourteen years ago he had left his wife and infant son in Belgium and had come to Africa to seek his fortune. He had found it here at the mission. He had found himself, been baptized, become a responsible and worthy Christian,  *and become most useful to us with his talents and experience with the blacks. . . . Van de Velde's wife was . . . suing him for a divorce. He wanted to return to Belgium. . . . Little Lydia noticed his change of behavior and prayed in her evening prayer: "Dear Lord, give Uncle Van de Velde some oil in his lamp."*

January 3, 1935. Today Van de Velde left us. . . . Now I was the administrator. . . . The village people say, now that the men are gone the mission work is over and done with.

February 14, 1935. The children return to school from their vacation but have reverted to their heathen customs again. Besides that they have caught a bad case of a cough.

March 25, 1935. Everything is in full swing: Our student membership is over 130. . . . When one has seen the threat of evil spirits, of torment and death so active among these people, one rejoices that some of them have reached out for salvation and how God has helped them. The doors are open and the possibilities are endless.

May 17, 1935. Miss Harder has a terrible headache.

June 8, 1935. Miss Harder is sick unto death. She's got a temperature over 105.

June 13, 1935. Miss Harder's health is worse today. Temperature is 105.4 and her speech is confused.

June 19, 1935. Miss Harder is still alive. The doctor was here and we are happy that she has shown signs of improvement.

August 5, 1935. We start classes again. We're quite surprised that the students have returned without difficulty and that they are so attentive. One reason might be that they are expecting Henry's return.

At the same time we have seen such violent people here recently. The natives call them "possessed." They rave and beat their bodies. When they whimper and shriek and howl and cry, it gives one the shivers.

In the village the people whispered quietly and the children spread rumors, "Henry has become unfaithful. Lusanganye has died. Why should we wait any longer for his return?"

I said, "Well, I guess I shall have to pack my bags and take my children and go too."

"No, don't do that!" they interjected. "Let's wait one more month." (I already knew that Henry's ship had landed at Matadi and that he would be on his way into the interior by now.)[29]

Dad's Return from America

My boat arrived at Djongo Beach at about 8 AM, September 17, 1935. A small landing had been made since we came to Bololo. A number of Dengese natives were there and stared out at us shyly from the bushes. When they saw me get off the boat, they all emerged from the forest—men, women and children, including very old grandfathers and grandmothers—and greeted me in a way distinctive to Dengese. The passengers and the captain on board were completely astounded to see a white man welcomed so heartily by these primitives, whom they had

---

[29] Anna Bartsch, *The Hidden Hand*, p. 155, translated by Arthur Bartsch.

learned to know from their newspapers and articles to be evil. I, too, was quite overwhelmed by their friendliness and the joy which surrounded me on all sides.

The first ones who greeted me wanted to tell me all the details about my family in Bololo. Everyone who had a chance to speak to me directly reiterated in one way or another: "You were gone a very long time, but you returned. Ikongo-Samu (our little Arthur) is well and is growing up." Then men and women came and asked if they could take my baggage to Bololo–a most unusual thing for the Dengese people. I normally had to beg for hours and make all kinds of promises to get carriers when I needed them. My coming was now such a great surprise that it inadvertently shook them out of their natural pattern of behavior.

It had been rumored here that I had died somewhere either en-route or in the land of the white man. They were all convinced of this, so that when they saw me they were altogether amazed.

I arranged for a part of my things to be sent ahead to Bololo. I stowed the rest of them in a shelter at the Sankuru River. Then I took my bicycle, which I had brought with me from Germany, and began my journey to Bololo. The distance from the Sankuru River to our mission is about 15-20 kilometers. The road, or better said the forest path, was very bad. It was so overgrown and crossed with fallen trees that I had great difficulty in getting through with my bicycle. Driving was impossible! The journey didn't seem to go fast enough. Even though it was morning and the sun was still low on the horizon I was bathed in sweat. My whole trip from Canada and Europe didn't appear to have taken as long as this final stretch toward my destination.

One hour before Bololo lies the village of Djongo-Sanga. Just a few kilometers before we get to the village, there is clearing and it can be driven easily. So the people here were not able to get ready to meet me. To everyone's fright, I suddenly whizzed by them on my bicycle. I just heard my name being called with a stifled shriek, and there was jubilation just after I had passed another group of people. The way out of Djongo-Sanga leads up a hill and I had to give up trying to ride until I was over the crest. My followers became aware of this and soon caught up to me.

Before long I was surrounded by a noisy, dancing throng, and I exerted myself to get to the top so that I could get away from them.

On the downhill stretch I gave my "blackie" (bicycle) full sway and it glided swiftly along, seeming to share my soul's delight. A number of stalwart runners, however, had enough energy to remain close in behind me, and in fact, continued running right until I was home. My carriers with the baggage, however, remained far behind so that no one was able to deliver a verbal telegram to Bololo.

I arrived on the yard in Bololo, at about 11:30 AM. I caught my dear ones and the local people by surprise, even though they had been eagerly awaiting me for a long time. They had often tried to anticipate my arrival but had always been disappointed whenever the ship came by and I had not appeared. Now however they were caught quite off guard. I suddenly was there and no one had been prepared to meet me at the boat.

When I neared Bololo, the first group of students recognized me and broke out in a tumult of rejoicing so that my dear Anna and the three children who heard it came out to greet me. That was a reunion of joy much too intimate to tell.

After a period of 360 days I again had my wife and family

in my arms. We praise God for everything and thank Him for His faithfulness. He keeps His promises as we had experienced. No evil had approached our dwelling place. Even our Erna thanked the Lord, in her childlike way, when she had not been disappointed in her faith and in her long wait for my re-

Dancing at Dad's return.

turn. In the dining room a large white cloth had been hung up on the wall. The wall hanging bore the following inscription in large green letters:

I have been with you,
I have protected you where you have gone,
I have brought you back into this land,
I have not forsaken you,
I have done what I promised.

Dad with Erna and Lydia after his return. Notice the wall hanging of the above Genesis 28:15 passage that mother had hung on the wall as a welcome.

This rephrased Genesis 28:15 was the text at our farewell service held a year ago on September 23rd, 1934. I believe the Lord will let us use this verse and apply it to us personally in this case. Out in the yard the passionate dancing continued unabated as the heathen displayed their praise to God in their own way over my return. At the evening service

Henry and Anna Bartsch family, with Erna, Lydia and Arthur, 1935 in Bololo.

that night I was impressed by the remarks repeated by men who had gathered. "Lusanganye has not betrayed us. He has come back just as Jesus will someday come again." The natives took what we said quite literally and looked to us as models so that in view of our human limitations we often felt quite helpless and were reluctant to set ourselves up as examples.[30]

Significance of the Trip to North America[31]

The primary purpose of the trip was to renew my parents' Canadian citizenship. This was accomplished in Ottawa with little difficulty. They could return to Canada assured that that was their country.

---

[30] In the two-and-a-half years, from March 1933 when they arrived in Bololo, to September 1935, when father returned from Canada, remarkable changes had occured in the mission. The white missionaries had won the trust of the Dengese people who had cannibalized the previous white person to enter their territory. They had established a school for 120 boys, a clinic to heal the sick, and had begun a program of evangelism in the villages. Distrust and fear melted with the birth of a white child on Dengese soil. Dad's necessary departure to Canada in September 1934, left the mission in the hands of three women: Mother (with three children), Katherine Harder and Lydia Jantz. The mission prospered, students begged to stay at the mission school, the clinic treated the sick, and teachers trained at the mission fanned out to spread the good news of God's grace in the villages. The Canadian Conference of Mennonite Brethern set up a mechanism to encourage prayer and financial support. A mission was begun. There was hope that it would continue to grow.

[31] *Der kleine Africa Bote* (The African Messenger), was published beginning in June 1936. That publication, and mother's *The Hidden Hand*, are primary sources of the events in Henry's life reported here.

There was another significant outcome of the trip, related to the support of their mission in Bololo. They had set out independently, with the support of a small group of former teachers and friends. Having established the mission in Bololo, the school, the clinic and the evangelistic outreach into the villages, Dad was now in a position to explain what they were about. Churches across Canada and the United States asked him to visit and tell his stories. For a whole year he toured Mennonite Brethren churches and told them stories about Africa that were remembered fifty years later. He reported the following:

We were not sent either by our Conference or any other committee. We were not called by man but by God, and this call occurred so powerfully to us one day that we could not resist it. Unconditionally we surrendered ourselves to the call: "Go into a land which I will show you." We risked our lives and the Lord kept His promises to us.[32]

In the midst of their struggle to survive, after regrouping from their escape from Soviet Russia, Mennonite communities across Canada found something to celebrate. Father's reports raised a ground swell of prayer and financial support they had not known before. The Africa Missions Society was formed in the summer of 1935. This Society published bulletins from the mission field and transmitted funds from the churches.

---

[32] Anna Bartsch, *The Hidden Hand*, p. 159, translated by Arthur Bartsch.

Chapter 5

Challenges and Perseverance
1936

Events in Bololo

By July 1936, three years after the birth of our son, many people claimed to have found peace with God and, with a few exceptions, demonstrated a new way of living. We were quite surprised to hear stories about conversions happening in the villages among people who had not come to the mission. We had often felt hopeless about preaching in the villages because no foundation had been laid for the seed of God. But we learned that God does not depend on the preparations we make, but can intervene without our assistance. The Lord has not let His Word return without effect. "The wind blows where it wills...."

Mother reports[33] that Henry's calmness and control over the activities was very comforting to her. After lunch, he often turned on the gramophone and played beautiful music: "Eine kleine Nachtmusik," "The Blue Danube" and other lovely records he had brought with him from friends he had met in Germany. He also brought toys for the children.

- Our health is very good. The children are well too. We tell ourselves that the climate here in the Congo is very healthy. The sun is directly overhead and the temperature is 30 degrees centigrade.
- The group of missionaries from California–Africa-Evangelism Association – that considered working in the Dengese district has decided to leave.
- The Dengese King, Ikongo-Samu, has made several visits to Bololo. He also came up to the mission. Whatever things his

---

[33] Anna Bartsch, *The Hidden Hand*, p. 161, translated by Arthur Bartsch.

Lordship sees in our house, he wants as a gift. In order not to appear inhospitable, we need to clear things out of the way that we do not want to give to him. The only blessing of such a visit is this: He orders his hunters to bring us meat. It takes a lot of meat to feed all of us, the 121 people at our mission. Since our hunting rifles have not arrived as yet, we are very grateful for the meat his visit provides.

Mother, Dad, Arthur, Lydia and Erna, 1936.

• The Belgian government has appointed an agronomist to this region. He is trying to persuade people to cut trees and plant vegetable gardens. The soil is very rich. When the thick forest is cut and burned, villagers can prepare gardens and grow crops. It is better for us to buy our food for the boys from the villagers, rather than supervise our boys in their gardening. That is a job that the villagers can do and they do it for a small fee. We are busy enough taking care of our own gardens and banana trees.

• We do keep in touch with world news. We read the Mennonite papers. Also, I was fortunate to get to know a fellow on the ship when I came back from Canada. He sends us the *Johannesburg Daily* and the *German Afrikaner*, once a week. We get the mail delivery every 10 or 12 days at Port Francqui. The mail comes by rail via South Africa.

• A terrifying event occurred on May 10, 1936: A rabid dog bit our two daughters, Erna (6) and Lydia (5). When dogs run around and bite people, they are usually rabid. Arthur (3) was very frightened but not bitten. Erna's wound bled profusely, while Lydia's skin was only scratched. So I took Erna to the doctor in Luebo. The trip took four days. I took food along for the trip since nothing could be purchased on the way. When we arrived at Luebo, no one could find any medicine. We needed Antiravin so the plan was to fly to Leopoldville the next day. The black congregation in Luebo prayed. A Catholic priest from the other side of the river heard of our ordeal. Since he had mistakenly received some Antiravin in his last shipment, he made it available to us. That night the medicine was brought across the river to Luebo and Erna was given the injections. I gave Lydia anti-rabid injections later, as the doctor instructed me. The Lord was good to us; He worked through the medicine and the kindness of the priest. No bad effects resulted from the rabid dog incident. We give Him the honor for this.

• Bololo, November 27, 1936: Our work continues in the same old way. A number of the believers who fell away have come back. The longer we are here, the more we realize that if our heavenly Father does not invite people, pressure on them only has negative effects. On the whole, native customs and practices have a very powerful grip on people. Even if Jesus' might is greater than anything in the world, it can only work in an individual who chooses to turn away from evil. People have choice. And yet, God invites to bring about the willingness and to do His will.

• We need to separate ourselves from the village life so that the temptations and opportunities are fewer for our students. We are therefore not building any new buildings now but are repairing the old ones.

• At our school we have had classes continuously for seven months. We'll go until Christmas, when the students will leave. After eight months of classes, we can certainly use a quiet retreat in the high mountains. Most missionaries do it after four months.

• Bololo, December 1936: In the previous mail I informed you that Margaret Siemens arrived here safely. She is staying in our house as long as the other sister missionaries are still here.

• Report from Ms. Siemens' letters.

In her first letter Ms. Siemens reported that she brought some seeds along from America. A week later these had begun to grow very quickly. Cucumbers and tomatoes do well, she says. Bananas and papaya are plentiful. Melons and lemons grow well too.

She also reports that missionaries do not carry firearms, though she says it might be good to have a rifle for protection against wild animals. Big snakes are particularly common and these are difficult to kill.

She also reports that the air is not as clear as at home in America where there is more grass. The smell in the air is quite bad, she says because the ants build their sand castles higher than six feet. These ants stink. Big snakes also live beneath the giant ant hills.

The mission is surrounded with sand that is swept every day. We are in God's hand and He will protect and carry us. Pray that we have health and strength.

- In the last little while, I have been alone with my group of students. We are planning to close the school for one or two months after Christmas. This last semester was too long for us. We had let 95 students go on vacation and immediately took on another 100. Now we give students a shirt, a pair of trousers, a bush-knife, and soap before releasing them to the villages. Some return to their old customs, but we cannot control that. If they want to go along the path that we have shown them, they can do so. They have received enough light that they can choose salvation in Jesus. For Christmas, we are practicing a number of new songs and a dozen Old Testament prophecies of the coming of Jesus. Aside from the many difficulties our boys have inherited, we continue to hope that a new generation of Dengese will arise.

Medical Conditions Among the Dengese[34]

The medical condition among the Dengese is terrible. The itinerant government doctor came into our district and determined that of 150 people, 53 had tuberculosis, 15 had skin diseases, and nearly all the rest had curable illnesses. He called this place a "living cemetery." If our work were not concerned with the souls of these people, we would fold up our tents and go home. This doctor, who had no religious faith himself, said

---

[34] *Der kleine Africa Bote,* April 1937, pp. 4-7.

we must have a much more satisfying job than his as a medical doctor because we worked with the spiritual life of the people.

I am really very concerned about the physical condition of our people. Some will tell us that the physical care of the people is the responsibility of the government; our responsibility is for the souls of the people. But I strongly disagree. We cannot care for the soul unless we also care for the body of these people.

Physical ailments trouble the people in this tribe like nothing else. Every village could have a hospital. Where are the ones to heal? In terrible desperation the sick person throws himself into the arms of the medicine man, and experiences even worse consequences. If we had even a modicum of medical assistance and care, if even small cuts or bruises could be cleaned and covered so insects would not crawl all over them, we could help a lot of people. Dirt and lack of understanding of basic medical care make little sores life threatening to the person involved and dangerous for others.

The death rate is much higher here than elsewhere. The itinerant doctor told me that several people were allowed to die just before he arrived because they feared the treatment he prescribed. Other seriously ill people are taken into the forest till the doctor leaves the village. Distrust is so high! Firstborn children are seemingly always killed. At least that has been our observation here at the mission. The child of one of our students was nearly killed. The child is still alive, but we wonder if it won't be offered to Moloch as an offering. One of the workers at our mission station developed  a bronchial illness. Since he did not want to be helped by us at the station, I let him go back to the village. He was dead in two days. His mother asked us to call him back but he wanted to stay in the village. Now people say he died because he left his home village. We hear so much anguish in these villages.

One estimate is that 70% of those who die would not need to if proper help were provided. In some cases, when people are really desperate with a very seriously ill member, someone covers the mouth and closes the nose so that the person cannot breathe. At the funeral of one of our students, people sang repeatedly, "The white man has let you go hungry and has killed you." One of the workers, who is not a believer, could stand it no longer. Enraged, he shouted, "You have killed him and now you blame the white man." People stopped the singing for a bit and then continued. Then they came up with even greater lies. They said we had given the student poison and that is why he died.

Nutrition plays a major role in the early death of many blacks. Two-week-old infants are fed hard "quanga," dough paste made of a root called manioc. The poor infants are left to fend for themselves. Poor kids! If the child gets constipated, they take cold water and force it into the rectal openings without pity. We are amazed at how many children stay alive.

Most of the Dengese people are undernourished. Sometimes they do not have enough food and at other times they have an overabundance. Nutrition is very erratic. They cannot plan for the next day. If someone captures a wild animal it needs to be eaten before the next day, or the dogs and rats or other wild animals will get rid of it. It seems very hard for the blacks to conserve food. It even seems it is a violation of a moral law. We often hear from believers, bothered by guilty consciences, that the sin they have committed is to hide food from others. I am sure that we will have a hard time instilling regular mealtime habits. It just counters their culture too much. People can endure unbelievable hunger, but they cannot tolerate someone who hoards meat.

A similar situation occurs with the building of houses. If someone builds a house that is better than that of the others, he will suffer. The sin of pride and greed is punished more than any other. These poor people would rather die of hunger or cold than be damned by the community.

The doctor says that everything must change for the people if they are to be helped. We try this at the mission. We build houses using lime and roofs that keep the rain out. The students must wash and keep themselves clean and sleep in warm but clear air. We seek to regulate meal times. They are not allowed to cut their bodies, because so many sores result from it and because scarring the body is not consistent with a Christian view of the body. We don't allow students to file their teeth. So there are many differences between our students and people from the village. Our students are much healthier than people from the village, but even so village life attracts so many back to the dirt. One gets discouraged with enforcing discipline.

Several days ago a student at our mission got pneumonia. I wanted to see to it that he was not constantly dowsed with cold water and that he could stay in a warm hut. But yesterday someone took the little boy away and I don't know where he stayed. I will be happy if he is alive tomorrow. I need so much patience and energy and courage to help these people!

Last week we did some work with lime in the old school building. Some water remained in a barrel. It turns out that the workers, who had worked with the lime, had washed themselves with that water. Early Sunday morning, we saw boys draw water out of the barrels to drink. It doesn't seem to bother people or maybe they are too lazy to get clean water. Many illnesses are attributable to dirty water, rotting meat and bad bread.

Yes, the field is wide open but there are few to work here.

Even though there are so few of us, and although we feel so weak to do this demanding work, the government doctor has inspired us with a plan. He will visit us once a month and will arrange to see sick people.

Travel to a Village[35]

This morning I left Bololo on bike with several assistants. When it's not possible to ride the bike, I have to walk. When I get too tired, I let myself be carried on the kipoy. I am heading to Bisonganda, a distance of about 25 miles. The trip will probably take us about six or seven hours. The weather was beautiful, almost too nice to travel since we have to travel through heavy forest most of the way. If we get thunder and lightening, I feel rather unsafe under the large trees. As we travel through the primeval forest, we often see where lightning has shredded huge ancient trees and dropped them on the path we are taking. The forces of nature remind everyone of powers greater than themselves. But when the storms are past, most of us carry on as we did before.

Travel by bike or kipoy.

A traditionally dressed-up woman.

---

[35] *Der kleine Africa Bote,* January 1937, pp. 3-5.

A Congo Village[36]

Strange, yet interesting are the sights of that native village deep in the heart of Africa. The huts of simplest style, the people of simplest dress, the village, as a whole, of simplest plan and structure are impressive and unforgettable. Diseases, filth, dogs and dirt characterize such a village in any part of the Congo basin.

The village is situated among dense jungles and forest. It is hard to clear the land and the native villages are an oases of light and air surrounded by the tall hot dark forest where wildlife is dominant.

An equatorial rain-belt forest covers the lower and the middle Congo. Gigantic rubber trees stretch hundreds of feet skyward. The entangled underbrush marks a thickened mass where snakes and tigers creep. Well-beaten paths lead through the jungle or forest from village to village.

Sometimes between the village and such a jungle lie the grasslands. Tall, sharp-edged grasses of about 10 feet high are splendid hideouts

Women pounding manioc.

for the sly fox and the laughing hyena. The thread-like path twists its way out and in and out again, around and through these grasses.

Following this path to its root, we find ourselves on the main street, for the plan of the village is simple, having only this one highway. The confusion of street names is not there, and it would

---

[36] This description of a Congo village was submitted by my sister, Lydia Bartsch Reimer as she remembered African villages when she was in high school, about ten years after our family left the Congo.

be difficult to get lost. Two, long irregular rows of mud houses face this pave-like path at the end of which the jungle path continues. In the center of the village is a large circle, which in our language can be termed as the "social center" of the village.

Now the individual characteristics impress us more. Close to the huts, we notice the mango-root in the gardens of the natives. Strange crops and spices are also visible as we draw closer. Bright but small are the fires that burned in the front of each individual dwelling. About these fires are the pots which contain the evening meal. The tiny, nude, black-eyed children playing around these fires catch our eyes immediately. Besides these children and the old grandfathers squatted near the fire are the women. Some, possibly inside the huts, but most of them assembled in an inconspicuous corner talking gossip and the like. Fierce, diseased dogs bark wildly, threatening the frightened stranger. Huss-buss, noise and unrest fill the atmosphere and the strange spell seems to reign.

As we come closer, we notice the structure and composition of the huts. These are made either of mud or bamboo walls and are only about a 5-foot square in area. The slanted roof is extended somewhat beyond the walls to give a porch-like protection from the torrent rains and the scorching heat. Four poles of about 6 feet height support the

straw-colored thatched roof which is waterproofed with mud and lime. A small, dark, square doorway, or sometimes a hole large enough to permit an ordinary man to crawl through is the only opening. Dark and dingy are the inside walls of dried grasses and leaves. Straw and bare-earth replaces our hardwood floors and linoleums. Simple and primitive are these huts, but they give protection from beast and weather to the native.

The lack of cleanliness and health of these dwellings is of the first-degree. A strong, irritating odor is prevalent in the huts. The smell of strong spices, medicines, rotten meat, filth and dirt is always there. The only ventilation is the single doorway where small amounts of light and air pass in and dark amounts of smoke and stuffy air pass out. Dark hidden crevices breed germs which breed diseases uncontrollably.

These are the "trademarks" of every Congo village. Grime and lack of sanitation are unforgettable facts of these villages. Thus in such a lowly state can be found the innumerable villages throughout the Congo basin.

Meal of manioc.

Checking for lice.

My Experience in Bisongonda Village

Bisongonda is a large village with about 600 residents. White people are not welcome and, so, neither Belgian government officials nor missionaries have much influence here. Of the fifty possible students from this district, only three have come to our school. The rest do not come because of the influence of the medicine man. He is afraid to lose his people. The mothers of the boys also warn them about coming to our school. The leader of the village is decidedly against white people. He served as a soldier for the Belgian army but never took on western civilization. His lifestyle is as "wild" as that of the people in the village.

A tragedy struck the village the day I arrived. An elephant had killed a man and then disappeared into the forest with a spear stuck in his side. If they find and kill the elephant, the villagers have meat for a month. The loss of the man is painful to the community but that pain is relieved somewhat with the increased food supply. In any case, this elephant has taken the life of one of the villagers. The custom requires that a potion be created from the remains of the killed person. This potion is only good for the hunt of this one elephant.

I called the people together for a worship service. I made some space in front of my hut for the gathering. Only old women and little children gathered. They cannot understand our message. There was a lot of noise, so the students that I brought with me interrupted the noise with a few hymns. I feel so hopeless about being of any value when I just travel through a village. I would like so much to bring them God's Word. The men and boys hunt all day in the deep forest. They arrive in the village late in the evening. When I see these poor people with all their sickness, I get the impression that I am passing through a gigantic hospital, much as the itinerant government doctor said.

At the end of the meeting several men came to the gathering. The leader of the village also came. He was very restless. He walked back and forth, went away and then returned. My students sang spiritual hymns, but seemingly without spirit.

Nevertheless, it did quiet the women and children. My best student, Ngunga, the one we are closest to, prayed. Then I told the story of the paralytic man. Ngunga explained to people what I could not explain in their language. Everyone was curious about things they had not heard before. We closed with a song and a prayer. At the end, I felt as though I spoke to the trees in the forest. They too remained quiet when I paused in silence.

As I and the group I brought with me left the gathering, a government officer arrived to give the gathering a message. He used our gathering for his purposes because it would have been impossible for him to get people together like this on his own. Suddenly, I heard a noise shatter the stillness. Whatever he said to them, stirred them up to frenzy. I heard people cursing and carrying on in ways one could hardly believe. My heart aches for these people.

That was the end of the village gathering.

As my assistant made a fire, I looked through my bags for something that was ready to eat since it gets dark very quickly in the tropics. The village people sit in front of their huts for their meals. They swallow balls of a dough-like substance they call "Kwenga." Their stomachs expand and then they seem satisfied.

I sat at my hut. Many of the villagers came by to beg for salt. As they did, they held in their stomachs, as though they had lost their breath. They came till late in the evening. They crave salt and I am glad to give it to them, as long as supplies last. I exchanged chicken eggs for the salt, though most of the eggs are not edible.

I sat outside in the moonlight and looked to the heavens in the evening. In the west I saw heavy clouds with silver lining. I knew a storm was coming. I could hear heavy thunder and soon saw lightening, clear signals of the coming storm. I withdrew into my hut, lit the lantern and read my Bible. I read Psalm 84. It is a Psalm someone referred us to in a letter.

Yahweh, hear my prayer:
Listen, God of Jacob.
God is our shield.

The longing expressed in the Psalm was mine too, but verse 8 did not match my experience. Then I blew out the light and poured my heart out to God, who, after all, is my sun and shield. Whether anyone has understood us here is doubtful, but the Lord understands my deepest intent. That thought encouraged and strengthened me. I have walked, ridden my bike and crawled all day, and now I am tired and want to sleep.

My assistants were housed in a hut about 100 meters away. I could hear them. They had a lot to talk about. I heard their laughter. Then I heard them sing. It's about 10 PM. The storm has passed, they and all the village people are very happy to have survived it. They dance and drum monotonously through the night. I fell asleep in the early morning. I woke up exhausted. I knew I had a nine-hour trip before me.

The Difficulties I Face in Travel

We left early in the morning. The assistants quarreled with each other about the heaviest and lightest baggage to carry. I didn't feel bad because I had taken only the most necessary things. The paths led over mountains, through valleys, and through streams. I couldn't ride my bike, couldn't walk and couldn't even be carried through the rough terrain. We just have to squirm our way through. I wondered if the assistants could make the trip, having spent half the night dancing. I wondered when a decent road would be built. My guess is never!

We arrived at the Sankuru River in two-and-a-half days and took a dugout canoe downstream for three hours. The boatman is very happy to take me for a little beer-money. But I can only take a few of the boys with me along with my bicycle. The rest had to take separate canoes. The canoe is small and rocks considerably. If we tip, we are children of death. Surely the Lord must protect us. Even those who usually scream and carry on the most are absolutely quiet as we ride downstream. All of them know what danger lurks in the river depths. We all sit on our knees and grab the sides of the canoe. Everyone has a job to do. If he does not know how to do it, he will learn it quickly; it is to balance the round-bottomed dugout canoe.

Getting ready for the dance.

Finally the canoe moves into high grass. We have arrived. We got out of the canoe. We haven't put on our shoes yet, because we still have to get through a heavy swamp. Then we hiked across land for more than two hours till we arrived at the Lutchwadi River, which empties into Kasai River near Port Francqui.

We had to kneel in another dugout canoe for another hour. The only difference between the two canoe rides is that there was only a little water in the other canoe. Every little ripple seems to enter this boat. Anything that is not waterproof had to be put on blocks or held in our hands. It didn't help to bail water out of the canoe. Fresh water always entered. Finally we finished this trip as well, and I arrived just a few hundred yards from Port Francqui. I hoped my assistants will arrive soon.

An Italian businessman, Guilvie, welcomed me in a most friendly way. He also invited me to stay at his residence and to eat with him for any of the meals I was to have in Port Francqui. I am happy with that.

I waited for my assistants to arrive. I have purchased and packed all the supplies that I plan to take back to Bololo. Finally, two men arrived and notified me that the eighteen assistants will not be coming because the boatman at the Sankuru River was afraid to take my people across the river. I was really in a dilemma. I began to get ready to go back with only a few of the most necessary items. The trip has taken eight days. The cost of these misadventures was considerable. But if I allow myself to get too frustrated by all the difficulties I have faced, I can't handle anything else, so I accept things as they are.

You see from the above report how we travel here. We must take these trips for supplies. When we make these trips we often think of resettling the mission to Bolombo, which has a road that cars can travel on to Dekese. We need to consider the cost of such a transfer and need to discuss this with the government officials. In the meantime, we remain here in Bololo and continue to do the mission work the way we began.

Do We Relocate the Mission? [37]

September 20, 1936

This week I went to Bolombo, about 25 miles from Bololo. A Belgian government officer is working on road designs that may affect our work. I had a number of things to talk to him about, including the transfer of our mission to Bolombo near auto and water transport. There are many things that argue for such a move and a few against. Contact with the outside world is a big factor. But we will pray about the matter and consider the issues carefully. (We know you cannot advise us from North America about such matters.) The downside of such a move is that we would lose a number of students because the distance would be too great from their villages. But the move is probably necessary for the future. The road will never come here to Bololo, and eventually people move to where the transportation possibilities are better. Lodi is located on the other side of the Sankuru River, across from Bolombo. We are somewhat frightened about the possible move. There is so much building to do. Then again, most roofs of leaves and buildings with walls of mud and lime do not last more than 3-4 years.

---

[37] *Der kleine Africa Bote*, January 1937, pp. 5-6.

In any case, if we wanted to build more solid buildings, we could not do it here because there would be no way to bring the materials here. Over there, there are connections in all directions.

The leaders of Bololo came to see us yesterday. Under no circumstances would they support us moving away. They wondered if we were displeased with them in Bololo. They wondered if we wanted to get away from them because of that. They wanted to do whatever they could to keep us here. This is certainly different than it was when we came three short years ago.

A metaphor comes to mind: There is fruit that takes a little time to ripen but it is not yet ripe; it is not edible yet, but we are happy about the fruit. Everything is going very well in the school in Bololo. The new students, 78 of them, are very punctual. Our older students are on vacation. (We only need school supplies in the local language. We don't even have blackboards.)

The government also has many doctors and is seeking ways to bring these to this place. There is a very good medical person in Dekese, whom the government pays about 20,000 francs monthly. This doctor provides free services for blacks and whites. If he goes on leave in January, government officials say another doctor will replace him. (I think the government is paying for these doctors because I was able to convince Dr. Van Hof in Kinshasa of the terrible medical conditions in the Dengese region.) So, don't worry if no medical specialist from America volunteers to come. That's my personal opinion.

It is hard to see so many helpless people and note how little they sense how much we want to help them. They have had terrible experiences with white people. Local people believe that we eat human flesh and that is why we have so much energy and intelligence. I'm sure it will take many years till the black people will trust us. And I don't blame them!

Work Among Girls of the Villages

Since the Belgian government has indicated a willingness to take over more of our medical work, we can spend more time on spiritual matters. Our special concern is for the girls of the villages. We believe that the work among girls should be approached quite energetically. If we don't, the mission-wagon we are riding will curve off the road and eventually topple. Until new female volunteers arrive, the work among the girls will be in the hands of Katherine Harder, who has returned from furlough, and Margaret Siemens, who has arrived here recently. They will be responsible for recruiting girls and setting up the work with them. It must be separated from work with the boys.

A Serious Catastrophe Averted

People are very hostile to the Belgian government in the region where we are considering setting up the future mission, close to Djia. The most recent incident is that the governor had sent 32 medicine men to the courts in Luebo. Belgian courts in such matters are predictable. It's not likely that they will ever return to the Dengese people. The Belgians take them to some distant place and leave them there to die a natural death. In fact, the Governor recently warned a Roman Catholic priest about the danger of travel through Djia. The priest went, despite the warning, but took two policemen along for protection. Local men made several attempts to kill the priest during his stay in a village. They would have succeeded, too, had the two policemen not kept an armed guard that night.

When we heard about this, we were stunned. We had planned to travel through that same region with our whole family at the same time the priest had traveled there. Fortunately, we could not go because we had too much work to do here. Now we see that the Lord kept us from that trip. Naturally, we would have forgone the police protection. If the Lord had not protected us, we would have been killed and become meat for the "wild ones." We fear, but do not want to be afraid. Jesus says, "I send you as sheep among wolves." We believe the Belgian doctor, who said that these people are not yet free of cannibalism.

Please pray for us and advise us as you are able. The work will go on. We have not yet baptized any of the 83 boys who claim to have a faith in God, though we were close to it once. Then we noticed too many untamed aspects of the boys ages 10-18. So we decided to wait. For us to rush things would be our biggest mistake. We need much patience and time to help them make their faith real. Many of them still seem to view it as magical medicine.

My Reactions and Advice Regarding Another Mission

On September 25, 1936, we received a letter from Mr. Siegler from Dekese. He presented himself as a missionary from the Four Square Gospel Mission (FSGM) in Luisa, Kosai. He said he came from Los Angeles, California, where about 400 churches had sent him to the Belgian Congo to explore the possibility of setting up mission programs. Amee Sempel McPherson, a popular California personality, heads the mission he represents. It has a lot of financial backing, but it represents a type of Christian spirituality that threatens to undermine the very solid program we have begun in the region. When the letter arrived we discussed and prayed about the matter as a group. We decided that I would go to Dekese to meet Mr. Siegler in person. I took ten local men with me.

Mr. Siegler greeted me and soon we were deep in discussion about my concerns. I presented my concern about the effect of his type of spirituality on the Dengese people. I told him that we preferred him not to enter into this region to set up a "competing" orientation to the Christian faith. Mr. Siegler responded by saying, "If there is a mission here, we do not need to be here." I was glad that I had decided to meet him directly in Dekese. I have not heard, as yet, how the Governor has decided about this mission, but the Governor told me, six months ago, that he would allow entry only to those missionaries that I recommended. That is quite a trust.

Summary Report, January 4, 1937 [38]

The work in the school was the main focus of our work this past year. This was the most productive aspect of our work: To create a community faithful to Jesus. We had 200 eager students that attended school. We had clear regulations which make it possible to teach. We had seven teachers shown here.

Teachers from other tribes refuse to come here. This tribe is unique in language, customs, and self-identity. There have been occasions when students threatened teachers with bows and arrows.

---

[38] *Der kleine Africa Bote*, March 1937, pp. 3-9.

Worship services continued daily in the school, morning and evening, and Sundays in the church building. If everything is quiet, we conduct services in the villages. We do this in villages that are nearby and those that are farther away. Travel to the outlying village comes at a cost because of the difficulty in getting there. There are places where one cannot drive, be carried, or walk. One must literally crawl.

People from the village seek to draw the believers back into their old ways. They are cunning, and sometimes use force. I often hear the expression, "I got tired of the pressure from the village. I gave up. Now I can't get away." These teenage boys, 10-18, need help.

The medical work is considerably easier. The government medical doctor works in and around Bololo several times a month now.

It is clear to me that if we want to help people deal with their souls, we must help them physically. Every time I walk through the village, I ask myself what we could do to help people deal with their illness. We don't do nearly enough to help people physically. I feel guilty about that.

Since the government medical doctor left this region for three months to see people in the north, I have been left with the responsibility to care for people here. Yesterday, a man was brought to me with a spear through his thigh. He had been hunting.

Although the wound was fresh, a watery substance poured out of the wound. We really don't know enough to treat it.

I've been asked about our progress in translation work. We have translated the Gospel of John and have given copies of it to our graduating class. We have a crude mimeographing machine to make the copies. We have also written 35 Old Testament stories in the local language that we want to duplicate. My wife Anna, has been working on this most intensely. As you can see, we have big plans that we have not been able to implement yet.

I'll close this report with a brief story to show how the Lord protects us in various dangerous situations. In November I was sitting at a table reading the mail in my room. Suddenly I heard my wife scream in the next room. I ran into the room. She pointed to a huge snake that had crept behind a box in the corner of the room. The snake had already swallowed a number of chicks and a European hen. We called for help and a number of our able-bodied young men came with their weapons. I ordered everyone to remain calm so that we would not have any accidents. In one hand I had a large knife, in the other a lantern. I was barefoot. We slowly pushed the box with more chicks out of the room so that we had more room to do life-and-death battle with the snake.

Snakes of this kind attack. Katherine Harder had previously experienced an attack by a similar snake. When it reared itself to attack, the only solution was to run. That was then. Now we had to do something differently.

I had the job of encouraging my black warriors who increasingly began to shiver with fright. As we shook its cover, the snake stuck out its head, probably to assess its enemy. At the sight of the snake, my warriors shrieked and ran to the village. So I remained alone with the snake in that small room. I had no one else to rely on and so the battle with the beast began. Because my first stroke met its mark, victory was on my side. I then pulled the whole body of the snake out and measured it. It was as thick as a man's arm and two meters long.[39]

---

[39] Henry Bartsch does not name the snake but it may have been a mamba.

The people spoke about my courage, but we say that the Lord has protected me in an amazing way.

Christmas in the Jungle, 1936

Christmas has always meant joy and festivity for young and old in our homeland. In central Africa, people do not know such joy. Perhaps the only joy that people experience here is the village dance, and I sometimes doubt how much joy that is for them. The event usually occurs when a wild animal has been slain, or when girls and boys arrive at puberty. On such occasions old people and children decorate themselves with red clay and with feathers of wild birds. Men dress up with their various weapons (spears, bows and arrows, and bush knives). They then begin to spin around in circles to the beat of a drum that seems without rhythm to me. To a white person, listening to such "noise" for days on end is difficult. But to somehow take this joyous activity away from these people, without replacing it with something more substantial, embitters people towards the whites.

The missionaries try to provide a Christian joy for the villagers. This does not always succeed because in the process we also seek to separate people from the sinful aspects of their lives. It is evident that many turn away from Christianity because of their attraction to their old ways. Nevertheless, many followed our invitation to join us at the mission station on December 25. The 200 or so students had dressed and washed themselves decently while the villagers had decorated themselves in their traditionally festive way. There was plenty of room for all. Since the church building is too small for such occasions, we covered a large place in the yard with palm leaves, drew lines so people could sit on the ground in rows. In the middle of the yard we placed a table with books and musical instruments. We, white missionaries with our children, sat in chairs behind the table.

Margaret Siemens' Reflections

Margaret Siemens, who had arrived in Bololo late in

1936, reported that the wives of 15 of the workers at the mission received several yards of cloth to make themselves dresses. They received this before the gathering. Arthur, age three-and-a-half, explained to the ladies, in their language, why they received the gifts. He explained that the Savior from heaven had come to us as a gift from heaven. Then we went out to where the people were gathering on the yard.

Ms. Siemens reports that the turmoil of people was horrendous. Two 5-to 6-year-olds bit each other in the stomach till the mother of one of them took her son away. On the other hand, students' eyes looked radiant. "One can see," she said, "what the grace of God can do."

I began by telling everyone about the meaning of the event, and asked everyone to remain calm through the proceedings. First we played a song on the gramophone. Then the 200 member student choir sang the song, "Christ the Savior Is Here." The woods and the valley echoed with the Christmas cheer, but the blunted hearts of the people seemed to have no pleasure in our song. Some even laughed. Then we prayed and sang another song.

The main theme of the event was to present the Christmas story, along with Old Testament prophesy. A number of our best students had worked out appropriate applications to people's lives. They presented these in their free style. People could hear about the marvelous acts of God in their own language, but most remained deaf and dumb in their hearts. Poor souls, blinded by the devil, do not want to hear about sin and hell. When I asked, during the service, if there were any guilty people present, they all said, "No." Nevertheless, each one knows about his or her own guilty conscience.

We closed with a song. Only the students really understood it. They were fully involved with body and soul and understood the meaning of Christmas. For the others the whole event was like a distant thundercloud. We made arrangements with the believing students to give each person a present, a small gift. We did this so that each one would get some idea of what Christmas meant. These gifts were given regardless of status or rank. What people here cherish and long for most is salt. So everyone, oldest grandmothers to littlest tots, was given a cup of salt. We distributed four sacks of the stuff. Then they left for the village in groups, as they had come, with a lot of noise and commotion. No one said, "Thank you." Only our wonderful students had learned to say, "Thank you." They learned in their classes that neither earthly material nor heavenly gifts are seen as automatic by Christians.

As I consider the masses of people here that seem to show neither hunger nor thirst for the Word of God, I think of Romans 1:18-32. Whoever reads these writings, please pray that the Lord will send hunger upon this land for the living Word of God.

— Chapter 6 —

Adversities and Fatigue
1937

Help Arrives on Time

The arrival of Margaret Siemens in December 1936, could not have been more fortuitous. Her ship came to Djongo-Beach, where I picked her up myself. She is healthy and her baggage arrived safely too, that is, everything except the writing tablets for the students. She went right to work, learning the language and caring for my wife, Anna, in her last month of pregnancy. The Lord stood at our right side with her help. We had made plans for the delivery, in the event that no nurse would be here. We are very thankful that she could be present at the birth of our son, Karl, on January 28. My wife and the little Karl are doing well.

We were supposed to start school again tomorrow. Most of the students have arrived already but we do not have any writing tablets. The books we are preparing are not ready yet either. I am also busy renovating our living quarters located with the 200 students around us. We won't move the mission in the next year. We would lose too many students. Besides, the main road between Lodi and Djia is not finished because the government ran out of money.

Katherine Harder is supposed to arrive in a day or two. Our plan is for Ms. Harder and Ms. Siemens to begin work among the girls. When

Margaret Siemens, Mother, Arthur, and Lydia the day before Karl was born.

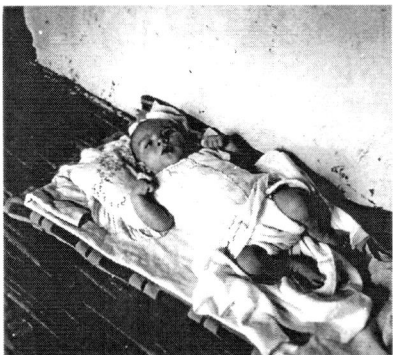
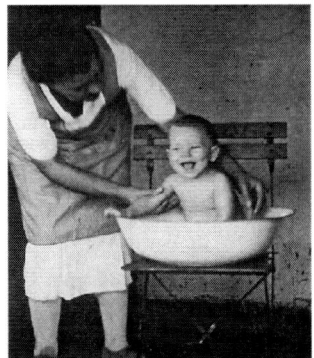

Karl, born January 28, 1937.   *Mother and Karl, 6 months.*

Ms. Siemens is ready to take on the work of the girls alone, Ms. Harder will take over all the work with the sick in the hospital. When I am not on some trip or other, I will help Mrs. Bartsch in the school. We feel a sense of hope in working with the 200 boys daily. It does, however, wear us out. But with an eye on the Lord and the year of furlough, we do what we can to bring these people light. Without your prayers we would not dare to do this work with 200 boys as they mingle with our four children. I can honestly say that people here both love and fear us. If this were not the case, then we would be in serious danger.

Our Family's Adjustment to the Congo

My health and that of the children is good. Perhaps the trip I took to Canada in 1934-35 renewed my strength. That is why I could wait for the furlough for several more years. In the wilderness especially, being cut off from all culture we have known, one gets very tired. I have not gotten to the point of relinquishing my own culture. I have a hard time adjusting to the wilderness here. I know that the Lord has sent me here to bring the good news to the people of the jungle, but if this region should, miraculously, become civilized overnight, I would have double the energy to do the work I am doing.

On February 20, I had to go to Dekese to register our newborn son, Karl. Because it is such a hassle to travel with the Dengese, I postponed the trip as long as I could. If you have never traveled through an African jungle, you cannot imagine when I say that it is a terrible thing that, in the 20th century, one has to wade through rivers and climb over mountains, often carried by others. I had to walk most of the way because even the bike had to be carried on a kipoy. Sometimes I could hardly stand it that the carriers puffed like locomotives, always waiting for an opportunity to take a break. It took us six hours to go from Jafa to Dekese. If you can imagine being without food, soaking wet, arriving in the village tired, hungry, finding neither bed nor food to eat, you know what I felt like.

On the way back I injured my left foot, so I could not walk. I had to take the long way around on the newly proposed roadway. I am sure that the people find it hard to put together my preaching of freedom and salvation when I put them through such ordeals.

When I met with the government official, we made glorious plans for the district, plans that would not come about for the next 10-15 years, if the Lord does not take us sooner. In spite of all the difficulties I will need to make several lengthy trips. It is as necessary

British Embassy in Dekese.

to me as breathing. Please pray for me regarding this.

Yesterday the carrier assistants came with a sack of flour. They came all the way from Port Francqui. I had provided them with a metal container to keep the flour from getting wet. When we opened the container a sour smell stunned our nostrils. Half the sack was soaked. My guess is that the sack got dropped into the water some-

Lydia is very sick, my parents are worried, and Erna is very sad.

place en route. I can't seem to get it through to the carriers that wet flour is useless to us. This is because their bread lies in water several days before it is ready to be eaten.

My wife's health is better now except for her teeth that give her a lot of pain and grief. We keep debating whether to have the teeth extracted before our furlough or to wait till we go. If we wait, she will experience a lot of pain. Brothers and sisters, please pray diligently for her in this condition. The Lord hears our prayers.

March 8, 1937

Katherine Harder returned on March 5. Her belongings came 14 days later. She ran short of money, but an American helped her out in Port Francqui. We had a special welcome for her. Students recited verses, King Ikongo-Samu was also present, but he did not say anything publicly.

We are saddened that the school supplies did not arrive. I had ordered unbreakable writing tablets. Now we see that the ones that arrived are rusted and totally unusable. So we adapt and have the lower classes write their words in the sand.

Church services are well attended. We separated the girls from the boys so that they could attend a little better. I spoke to the boys and Katherine Harder and Margaret Siemens led the girls.

We get together with the believers twice a week. Every so often someone who has been a believer, but has fallen away, returns. That is always a joyous event for us. Each morning and evening, we missionaries get together for worship, led by one of us. We often plead for patience and wisdom.

Six days ago, the wife of the Belgian Governor came to visit us. She stayed as our guest for a whole day. We don't know if the Governor sent her here to give us advice or to check on what we are doing. But she was very wise and gave us good advice. Among other things, Mrs. Rocquet said, "You are doing a lot of work. It is too difficult for two people to run the school. What will happen to the mission when your strength fails you? When will new missionaries come?"

Mrs. Rocquet with Karl.

Our health is still okay. Our children are well.

Reports by Katherine Harder and Margaret Siemens

After Katherine Harder arrived on March 5, 1937, she reported to Der kleine Africa Bote *on her trip and added that both Henry and Anna Bartsch were under considerable stress. She said they were happy in their work, but the strain in their faces was very evident. She also reported that the people had made a big shift in attitude. In contrast to her previous experience in Bololo, when no one seemed to understand what we were saying when we talked of the Lord, or when it was difficult to find anyone to help us in any way, now people were eager for more Bible stories. "I brought a Bible story book with pictures," she says. "When I began telling them about the pictures, they knew the end of the stories. Before when we showed them pictures, they only saw the colors in the pictures. They didn't distinguish between animals and people. Now they distinguish these. It is such a pleasure to see 200 boys in the school. The Lord has done marvelously in Bololo."*

On April 4, 1937, Margaret Siemens writes that Mrs. Bartsch does most of the translation work but has had malaria fever several times, so she looks very tired. *"She needs to go home,"* Margaret writes. *"But there is so much to do before night falls."*

Opposition to Our Work

Recently, we have begun to experience opposition from the Catholics. King Ikongo-Samu along with some of his men, came to get some of our students. Some of them were believers. The child of Mpembe Ndedji, the only believer with a wife at the mission station, was killed. The King heard him speak on Sunday as he made a very clear statement of his faith in Christ. By nightfall, his public declaration cost him his child. We know that we cannot appeal to the government official in a case like this. He just says, "Those are the customs of the Dengese people."

We began classes on March 15 with 175 students. Later there were 200. We were just in the flow of a successful school operation when the enemy appeared. The King appeared and took a lot our students to the Catholic school. It became hard to discipline our students. The 100 remaining students gave us trouble but they have accepted their punishment. The 100 students who left, come from neighboring villages. The Lord can restore things again.

King Ikongo-Samu.

My Recent Trip to Port Francqui

I had planned a trip to Port Francqui to get some business done. Since Katherine Harder's shipment was due to arrive at Basongo Beach on the Sankuru River on March 26, I planned to pick up her things as well. I also made plans to make this an evangelistic trip into the villages along the way. I left on the 25th and spent the night on the beach by the river. The riverboat arrived at 8 AM. I picked out Ms. Harder's belongings to send them to Bololo. The captain of the riverboat was very friendly. He offered and I accepted his invitation to ferry me, along with the things and carriers, to the other side of the river to Butala. My helpers were so impressed with the boat ride that they talked about it for a long time. My immediate assistant was so excited by the whole thing that he lost my coat. We found it later on. When we arrived at the other side, my carriers begged to be able to continue riding the riverboat. They didn't understand why. I practically drove them onto the shore. We walked to the village of Musungu. On the way, they talked excitedly about the excitement they experienced on the boat. It didn't even bother them that they had to sit next to the boilers on the boat.

In Musungu, people gathered from different tribes to do some work for a white businessman. The town chiefs were friendly. In the evening I got the workers together and explained the Good Friday stories from the Bible. They listened well and understood what I explained to them. My student assistants sang some songs and were surprised how much I could speak Kikongo. After the meeting, I discovered that many of the workers had been at other missions earlier. As I went to sleep, I heard songs that they had learned many years ago at the mission schools. I was impressed that these people, who came from many different tribes, who in past times would have attacked each other now, sang Christian hymns on Good Friday. I spent a long time gazing at the bright moon. I thought, *He gave himself for our sins. When will these poor people be given the message of release from captivity again? Maybe never!*

We went to Mongono early next morning. There I wanted to meet with a white man with whom I had corresponded. Sadly, he was not home. I went to a poorly attended meeting. Actually, the Lord is present where two or three are gathered.

On Easter Sunday morning we had a meeting at which I told the resurrection story. Then I got on my bike and let my assistant carriers bring the supplies. As I approached a rather large village, I noticed that a lot of people were going to a church service. The preacher came out to greet me. He was an American Presbyterian. He earnestly invited me to come to the service with him. I did and found a large congregation. After a welcoming introduction, he asked me to preach. I did. I spoke about the theme, "Why did Christ have to rise from the dead and why do so many people not have a living faith?" We had a lively discussion after the sermon. I was glad to have had the opportunity to talk to people about Jesus.

I then traveled on to Port Francqui where I did some important business.

I made my way back along the Sankuru River in order to visit other Dengese villages. I was able to share the Word of God in all villages except one. One student, who had previously been excluded from the group of believers, was a tremendous help to me.

Experiences in Bolombo

We arrived in Bolombo, a fairly large village. I thought of Bolombo's people as most unreceptive to God's Word.

Bolombo village has two parts separated by a field of high grass. Since I had had meetings at the one side of the village the previous time I was here, I decided to hold meetings on the other side this time. But, seemingly, no one was home except women and a few old men. With my student assistants, I sent word out that we would be holding a meeting. An old mother came fairly soon. She gave a number of reasons why I should go to the other side of the village. She said the men were all over there and, besides, there weren't enough people in this part of town to hold a meeting. I did not leave. I said we would hold a meeting when everyone had come out of their huts for the meeting. With that, the old woman shouted something, and people came out of their huts for the meeting. When I started to speak, the dear old mother said she could not understand my speech. I told her that one of my students would talk for me. Now they had no excuse, so I asked for calm. My student assistant, Bokiri, began with the creation, the fall, and promises of redemption. The young student made appropriate applications. He could explain salvation in Jesus Christ very well. Everyone listened intently. When Bokiri had finished, the dear old woman repeated everything that the student had said. I was amazed at her memory. When she finished, she said she wanted to be a friend of Jesus and not of the enemy. As we parted, she said she wanted to go to the other side of the village tomorrow to tell people what she had heard.

How good it would be, I thought, if people such as this lovely old mother, were taught so that they could minister to their own people.

My experiences in the other villages were similar to that in Bolombo. My carrier assistants had already made their way home. I got home on April 4 to see my loved ones.

Conditions Among the Dengese People

Give thanks to the Lord because He is gracious and His goodness endures forever. We close off the month of April with these words from a Psalm. We recognize that this language has no word for "Thank you." When someone recognizes that the other has good intentions, the Dengese says, "Ombonanba bolo." This means, "You have done well."

• Today we taught a man to say "Thank you." When he finally left he said, "I have done you well." He meant, "I have received your gift." This mentality is characteristic of the whole tribe. Romans 1:21 says this very clearly, "For though they knew God, they did not honor Him nor did they give thanks."

• In the last little while we have experienced the depth of people's depravity. A young girl, about 12, was recently brought to us. She had eaten some poison. (They offer the healthy girls to Satan as a sacrifice; we are supposed to awaken the dead.) Because the poison had been inside for so long, all attempts at rescue failed. The mother had begged to bring the girl in earlier, but there had been too many delays. The girl died. We know the man who gave the poison and also the kind of poison given but we can do nothing to help. That is the hardest thing to bear.

• Our nurses, Katherine Harder and Margaret Siemens, have been called on many times this month, to provide care for women in the villages. They get called when all hope of helping them by local methods has gone. Thank God, some women have been helped. For some, the help came too late. There is so much need and darkness among these people who are made in God's image! Often we pray with the prophet, "Guardian, is the night almost over?" Since we live only about a half-mile from the village, we hear people wailing about the death of loved ones. Often so many people die, one after another, so close in time that the death wails go on for days. Naturally that disturbs the students when they study. The good news of Jesus works only where faith has taken root.

• We have been able to teach about 95 students this month without interruption. The 100 students who in the previous year had been so eager, and had learned so much, left under pressure of the King. We taught the remaining 95 students some new songs. The translation of the Old Testament stories is progressing. We are up to the Fall of Jericho. The children pointed out to us that Rahab, through wisdom, had saved herself and her family but Achan, because of his lust for things, ended up in defeat.

• In spite of all the important discussions, there are some students who simply fall asleep. We simply let them dream on, since we cannot force them into life. That really bothered one student. Today he prayed that God would give him open eyes. We can usually tell during classes which students live a sober life and which are caught in their sin. God has given light and salvation to so many of the students. The child of truth will hear the voice of the shepherd.

• The believers have to face major trials. Many do not withstand the temptations and become very unhappy. Recently, some have returned after taking the wrong paths, and shared their stories. One such man had a very sore foot. As he sat in front of his hut, allowing others to treat his wounds, Erna, age 7, walked by and told him that he should really pray. God could help him. He said later that he "came to himself," that he had not been able to sleep that night. So he committed himself then and there to join the Lord and His people and became very happy in the Lord.

- One of the teachers confessed at the last prayer meeting that he had had a bitter fight with a fellow Christian. He asked us to pray that he would go on the right path. He knew that if he fell out of the experience of love, he could fall into sin. He has become happy again.
- A man was brought to us with deep wounds this morning before classes began. He has been opposed to the mission in the past. His son, who is antagonistic like his father, had driven a spear into his father's head. A son can kill his own father out of revenge. That is the way it is here.

We have let you see into our joys and successes, but perhaps have not let you see into our suffering and temptations. Maybe you don't need to see all our dark sides. Nevertheless here are some of them:

- Three students ran away again. The King does nothing about it. In fact, he may have helped the students to do so by enticing them to stay with the teachings of their fathers. He does not let us teach the girls either. He has decided, in council with the village leaders that the girls and women should do the work of the village. Although the children would gladly come, the older folks are cautious and warn the children not to go. Many girls die in the village. The medicine man uses them as offerings so that the white man cannot take them to teach them about Christianity.
- It is more difficult to enforce discipline in the school in the last few months since the King took the other students away. We seem to have returned to the state we were in at the beginning of our mission. We, however, serve these people at the call of Jesus.
- Of the many that we rescue from sure death, not one comes to say "Thank you." When Jesus healed the lepers, at

least one came back to say thank you. At least the other nine did not create trouble. Here those who are healed seek to keep their children from God's Word. The Lord will speak earnestly again.

• Our nurses, who have never been very strong, have a high fever again. One fever is followed very quickly by another. We have the right medicine to fight the fever. But the Lord knows the best solution. This morning Margaret Siemens' fever dropped.

• My wife Anna is back on her feet and is working hard at translating the Old Testament into Dengese. She is so anemic that she can hardly bear to take the quinine. We hope that the Lord will help us through this time. My health is good. The trip I took in 1934-35 was not a vacation but my body has appreciated the change in climate. How could we survive if I too were suffering with fever and anemia? The children are well and the oldest two help around the house. We are not discouraged.

A poem by Wilhelm Lehe expresses our attitude at this time.

What do I want?
   I want to serve!
Whom do I want to serve?
   The Lord's suffering and poverty ridden people.
And what is my reward?
   I serve for no reward or thanks
   I serve out of thankfulness and love;
   This is my reward: That I may serve!
What if I perish through all of this?
   "Then I perish! Then I perish!"
   So said Esther, who didn't know the One I know,
   The One, for love of whom, I might perish.
   But I know he will not let me perish.
And what if I grow old through all of this pain?
   My heart will blossom like a palm tree.
   The Lord will shade me with grace and pity.
   And I will live in peace without worry about anything.

Care for the Body and Care for the Soul

Earlier I wrote that the terrible physical condition of the Dengese people is what first greets the foreigner. This can overwhelm the missionary with pity to the point that it incapacitates him from carrying out his higher calling, namely to care for the soul. One must master the feelings of pity. Anyone who has been on the battlefield knows that medics are no good if they are too sensitive. The same principle applies here. We cannot mourn the fate of the person who is still living. When Dr. Pili came to visit us at Bololo the last time, he said, "My work as a physician is hopeless with these people. But at least you can do soul work." We seek to do both body and soul work as much as possible. We must meet the bodily needs in order to work with the soul, and the soul must be healthy if the body is to be healthy in the long run. A healthy soul lives in a healthy body and a healthy soul enhances a healthy body. That's what the physicians tell us. That is our experience here. So Africa does not need only physicians and nurses, but also people who can attend to the soul of the Dengese people.

To meet a person's soul needs, we need to earn the full trust of the patient. That is the most difficult task in the work of the missionary. The Dengese people will trust the white man with his bodily ailments fairly quickly, even though the white man knows little about physical care. The black man quickly promises to do what the white man instructs him to do. But to open up his soul, or to trust the white man, that is another matter. The inner life of the Dengese people and their inner needs are kept hidden. It is guarded and watched over very carefully. That's why it is so hard to learn the language of the Dengese people because that is how the soul of the people is exposed. Those who have become believers tell us now how the older people punished them if they gave us the right words for things we asked of them.

Everyone here knows that the soul is invisible and that it lives on after the body dies. That is why all kinds of objects and pieces of clothing are thrown into the grave when a person dies. One set of parents were very distressed because they could not drop any money into their dead daughter's grave. I saw how distressed these poor people were and gave them some money so that they could put it into the grave of their daughter. The parents breathed a sigh of relief and then gave us the exceptional privilege of going to the graveside with them. If the dead person is not provided with enough supplies for the beyond, then, after evaluation of the soul-searcher, the soul of the departed rises up and tortures the relatives on earth. These spirits usually arrive at night and choke the living till morning breaks. We often hear screams from the village, half a mile away, that awaken us in the night. It is very difficult to undo the evil on earth. If a person has not been reconciled with the dead person, the living person bears a curse that can drive him to insanity. Even when two living persons quarrel, everyone seeks to bring them together so that the dead spirits will not implant their rage in them. Dances and drinking parties are there to anesthetize the needy souls. The white person can sense the meaning of words when the black man sings, but seldom do you get the real meaning directly from spoken words.

The Dengese people appear happy only in a group. When they are alone, they are sad and unhappy. When a black man finds himself in the forest alone, fear and terror grips his soul. Every sound is a signal from the spirits of the deceased. Since so many of them have guilty consciences, they take messages from the "other side" as threats.

It is difficult to work in this climate. We experience this often when we talk to those who have come to the faith. Even though they believe in Christ, it does not mean that they are free from superstitions and the belief that spirits inhabit nature. Our task is to help the young people differentiate between the fundamental assumptions of Christianity and of their heathen heritage. Their heritage is filled with fear and despair under the control of the prince of darkness. It is being in the world without God and without hope that drinks from the pool of lies and witchcraft. Christianity is the experiential assurance from the conqueror of all forces and powers of darkness, namely Jesus

Christ. The more our young Christians learn to grow into the knowledge of the son of God, the more all aspects of life will be pervaded by the spirit of Jesus Christ. The spiritual release of the "old person" and the spiritual acceptance the "new person" takes as long as the growing up of a child. Let us continue to pray and act on behalf of these people that they may be rescued from their spiritual needs. The Lord can give us understanding in all things.

Last week I wrote that a fever had broken out among us. Now all of us are past that. The fevers have left us. My wife, Anna, had the fever first and recovered when she took the medicine. But now she is anemic. She can walk but is weak. She does the housework and is back at translation work. Katherine Harder and Margaret Siemens got sick about the same time. Ms. Harder had a fever of 101-102. I was up four nights to help her through the night. Ms. Siemens and my wife Anna could look after themselves. On top of that, our little son got the measles but has recovered from that, too. That was quite a week.

In spite of all of this we did not close the school. Everything went well. Only the singing seemed to suffer. I can't help with that part. Ms. Harder is now free of fever.

The climate has turned very dreary. The students count on the dry season coming. There are another 14-20 days till the end of school. I plan to do some travelling then.

The Africa Committee Reports on Replacements

Two couples, one from Canada and one from Germany, were selected by the Afrika Verein to replace Henry and Anna Bartsch. In August 1937, Hermann and Tina Lenzmann prepared to leave Canada. Churches in Winnipeg had departure celebrations. Maria and Karl Kramer had similar departure celebrations in Wiedenest, Germany. Although Henry and Anna felt increasing fatigue, they felt optimistic that their replacements would arrive soon.

July 20, 1937

Some Trials We Experience Here

I have told you of the difficulties we have experienced recently. I told you that the King had the infant son of our leading teacher killed. This was a difficult time for the teacher. But his faith withstood the trial. But then his relatives took his wife to the village, where they compelled her to practice the old customs. As difficult as this was for the dear brother, he continued in the faith, continued to teach in the school and in the preaching of God's word. After we dismissed the students and teachers for vacation, the secret society from the village persuaded the same dear brother to renounce his faith. This was a heavy blow for us. We continue to hope that the Lord will claim victory, even in the enemy's camp. We don't know why our newly begun work is tested so severely so soon; we do not know. Other missions seem to experience these onslaughts after ten or so years. But the onslaughts must come!

On Saturday we met with the believers in Bololo for a prayer and testimony meeting. We heard a number of moving testimonies. We were especially saddened to learn that Basongo, the lad that had worked in our house for three years, who had come to the faith, was forbidden by his father to attend. He is planning to get married and so must comply with all the practices of the village. If he does not comply, he cannot get married, which is a great shame for the Dengese people.

We still have no girls in the school. Katherine Harder is to take over the hospital work again in the last half of this year. I have seen about 1200 patients this year. I do not treat women's concerns or severe injuries.

Last week the Lord put me down. I was very sick. I had a tropical fever for 62 hours. Since I was in such pain, we were fortunate that the medical doctor was nearby and came to my aid. Now I am well again. Malaria is a terrible illness. We plan to take the long delayed trip to Luebo in August. We want to save what can be saved here. Thanks for your prayers and support.

June 1937: Dad's Sermon

I greet you with the verse from Matthew 10:16: "I send you as sheep among wolves. Therefore be clever as the snake but harmless as doves." We have never experienced the truth of these words of Jesus as much as we have now. We didn't understand the length and depth of our Lord's call when we made the decision to go into the mission field, as we do now. The Lord permits us to see into the depths of Satan's world only to the extent, at any given hour, that we can tolerate it. I marvel at the goodness of the Godly wisdom available for his children! The verse I quoted seems most appropriate for us today. It contains Jesus' command unmistakably, and simultaneously clarifies the character of the messenger and the spirit of the heathen. Jesus' command to his disciples is very clear. Even an uneducated person can understand it. The one who doubts the words, "I am sending you," or who misreads the command, or turns away from it, does so at his own peril.

Jesus sent His disciples to do mission work. The disciple must go, without asking what the result of going will be. We are not responsible for the results of the work. Only the Lord is responsible.

It doesn't matter where the disciples actually go themselves, or simply enable others to go. Whether the messenger hears, "Come over and help us," or "Why have you come to torture us," does not matter. What matters is that the messenger hears the word, "Obedience is better than sacrifice."

When Jesus uses the term "sheep" or "lambs" He describes the methods that the messenger must use, namely with the intelligence of snakes and the faithfulness of the dove. He did not mean to stifle His disciples spiritually by referring to them as sheep. But He did mean they were to have qualities of relinquishment, dedication and readiness to follow. Jesus has never uttered a spiritually restrictive phrase. In contrast, He asks, "Why don't you understand?" If spiritual development is necessary anywhere, it is needed among the wild people that literally eat each other up. I would sink into chaos if I did not love to read books and was not interested in spiritual matters. I would lose myself in trivial matters and get enraged by little things. It is our experience that piety is no shield to despair. We need to be spiritually grounded.

By using the example of the sheep, Jesus means to tell us that we are to serve without external supports. In the past century, mission work has relied on the power of the state and the power of money to evangelize and pilfer heathen people. I am no spiritualist dreamer who goes into the mission field and ignores every governmental control and every missionary organization. We live in the realities of government and organizational structures. In these we rely "Not through power or might but through my Spirit, says the Lord" (Zechariah 4:6).

On the other hand, mission work done with the power of the state (colonial powers), that Christianizes large districts of people with financial power are now in difficult straits. They have large numbers of baptized "heathen-Christians." One needs only to read the mission and church reports that come from abroad. What becomes even more evident when one meets such "Christians" directly is that everything but the Spirit of God governs their lives. We are saddened to read in these reports that many baptized believers have been put out of the church. The missionaries wanted so badly to believe that they had been converted and so they baptized them. We cannot allow ourselves to be blinded by native people who have been in the depths of Satan's grip for these thousands of years.

It is wrong for us to seek to tally large numbers of believers so that we get more support from you in the homeland. That is why Jesus has commanded us to have the intelligence of the serpent and the faithfulness of the dove. These must go together. Without wisdom from above, nothing works well among the heathen; and without faithfulness, intelligence is a curse. When the devil cunningly seeks to disturb the work of God, we need to be clever like a snake paired with wisdom from above. To do this the missionary must become even more faithful in prayer, in self-evaluation, close to the truths in the Scripture. Then we need the advice of our brothers and sisters at home. We need your prayers and words of encouragement. The messenger must be smart and faithful enough even when he cannot report massive following from the field.

Many of the difficulties of young Christians weigh heavily on us. If we report only successes, we would not be faithful to the truth. We see the boundaries of our efforts and also the boundaries of our presence. If that were not the case, we would become proud. If we only report successes, your prayers would likely diminish, to the detriment of the work we are doing and we would experience greater frailty. We are really only very weak vessels. This is to say we need your prayers on our behalf, your wisdom and intelligent response and faithfulness. So please do not let up in your support for us. We require more than our own strength to be among wolves. Our Lord says, "Ask and you shall receive...."

The Lord sent his disciples among wolves. Actually that is an insufficient term for this situation. Wolves are not dangerous animals here, but leopards are. When the Lord sends us we should read "leopards" instead of wolves. That would characterize our situation among the Dengese. The King has the leopard as a symbol of his power. I had to bring him a symbol of a leopard from Germany. Leopard skins adorn the King's council chamber. His council members and advisors have leopard skins draped around themselves or on their heads. A man who was attacked by a leopard in the forest, and was fortunate enough to be able to kill the leopard, was brought to trial by the King. He was put in prison and was soon found dead. He did not belong to the King's secret society and so had betrayed the soul of the leopard. The belief is that if someone dies through one of the secret society's members, that person enters a leopard's body. Members of high rank of the "leopard society" turn into leopards in the dark night and then kill people, goats and dogs.

Last week we had a lot of excitement. We woke up one morning to discover that one of our milk goats was slaughtered. We noticed the bloody tracks of the leopard around the fence. The leopard had jumped over the six-foot fence, dragged the goat into the nearby field, and eaten a large portion of it. When I noticed the tracks of the leopard around the fence the next morning, I decided to hide behind a cover and shoot the leopard. We did not think of a human leopard, but of a small leopard from the forest. I waited for the leopard for two nights with my rifle, with no luck. No leopard appeared. I was sorry that the Lord did not give me this opportunity to shoot a leopard. Then we discovered that it was not a wild animal at all that had killed the goat. We discovered that a man from the village of Bololo transformed himself into a leopard at night on a regular basis. He killed goats and dogs and ate them. I was thankful that God did not let me shoot the man. And I was happy to have sat up two long nights. That's how things go here.

Students have tried to persuade me that human beings can be transformed into wild animals. All my arguments against that were useless, even among believers. They say people can make it rain, can call down lightning onto certain people, and many other things. When we say that God is the only almighty one, the old and young ridicule us. I don't know what the outcome would have been, had I shot that "Leopard-man." No doubt we would have been in even greater conflict with the King than we are now. He may have sent us the "Leopard-man."

We believe that the seed we have sown here will bear fruit but we don't know if we will see it in our lifetime. Our believers are so weak and so dependent on the influence of the village. When the relatives notice the changes in their children after coming here, they do anything to influence and control their children. God's word gets presented and explained as much as little minds can understand. We notice again and again how far we fall short of making appropriate applications of the gospel. Nevertheless, the 100 youth that we have in school are the only field in which we can sow the seed. In other missions, the focus is on the establishment of faith communities. Their pioneer work was done 30-40 years ago. Practices that are commonplace here, are no longer even considered in those other tribes.

Nevertheless, we are thankful that the period of grace is here and that salvation can be brought to the Leopard-people. We don't know how long we will have the opportunity to do this.

We close out the school at the end of this month. It was a difficult year. But we kept at it and had classes with about 100 students. In the Bible Study curriculum we have gotten to the reign of King David. We have also studied the Mennonite catechism in most of the classes. We often tell ourselves that we have sown God's seed here and that people could believe if they wanted to. Students have also made good progress in reading, writing and arithmetic. The beautiful songs, too, that contain the pure gospel can only be a blessing to people here. The Lord has also preserved us from serious illness. That could have disrupted our teaching schedules.

Mother's Medical Condition

After the delivery and early months of care for the infant, Mother's health continued to deteriorate. They decided to seek medical help from the medical facility in Luebo. She writes about her travel to Luebo as follows.

Mother's Report [40]

On August 17, 1937, we were on our way to the dentist in Luebo. We left our children in the care of Margaret Siemens and Katherine Harder who had returned to the mission in the meantime. We made it to Mweka. After that I could not continue on the kipoy. We managed to get a two-wheeled cart with a chair in the middle and two long poles on either end. One man pulled, the other pushed the cart along. We came to the forest where there was only room for

---

[40] Anna Bartsch, *The Hidden Hand*, p. 163, translated by Arthur Bartsch.

one vehicle. Suddenly, out of the dark, a large truck with bright lights glaring appeared directly in front of us. Paralyzed with fright, the men heaved the entire carriage with me in it onto their shoulders and just stood there, frozen. I couldn't tell them to do a thing, so I climbed down and pulled the whole contraption off the road, allowing the monster to crawl by. They had never seen such a beast. They just stood there, dumbfounded, and didn't say a thing. I laughed. My presence of mind calmed their nerves. I stepped into the vehicle again, and slowly and carefully, they continued on the journey. Understandably, this was not their world, and they felt very uneasy in it. They told and retold this story amongst themselves as they sat by their fires. I arrived for the appointment with the doctor in Luebo.

In the hospital at Luebo they pulled all my teeth. After a month I was allowed to leave, but only because Dr. Poole would be going along with us to Dengese. Dr. Poole wanted to see the land and the people there.

September 26, 1937: Report on Our Condition

I am writing this report about our situation here.

We returned from Luebo two days ago, where my wife had all her teeth extracted. This was very necessary because her mouth was highly infected. We didn't have an opportunity to get there sooner. She will remain without teeth because we don't know, at present where she will get a set of false teeth. Since we were in Luebo, where medical attention was available, she had a general physical exam. This is so that we are not dependent on our general impressions and expectations. Dr. Stirrund, an elderly gynecologist, did the examination. He was very clear on his recommendations: To recover, my wife should leave the tropics immediately for at least a year. He said she needed a major operation or she would be in great danger. He insisted that the medical procedure be completed within six months. This is not something that could be done in Luebo because her blood levels were too inadequate and the infection from the teeth had spread too widely.

Dr. Poole, a young doctor and a man of faith, brought us to Lodi with his car. It was dark when we arrived at Djongo Beach on September 14. It was dark and the men wanted to stay overnight but my wife felt anxious and wanted to get home. So we continued in the dark, through jungle and grassland for three hours until we arrived at home in Bololo at 10:30. The Lord had led us to press on. At home little Karl lay deathly sick with a high fever. He probably would have died had not Dr. Poole been there. Not even bothering to take off his jacket, the doctor prepared an injection and gave the nine-month-old child a shot of quinine. Every minute was critical. The Lord leads in wonderful ways.

We have concluded the following regarding my wife's health and our work here. We will keep you informed of the way things are here. We will continue the work here as well as we are able till the new missionaries get here. Then we can introduce them to the relationships we have here and to the language. Then we will return to Europe, and then Canada. We would most like Professor and Doctor D. Olpp, in Tubingen, Germany, to treat Anna, though we don't know if that will be possible. There are people in Germany who will financially underwrite the false teeth for my wife. They have made that offer some time ago.

October 27, 1937: Mother's Condition

My wife is getting weaker every day in combating tropical ailments. Above and beyond that, a mark on her face has appeared which the doctor suspects is cancer. Knowing this we plan to leave the mission field at the start of the New Year. If further tests in Europe should prove our suspicions of cancer to be correct then we shall consider our work here to be done. We have undertaken it in faith and in love for Him who has forgiven our sins and had called us as witnesses into Africa. We leave to God what we have ventured in faith. I have resolved the question within myself that God is taking charge of the Ark of the Covenant. The Lord is holding the Dengese people in His hands, and that is enough for me. On the basis of a strong recommendation of the physician and our people on the mission field I shall undertake our trip to Europe with my family in the New Year.

Some Remarkable Events on the Mission

The Lord continues to work at our mission in some amazing ways, in spite of all that has gone on with our health. After the King did all he could to disrupt our mission, his wife got very sick. Katherine Harder was called and was helpful to her. This seemed to change his attitude completely. The damage he did to the souls of the believers can't be undone. Many have fallen into the hands of Satan and his henchmen. But a new beginning is possible. This is certainly easier, given the King's positive attitude towards us.

Then the King's wife died. She had apparently gotten up too soon. Dr. Poole, who was with me when I met the King the next day, said that her life could have been saved if he had come a day sooner. We thought that the King would turn against us again, since his wife had died. But that was not the case. He asked me to raise his dead wife's infant on the mission station. When I accepted the child, he promised all kinds of help.

Margaret Siemens Writes About the Same Incident[41]

September 1937, was a very eventful month for us. Mr. and Mrs. Bartsch left on August 17, so Katherine Harder and I stayed with the four Bartsch children. Soon we received a message from the King that his wife was very ill and that Katherine should come immediately. I stayed with the four children. The children said repeatedly, "We feel abandoned." Little Karl then got a fever and then Arthur. They older ones prayed so heartfelt for their parents and for Katherine Harder. Katherine came back in two days, pleased that she had been helpful to the King's wife and that she was recovering.

The King was very thankful and promised to send girls from the village to our school if we wanted them. Soon his servants brought us 26 girls. We began immediately to have classes for them each morning. The servants who brought them are eligible for marriage so they did not bring all the girls that had been sent. They said they wanted some to become their wives. Men have many wives. The number of girls at the mission rose to 41. We have to carefully oversee them and urge all the girls from the village of Bololo to come. There are 92 girls in the village altogether. They are eager to come here but the older folks do not want them to come.

Brother and Sister Bartsch came back happily on September 14. Fortunately Dr. Poole came along. The little Karl had a fever again. Dr. Poole was very helpful. Now the fever has gone.

Dr. Poole and Brother Bartsch went on a trip on September 18. They wanted to meet the King and Dr. Poole wanted to see the land and the people. On Sunday they heard that the King's wife had died. We were very sorry that she had not come to the mission to get help. We became afraid that the King would take the girls away again and so waited eagerly for Brother Bartsch's story. Then the rumor reached us that the King wanted to send his child to Katherine for her to take care of. We couldn't believe it, because the Dengeses do not give up their

---
[41] *Der kleine Africa Bote*, October 1937.

children. Then suddenly we saw Sister Bartsch come with a baby in her arms. People watched in amazement. What would we do with the baby? As the story unfolded, it turned out that Brother Bartsch had advised the King to bring the child to the mission so that it would get whole milk. Everyone watched as we gave the infant a bottle of milk.

The infant was restless the last few nights. It had a stomach trouble but it got better soon. The child's grandmother came every day to see what we would do with the child. The first night she wanted to have the child herself, but the King had expressly ordered that we should not give it to any of the women.

On Monday, 12:30 PM, I came back from the place where all the girls stayed. The child had not slept well at night, so Katherine had lain down with the little baby. All was quiet. I looked up and noticed that several servants came rushing to the house. I thought that the King had sent us more girls, but the servant girls asked about the baby. They wanted to see it. We brought it for them to see and they begged to hold it. We resisted because they were so dirty. One of them was so bold as to grab the child. She then ran down to the village. We knew that they would want to kill the child and screamed at them to stop but they kept running. We told the Bartsches immediately. Brother Bartsch got on his bike and retrieved the little child. This little "princess" really stirred us up. My, how thankful we are to have saved another life. The male students now tell us that the girl should die because the mother has died and because it is the firstborn. What superstition and dreariness these people have to live with! We are much more careful now and do not show it to others. We had the audacity to give her a name. Her name is Maria.

When Replacements Come

This is what can happen when the Lord intervenes. People are very friendly towards us again. But whether we stay in Bololo is questionable. We have to move to a less remote area. When the Lenzmanns come, we will move at the advice of the Governor. The road from Bololo to Dekese and Djia will soon be complete. The

Governor has already received funds to build that road. Sooner or later the people need to come out of their hidden villages and connect to the outside world. We have spread a lot of God's seed here. Maybe we or others will harvest the fruit. Christians here are certainly going through difficult trials and we are scared for many of them.

Two days ago our replacements, the Lenzmanns, arrived here. They are healthy as is their daughter Mary. Today I went to the next village, a distance of about 8 kilometers, with Brother Lenzmann, where I preached to the villagers.

Everyone here is healthy except for my wife. We are grateful for the well wishes you have sent with the Lenzmanns. We have felt encouraged by your prayers.

Brother Lenzmann, Mary Emma, Sister Lenzmann, Mother, Karl, Margaret Siemens, Maria, Katherine Harder.

Maria, age 13.

October 21, 1937: Update on Our Condition

We gather from your most recent letter that you are very concerned about us. That is a sign of our close relationship with you. Right now we are seeking to guide the mission to a place where it has a stable future. The Lenzmanns are learning the language and seemingly are making good progress. The Governor is pressing us to move our mission, so I can hardly ask him for workmen to rebuild our buildings here. The roadway from Bolombo to Josa to Dekese is supposed to be finished this year. We should be closer to that roadway.

Given the complications of moving, I cannot do that along with getting new students started and introducing the Lenzmanns to the running of the school at the same time. It is better that I introduce Herman Lenzmann to building procedures and then move to Josa where everything can be arranged better. We want to make the Lenzmanns' entry to the work as easy as possible. We have prayed a lot about this matter.

The girls from the village are still here. I don't think we will be able to keep the girls in the school if we move to Josa. Although, on second thought, it is possible if the Governor supports the move.

Katherine Harder continues to care for the King's daughter. She is quite taken with the child. She also homeschools our children. The King seems to be in a good mood these days.

Now to our personal circumstances! My wife is getting weaker all the time. Her body fights off tropical diseases less and less. In addition, doctors think they detect cancer in part of her body. They have not told us this directly, but have mentioned it to others who have passed it along to us. Now that we know this, we plan to leave the Mission after the New Year. If the suspicion of cancer is confirmed in Europe, then our work in Africa is complete. We did it in faith and out of love for our Lord, who forgave us our sins and called us to be witnesses for Him in Africa. The outcome of the work that we have begun is the Lord's concern, not ours. The Lord used us to build the foundation among the wild Dengese people. It often reminds us of Nehemiah's building of the temple in Palestine. We are confident and look up, from where help for my wife must come, whether it is to suffer or to be healed and to serve. Your intercession strengthens us. You took on our support when we were healthy. You will not desert us when we suffer deep pain. With best wishes from the other brothers and sisters here we remain in fellowship with you.

October 1937: Katherine Harder's Report[42]

We are happy that the Lenzmanns arrived. The carriers brought their belongings but much of what they brought was soaking wet. They needed to learn patience immediately and not get too attached to their things.

Mrs. Bartsch is very preoccupied with the translation of the Biblical stories. Margaret Siemens trains and teaches the girls. It is not easy to keep them here, since the parents do everything they can to get them to go back to the villages. The Lord has arranged for us to have a little baby, the King's daughter. The little child is growing well, so the King is very much in favor of the mission. We are very grateful that the Lord has arranged matters in this way.

One day the King came to us with a little girl from the neighboring village. He asked us to tell the girl to be his wife. We asked him how many wives he presently had. He said three. We said that the Scripture says a man should have one wife. He was not impressed and took her away. The King's son finagled the girl away and brought her to the mission. Her face beamed as she came to us. She was also glad to get away from that old man. How we long to help the girls get free of their servitude to the men. We have no idea of what kind of sin and degradation these girls have experienced before they come to us.

Someone recently brought us a little boy who was only skin and bones. He couldn't even swallow. We put a tube down his throat and poured milk down. He is recovering.

As I write this, Mr. Bartsch has a very high fever.

November 7, 1937: Travel with Brother Lenzmann

Last week Brother Lenzmann and I took a trip through some of the neighboring villages. The carriers rebelled in the

---
[42] *Der kleine Africa Bote*, October 1937.

next town, so we had to stay in that village overnight, even though we were only an hour from home. I felt a fever coming the next morning. Now we realized why we had to return home. The Governor had died, so we would not have accomplished anything, even if we had traveled on. He had bronchitis. Now we also know why there seemed to be a state of anarchy here for the past six months. Now we cannot begin a new school, nor can we get men to help us build a new mission. Everything depends on the attitude of the administrators and they are beholden to the Catholics. We ask for help to build the mission in Josa, but are told that we need to get the Governor's approval. We notice that the Catholics have sent a teacher to Josa. We will go there and see what can be done. The Lord can help us.

Reports indicate that, since 1931, Catholics have tripled in number. The Catholic missions have received instruction to set up missions wherever Protestants want to begin a new mission or where their number is small. They call themselves the National Belgians to get special privileges from the Belgian government. We are told that there are two-and-a-quarter million Catholics, one million Protestants, and eleven million heathen in the Belgian Congo.

November 25, 1937: Last Travels

I went to Dekese with Brother Lenzmann to arrange several matters for the mission and to introduce my replacement to travel here. On the way we heard that the District Commissioner was to arrive in Dekese. When we arrived, we discovered that the honorable Commissioner was to arrive the next day. That was our real fortune because it is not so easy to stay in Dekese a long time. We greeted the Commissioner when he arrived, and he promised us a half hour to tell him our situation. This happened very soon and so we were able to tell him about our mission. We left the next morning happy that we had accomplished our purpose. We held a number of gatherings, both on the way to and from Dekese. We were quite surprised that about twenty believers from various denominations took part in our services in Dekese. They even asked us if we would baptize them but we declined because we did not know how seriously they really took their faith.

When we returned to the mission in Bololo everyone seemed to be in an uproar. After Governor Rocquet died, all his misdeeds got published. One of these was the plan to destroy our Peniel Mission. In marvelous ways the Lord heard our prayers. We are very thankful. There are 125 students in the classrooms, hard at work. Now we can introduce the Lenzmanns to the practical sides of running the school. The new Governor will visit us soon. The former students are expected to return soon as are a number of girls from the villages. We are not sure who will teach the girls but perhaps it will be Katherine Harder. Her strength is returning.

My wife is very concerned about teaching the new missionaries the language and translating the essentials so that the work can progress when we are gone.

We are thankful that you give us so much leeway to handle things as we see fit. My wife is eager to go home. The women are sewing things for the trip. Our children are all well and bring us much joy. I am sad to leave here.

We have seriously prayed about the present situation. Everyone is convinced that Mrs. Bartsch is not strong enough to go home alone. Since we learned that she needs an operation, I have given up the notion that I could stay here. It became clear to me that God carries the Ark of the Covenant and that He does not need people for that. If the Lord wants to, He can bring us back here soon. If the Lord wants to bless the work here through others then we want to step aside. The Lord has His hand in the work among the Dengese people. That is enough for me. Your prayers and support encourage us to take the trip to Europe. Thank you for the love you show us.

December 9, 1937: Some Parting Comments

Much has changed since we wrote last month. The Lenzmanns have been here for about two months. They began with the study of the language. They made good progress. Also I am amazed how well they have adapted to the circumstances here. Mrs. Lenzmann works in the kitchen of the girls' residence and helps my wife as much as she can to get things ready for the trip. She also planted a garden. They will live in this house when we leave. Mr. Lenzmann has reviewed operations at the school, how to keep order and school discipline. He seeks to step into my shoes so that the work goes on unhindered.

Katherine Harder is sick again. She seems to get better for several weeks and then breaks down. She says this has always been her condition.

Margaret Siemens is not too well either. She is presently working with the girls. These are the ones sent by the King. They are the ones that arrived on the morning in August when we went to see the doctors in Luebo. I could not get enough commitments from the parents. Everything went too fast. We couldn't get their names and ages, etc. Many of them ran away. Last week about 40 returned and are committed to stay.

The Commissioner has asked us not to move from Bololo. He has ordered all the students to return. He has paddled, in a fatherly way, the ones who created the trouble. They have all come now and have promised to be obedient. He has also threatened the medicine man in the village. We are operating at full capacity since November. We will work together till into the New Year and then, we wish for all the best.

At the urging of the doctor, the Governor, and our brothers and sisters here, I will take my family to Europe on January 11, 1938. The ship is the *D. Wegrei.* It should arrive in Hamburg on February 5. We expect to come to Canada in May and can discuss everything with you then.

The Kramers (from Germany) wrote to us to say that they are on the way here. Too bad we could not meet with them here. We will pass them on the high seas. We were quite concerned about the future, about a lot of things here, but have become settled regarding these matters, too. The work will likely suffer at first, but then it will likely be done better than we could do it.

Farewell to Bololo: Mothers Comments[43]

    On December 29, 1937, we stepped aboard a small boat at Djongo Beach on the Sankuru River. The boat would take us to Port Francqui where a larger boat would take us down the Kwilo and finally down the Congo to Leopoldville. After seven days' journey we arrived in Leopoldville and found a friendly reception in the Salvation Army. We had to leave our parrots there. They could jabber like the girls and laugh like them so that we were often fooled. They used to call out the names of our children, a feature they retained while they stayed at the Salvation Army – so we were told many years later. On January 12, 1938, we took the steamer "Tanganika" to Hamburg, Germany. A day before we were to land, the sea began to get very rough. As we headed up the Elba estuary the captain feared that if the coal would shift in the storage bins the ship might not be able to right itself again. Port holes were smashed, dishes crashed on the floor. Finally, after 24 hours the storm began to die down, and we could land in Hamburg. It was February 11, 1938.

    Some people we had never met, the Paul Kempfers, met us at the dock and took us in till we could find a place to stay. I, Anna Bartsch, participated in a hospital recovery program.

---

[43] Anna Bartsch, *The Hidden Hand*, p. 173, translated by Arthur Bartsch.

Mother and Dad in Germany.

Bartsch family in Germany, 1938.

Karl, age one.

Erna, Lydia, and Arthur were taken to different homes while Karl and Henry and I stayed at the Kempfers. Henry was invited to speak in a variety of churches and organizations. He received a great response in reporting that the natives of the primeval force of Africa were reaching out for God. One printer, who would not disclose his name, printed all the materials, such as the Bible stories of the Old Testament (65 in all) which I had translated

into the Dengese dialect. He produced a hundred copies, and we sent them to Africa to the Bololo mission.

Germany was clearly preparing for war. Jews were persecuted. Henry had to convince authorities that he was not Jewish.

After the listing of the children the document reads, "Whether the parents are Aryan has not been proven. He reports himself to be a Mennonite. Mennonites are pure Aryan, historically."

We arrived in Halifax in May, and arrived in Winnipeg, Manitoba, Canada, on June 8, 1938. We were greeted and warmly received by the committee members.

— Chapter 7 —

Furlough and Recovery
1938-1939

June 28, 1938: Reflections About Our Work in Bololo

I greet you with Romans 14:7-9:

"We do not live to ourselves and we do not die to ourselves. So whether we live or die, we are the Lord's."

It has been five months since we have left our place of work to make our way to Canada. We have had a string of heavy, hot and cold days, but we were always surrounded by loving friends or enemies. Often we experienced danger and recovery from danger in such rapid succession that it was difficult to adjust either within or without. When we review the past five months, we are compelled to say that our sorrow and pain was carefully meted out by our Lord and master. He knew our condition and knew what we needed to become His witnesses. This Lord who loves us so much is the One we want to serve in a manner that pleases Him, whether at home or abroad.

I begin in Bololo where we had our assignment. (As you know, we settled there in February 1933, when the mission project was founded.) We were quite settled in Bololo but the physical health of my wife continued to deteriorate in the last year. We had to seriously consider a trip to Europe or Canada. Many in Africa and abroad prayed to heaven on our behalf. Many gave us advice and financial support.

We were greatly relieved when Katherine Harder and Margaret Siemens received the support of Brother and Sister Lenzmann. They came from Canada as your representatives. Our greatest sorrow and source of stress was that we had such a brief time to introduce the new missionary couple to important relationships here, to the way of life and to the learning of the language.

We considered various options. Everyone, both here and at home, was of one mind: We should leave with the family as quickly as possible to get medical help in Europe and Canada.

Everything was ready after Christmas 1937. We had a farewell service in the church with our beloved students, who had been with us for such a long time and who had heard the Word of God so often. We made many requests and gave warnings to students and workers. Many prayed for us. Our concern was that our replacements be able to carry on the work of the school in our absence. The six teachers could certainly do excellent service in the school. On December 30, 1937, we boarded the riverboat at Djongo Beach.

Herman Lenzmann and Katherine Harder, along with fifty boys from the school, accompanied us to the Sankuru River. When the riverboat finally came, our hearts beat heavily. The time of departure from the Dengese people had arrived. Katherine Harder and the fifty boys continued to wave handkerchiefs till we could see them no more. It must have been hard for her to be left alone in the African wilderness. And yet, it had been very different than it had been six years earlier when we landed at the same spot from which we now departed. At that time, the blacks fled in panic at the sight of the white person. Now many cried as we left. Many asked us to pass on greetings to their brothers and sisters abroad who had carried the weight of the mission.

After seven days on the Sankuru, then the Kwilo and then the mighty Congo Rivers, we arrived in Leopoldville. On January 12, 1938, we boarded the *Tanganika*, a passenger ship from Australia. The ship was headed for Hamburg, Germany.

Once aboard the ship we had a lot of time to reflect, not only on the year 1937, but on the seven years of mission work in Africa. It had been seven years earlier that we had landed at the same place that we now left. Now we had to leave the land that we had learned to love so much. So much had happened! When we arrived we were filled with fire and energy to witness for our Lord. We made our way into the depth of the African jungle.

Our Approach to Mission Work in Bololo

We had a false impression of the African people at that time. We had thought they were cruel. I thought that the gods of the people were like Moloch, the god of the Philistines who stretched out his arms to mothers to throw their living children into a body of fire. But I found out differently. My prejudices were not true. I could find no gods. There was no temple either. The people did not seem as hostile as I had imagined. Also, I could *not* sense that people sought Jesus or peace for their souls.

I remember a picture that I saw when I was a teenager. It had a missionary stepping off the ship, holding up a cross and natives kneeling down in prayer. This image in no way matched my experience in Africa.

Reality was quite different. "Heathenism" was different than I expected. When people sought salvation, this too, was different than I expected. The central themes of what we call "heathenism" are fear, deceit and lack of knowledge. The means of making these darkened souls into disciples of Jesus did not consist of holding up a cross, or even hanging one around their necks. It consisted rather of bringing people closer to the character of Jesus who was crucified and resurrected.

In my work, in my interaction with the people, I learned that "heathenism" is distance from God; Christianity is coming closer to the character of Jesus. The distance between these two poles is as great as the distance between the North and South Poles.

There are many obstacles to traverse the distance from one pole to the other, but the "Spirit-led missionary" is able to bring the people near to Jesus. One cannot do this with emotional intensity and excitement. One needs to possess proper qualities as a person, in one's character. And one needs to use Biblical methods and not get distracted by any other goals or objectives than those given to us by the Word. For both long-term and short-term goals we relied heavily on the biblical teachings and the Lord's help. He has not let us down. We praise Him and honor Him for His continued presence. We are also thankful for the many people who have prayed for us and not let us down.

We have learned that mission work is not like a military campaign with storm troopers. Rather it is more like a process of settling in, like a long-term siege. We do this till the old ways capitulate. We recognize that many missionaries have done it differently. Many have also been defeated. A new mission program requires continued self-sacrifice. In fact it requires more than we have been able to provide.

Our Trip to Germany and Canada

We arrived in Hamburg after a terrible storm. After a beautiful trip the storm hit us in the North Sea, one day before we were to arrive in Hamburg. Four ships sank. One ship had no survivors. We were met by friends in Hamburg. They received us warmly. Our three older children were farmed out to local caring families. Anna and one-year-old Karl stayed with the Paul Kempfers, while she went to get treatment in the tropical medicine institute. I spent a lot of time visiting churches that had supported us.

My wife received dentures, paid for by Dr. Hoenish of Poland. I should note, too, that Anna had skin allergies and not cancer. Mostly, she needed to recuperate.

In May 1938, we arrived in Halifax, and then traveled by train to Winnipeg, Manitoba, where we were met by Franz Thiessen, C. F. Klassen, and C. A. DeFehr of the support committee. We rented a place in Winnipeg, Manitoba.

Now we are in Canada, where we want to renew our strength and courage in order to serve our Lord abroad again. Erna was placed in Grade 3, Lydia in Grade 1, Arthur in Kindergarten, and Karl, (one-and-a-half), stayed home. We pray that more light will be spread among the Dengese people. As you know, presently there are two couples (Lenzmanns and Kramers) and two single women (Katherine Harder and Margaret Siemens) at the Mission station. Katherine Harder is the only one who was with us from the beginning. We were together all the time. In the early years, when obstacles threatened to overwhelm us, we learned to appreciate and love each other. Katherine Harder has returned to the Mission a second time, even though one cannot see the fruit ripen yet. Everything is still in the beginning stages of growth. Nevertheless, she has responded to the call of the Lord to serve the people there. Let us pray for the work in Bololo. Someday the Lord will reward the faithfulness and endurance of His workers, even though there are many changes on the field. The Lord will lead everything to the welfare of His Kingdom.

Executive Committee Report of the Africa Bund[44]

This was a very special meeting of the Executive Committee because Brother and Sister Bartsch were present. We recognize, to God's glory and honor, that much has been done in Bololo.

• In contrast to when they arrived and all the people fled in fear, at their departure, fifty students wept to see them go.

• We have before us all the copies of the translations that the Bartsches have completed. It certainly was a big accomplishment: Hymns, Old Testament stories, Proverbs, many Psalms and the whole Gospel of John and The Mennonite Catechism.

• Seven years ago a couple went to Africa. Today Lenzmanns, Kramers, K. Harder and M. Siemens are there.

• We keep considering a move from Bololo to Djia, a place more accessible because it is on the main road. We would construct a more permanent mission, school, and hospital there.

• Financially, we are also doing well. The more the demand, the more the money comes in.

• We will support the Bartsches while on furlough. We have found a nice inexpensive place for them to live.

The question came up repeatedly whether the Bartsches would return to Africa. We have not posed the question directly from the committee, but their attitude is expressed in the following words:

"If we felt God was calling us, if God wills, and we are alive, and see ourselves led to go abroad, then the question of staying here, then our concern for our children would be very

---

[44] *Der kleine Africa Bote*, October 1938.

heavy. But in this matter we want to wait on the Lord. He will make all well."

We are pleased that the interest in the Africa mission work has grown in Canada as well as in Germany. We are thankful that they have shown such kindness to the Bartsches. We are happy to work together with them.

End of Committee Report.

Letters from Students in Bololo[45]

Der kleine Africa Bote published excerpts of several letters from students in Bololo. The editor reports that these were written to Brother and Sister Bartsch. He goes on to say, "When we consider that the Dengese tribe had no written language when the Bartsches came, and when we look at the beautifully written letters, then we are amazed. We offer thanks for the wonders and transformation that has already taken place."

Lusanganye (the name given to Brother Bartsch)
I am sending you a letter. Sadly, I am in the village, but soon I will come to the Mission again! I pray for you to God and cannot stop thinking about you, even now. I also think of Mama and children. We wait now till you come again. . . .
I continue to pray for you. Now I have returned to the Mission. God has called me in my heart to come back to the Mission. I think about you and the lovely songs. Can you send another song? I can't stop thinking about you. I am
Mpembe Nto (approximately 13 years old).

Mama Mpembe (name given to Mrs. Bartsch)
We were very delighted with your letter. All the children have left the mission. I left after four months. . . . I love you a lot, because you have done us much good. The Word of God that you have brought us is true, but our hearts are sinful. Please pray to God for me. I think of Lusanganye all day because he loved us so

---

[45] *Der kleine Africa Bote*, November 1938.

much. I wish you and your children all the best. I am lonely for you. I love you very much and think of you every day.
    Ngunga Djo

    . . . .There is only one thing I want to write about: We have all fallen away from God. I am at the Mission, but we have no school. Things do not look good in the village. Many people are dying. The missionaries tell us a lot about God's Word. We hear it and will return to God.
    Etschinda

    . . . . Lusanganye, I think about all the good that you have done for me, that you freed me from the governor. . . .
    Dpema

    The letter that you wrote to us was read in the village. Many people gathered and were happy for the letter. . . . I bow before God, because He is Lord. Etschinda and I want to believe in God and will do what is right. He definitely is our God. We won't pay attention to the people in the village, because they just pull people into eternal destruction. If the two of us start to believe, then it won't be long till others join us. Faith makes our hearts happy and peaceful. We are happy to hear that you are coming again. We do not stop praying for you. Please also pray for us. Your letter brings us peace.
    Enough. Our Mama, Lusanganye, children, remain in peace.
    Boto

Report from Bololo

- *We have started school again–only 17 students. No new students have arrived. (H. Lenzmann)*
- *Karl Kramer reports that he was standing next to a palm tree when a snake dropped beside him from above, striking his hat. He ran away and the snake fled.*
    - *There is a food shortage and starvation is setting in.*
    - *We need to set up our own farm to feed the students.*

- *The most powerful medicine man in the district was caught, bound and taken to the Governor. He had mixed a particularly powerful potion that people said would kill them immediately. Mostly people die of fear that the medicine will kill them.*
- *Kramers killed four snakes in their house one month.*
- *A mad dog entered the compound but fortunately no one was bitten. A boy in the village died of dog bites.*
- *By June 1939, the school had 110 students.*

Our Activities During Furlough

- This is to let you know what we do during furlough. We live in a nice little house that was furnished for us. We try to keep it as warm as possible in the cold winter. Not an easy task in the city of Winnipeg.
- We appreciate the visitors we get. Once we are back in Africa, this will not be possible.
- We have been well received in the churches. There are three provinces where we want to visit churches: Ontario, Saskatchewan, and British Columbia. We have a few invitations to go to the United States.
- People, old and young, have received us well, have prayed with us and have given generously. We told people about the joys and pains of our work with the Dengese people. We asked for their participation in the continued work of saving souls and time permitted, we preached salvation to the audience.
- I have two stories. A very poor family that had supported the mission had a failed harvest. The mother of the family told us that she prayed that the chicks would survive. Of 100, not one died and they were able to sell them and make a donation. With support like that, the mission cannot fail.
- In another situation, a non-Mennonite man came to visit us. He confessed that they were very poor and, together with his wife, wondered why. They decided it was because they had not given adequately to the mission. They picked out their best heifer, sold it in Winnipeg at a surprisingly high price, and gave the money to missions. They have ten children.

• Please don't think that we tell these stories to get more money. We do share with you the joy of people committed to mission work.

Suffering of the Dengese Children[46]

People have various impressions of people in uncivilized or primitive worlds. The Dengese people are such a people. Everyone makes judgments from his or her own perspective; the Governor always has a different opinion than the businessman about conditions in the primeval forest. The hunter or adventurer has a different opinion than the missionary.

The opinion of many in America or Europe is that people of the primeval forests, living in God's heavenly nature, must be healthy and strong. We often hear and read that our culture and civilization has made us into such fragmented people.

But this is a false impression of the world. The suffering that comes out of the primitive and superstitious tradition weighs like a demon on the black people of Africa. We stand in horror and sympathy for the people sacrificed by the barbaric ceremonies and child rearing methods.

I want to share with you some of the inhumane horrors of African customs, particularly as it affects children. These customs affect the children of this "wild paradise" from day one of their lives and result in so many tears for these poor little black babies.

The torture of Dengese children in the primeval forest begins with birth. Ignorance and misguided taste about what looks pretty to the Dengese people result in many navel ruptures for these little children. Every birth arouses a lot of excitement in a native village. They never know if the newborn embodies the spirit of someone who has died. And so, they never know if bad people have returned to the world. If so, terrible trouble and fear pervades the village. Some men and women are designated to determine whether such an evil person has returned. Their role

---

[46] *Der kleine Africa Bote*, July 1939.

is to discern the spirits. They examine each newly-born child, according to their criteria, to determine whether the signs are favorable or unfavorable for the child. If the child is considered to be dangerous for the tribe, they choke the child to death or give it poison. One can only understand how a mother can relinquish her child to these murderers if one understands the tremendous fear of the evil spirits that plague these poor people all their lives. A number of children were born at our mission site, but none of them survived because they were the "firstborn." We do not know, even after considerable study, whether this killing of the firstborn children relates in any way to the biblical command to kill the firstborn domestic animal.

The arrival of twins is greatly feared. They say that only one of the two has a right to live in the village. It is hard to describe the superstition surrounding the arrival of twins, because everything surrounding the event is so secretive. People also fear the arrival of twins because they must then catch a number of wild animals, which is rather difficult for the hunter with their primitive weapons. Katherine Harder was present at the birth of twins. The birth process was quite normal but both infants died soon afterward in her presence.

Many exorcisms accompany the birth of a child. If these are not followed, people believe that trouble will follow trouble. As soon as the child enters the world it is painted with a red paint, derived from trees (Nkula). If an adult is painted with this red paint, it stings like disinfectant. What torture the poor little infant must experience when the whole body is covered with this paint. If the mother is not able to produce milk for her infant, they feed the infant large balls of "quango" that are forced down the throat. This is food that grownups eat and that often creates a lot of stomach problems for them. No wonder so many children die in their first year of life.

The name given to the child depends on the circumstances surrounding the birth. If, for example, it happens to be raining at the time of birth, the child will be called "Rain," regardless of the sex of the child.

The little infants are very beautiful. Since they have the skin color of a white child at birth, one cannot see the curly hair or the dark eyes at first. The body turns dark after about fourteen days.

As soon as the mother is fit to go to work, the baby is taken to the forest with her. The mothers carry their children on the back, held by a woven towel-like material. The children are transported like this till about age five. The legs dangle on either side of the mother. Often the child's body is twisted in ways that affect it for life. One seldom sees the little child sitting or crawling on the floor. Since they do not wear clothing, the little children get a lot of colds. The child hangs on the mother, whether it is sleeping or awake.

When the children get permanent teeth they begin a new set of tortures. The Dengese people belong to the Basongo people, meaning "the tooth filers." Between ages 8 and 12, their teeth are filed with a rough piece of iron. We can only imagine how painful this must be for the children. They do this so their protective spirit will recognize them in the forest. Otherwise, they are subject to the whims of the evil spirits. They also consider this to be sign of beauty. What people will do to appear beautiful!

There are many other practices that I cannot or do not want to describe. These hold the people in their grasp. These customs are tragic for the African people. They enclose every newly-born like a net, the fate of the wilderness. The unbounded ignorance and the incredible fear of unexamined powers of nature show up in their imagination and superstition. One can hardly grasp it. I will never grasp the many tears of the tiny babies.

My dear reader! Can you allow yourself to enter into this pervasive suffering? Having seen it, I can never get away from it. May more able people bring relief and enlightenment to these poor people!

"What you have done for the least of these, you have done for me." The Dengese people belong to this group of people for whom our Lord Jesus has died and to whom He calls us to go to tell them about relief and salvation. But you, dear friend of the mission work, please pray that the Lord send out more workers and that they are fruitful.

— Chapter 8 —

Recall and Recommitment
1939

Events in the Summer of 1939

My parents' plans were to go back to the mission field which they had left in 1938. Their departure was to take place on August 6, 1939. The announcement in the Afrika-Bote *read:*

The Bartsches have visited about 100 churches in Canada. They have shown us something of their pioneer activity. Their reports have been received with the greatest of interest as evidenced by the money collected.

Everything indicated a successful new term in the mission field. However, things turned out quite differently.

Dad, along with other brethren had gone to the Mennonite Brethren Conference in Coaldale, Alberta. Mother was busy cleaning and making preparations for the trip. Dad and others returned to Winnipeg earlier than they expected. He carefully and calmly tried to prepare Mother for what had happened, why they had come home earlier and what had been decided. Telegrams had come from Africa: "There is an emergency on the field and Mr. Bartsch must come back."

A Summary of the Africa Committee's Response to the Crisis, by H. H. Janzen

I called this special meeting of the Africa Committee because we face an emergency in the Mission in Bololo. I've sent all of you copies of the telegrams that I received from the Kramers, who arrived in Bololo after the Bartsches left in January 1938. The message is clear. It read, "Beg the Bartsches to return immediately. Katherine Harder has a lung disease and has to leave the Congo. Sister Lenzmann has the same disease and must also leave, so the entire Lenzmann family has to leave. Brother Lenzmann cannot care for both sick women on the trip, along with his two little children, so Margaret Siemens will need to accompany them. That leaves me and my wife, and we hardly know what to do with the school and the clinic. Furthermore, the King of the Dengese is more antagonistic everyday. He is openly defiant of the missionaries. Please advise us."

This put all of us in a somber state. It seems impossible for the mission to continue. The situation is desperate. But the mission must go on. We are committed to follow the call of God in the future.

Brother and Sister Bartsch have talked this over before our meeting. As you know they were supposed to return to Bololo on August 6 but they cannot get everything ready that soon. Besides, Sister Bartsch is still recovering. So they have decided that Brother Bartsch will go alone now using the quickest possible transportation. Sister Bartsch will follow in several months with the four children, Erna, Lydia, Arthur, and Karl. Henry said it was like a ship in distress. "Who can sit idly by?"

The Africa Committee met at C. F. Klassen's home along with both Dad and Mom present. Dad said, "There is a ship in distress. We have heard the cry for help. How can we sit by, idly?" Dad would go alone as soon as possible.

They walked home from the meeting, arms linked but minds in very different places. They made preparations, he to go and she to stay.

On July 25, at sunset, at the train station, they gathered with the children and many others. Mother says they "stood there speechless and silent with nothing left to say. Erna was 10, Lydia, 8, Arthur 6, and Karl 2-1/2. Karl was sick so I held him in my arms. The train rolled in. A quick embrace, Henry stepped on board, waved once more and disappeared quickly from sight."

Chairman H. H. Janzen's Report[47]

Our regular, yearly meeting of the board overseeing the mission work in Africa was to take place on July 25 and 26. But

---

[47] *Der kleine Africa Bote*, August 1939.

an emergency arose, necessitating an earlier meeting. I want to tell you about the events as they happened. It all began with a telegram from Germany, from Brother Eric Sauer, a professor at the Wiedenest Bible School. The telegram came on July 7 and read: "Kramers are in desperate need. Beg Bartsches return to Africa." At this time we didn't know what desperate need the Kramers had. People's courage or lack of it is not easy to describe. I sent the telegram to the other members of the directory, many of whom happened to be at the Coaldale Conference which was dealing with the issues of the mission work in Africa. As an aside, I note that the whole conference was very supportive of the mission work in Africa. That is the Lord's work and we thank Him from the bottom of our hearts as well as the brothers who allowed themselves to be led by the Spirit.

On July 16 both I and Brother F. C. Thiessen received two airmail letters: One from the Kramers and the other from the Lenzmanns. These letters were "Job" letters: They were that tragic. Katherine Harder had a disease of the lungs. She was to leave Africa within three months. Sister Lenzmann got the same disease and is to leave the Congo within two months. The letters were written on June 25. The doctor says that Mrs. Lenzmann needs to go to a cool climate and may be able to return in a year and-a-half. We do not know how seriously ill Katherine Harder is. The attitude of the King of the Dengese gets worse every day. He is more openly opposed to the missionaries: He withholds carrier assistance and provisions from the mission. These conditions make the work at the mission difficult. Brother Lenzmann asks for permission and support to return home. Brother Kramer asks for advice to deal with the difficulties that have mounted up. These difficulties will increase when the Lenzmanns leave. What is to be done?

I decided to take the train to Winnipeg immediately and telegrammed Brother Thiessen of this. He called other members of the committee. Only five were missing. The mood was somber. It seemed impossible. Our hearts were very heavy.

We met. We lacked courage, comfort and wisdom. We reached into the well, the Source of all our hope, the Word of God. I read

Isaiah 50:4-10. We focused on verse 10. We read these precious words there:

> *Who among you fears the Lord*
> *and obeys the voice of his servant,*
> *who walks in darkness*
> *and has no light,*
> *yet trusts in the name of the Lord*
> *and relies upon his God?*

That's it. That's what we need. As a committee we knelt to pray. Every soul opened itself to God and when we sat down again, everything had been settled. We had regained our confidence. Even though we don't know exactly what we would do, we believed that the Lord would give us light again. For the true believer the light will always return. We ended our meeting late at night. We have found the direction for our work that will help us in the days ahead.

The Bartsch family before Henry left for Africa, 1939.

We are all clear again about one thing. The message has taken on particular form and in our hearts has become a definite command. It is this: As long as the Lord gives us the work to do, as long as people pray for the work, as long as He sends us financial support through His servants, the work in Africa will not be given up. We may leave the mission station in Bololo to find another. St. Paul has had to do that more than once. That does not alter God's commission to preach the gospel on the "dark continent." We are committed to follow the call of God in the future. That was the firm decision of Brother and Sister Bartsch as well as the Brothers on the Committee.

The Lenzmanns and Katherine Harder are to come home immediately. We were able to find the necessary funds for the trip. It will be too difficult for Brother Lenzmann to look after both women as well as two little children if the women are confined to their beds. In that event Margaret Siemens should travel with them to help. The Kramers will also have to leave the mission station for a while in the fall to see the medical doctor in the next town.

So then the mission station would be without workers. We cannot allow that. But whom shall we send? Under the circumstances we cannot send the Bartsches with their family. We need more order in the situation before we do that. On the other hand, we know that it is necessary at this time that Brother Bartsch go to help the dear brothers and sisters, with advice and initiative based on his experience in the field. And so, after much discussion, a proposal was presented to Brother and Sister Bartsch. "Would you allow yourselves to be separated so that Brother Bartsch could go alone in order that he could organize the work?"

We know that the request requires a big sacrifice. They have already had the experience of being separated once for an extended period of time. They responded: "The die was cast long ago, when we first were called by the Lord to do the work. Now there is no return." The decision is made.

Brother Bartsch will leave Winnipeg on July 25–that is today, as I write this. He will first travel to Ottawa to make sure his passport is in order. If possible he will catch a ship on Saturday that will take him to Europe in six days. From there he will fly to Africa. He should arrive in the Congo in four to six days after that. With these plans we get him there about five or six weeks before we would without the flights. He goes with our full authority to do whatever it takes to further the work of the mission in Africa. When he gets on the train today, to begin *the lengthy and dangerous trip, then he must know that we stand behind him with our prayers like a wall of support. We go with him. What is more, the Lord goes with him.*

The next few weeks will place a lot of demands on our financial resources. We are thankful for the many people who have given generously of their meager earnings so that we could deal with these emergencies. We believe that the Lord will assist in the future as well.

Henry's public statement of his mission was given in a letter.

"We heard the S.O.S. of a sinking ship. Who can remain unaffected by this emergency situation? In view of the developments in the mission field I and my family have taken leave from each other for an undetermined period of time. Mrs. Bartsch will stay with the children in Canada and I am on my way to Africa in order to help."

On Board the *Empress of Britain*

Dear Brothers, Sisters and Friends!

The ship was supposed to leave Canada today. But it took till three o'clock for everything to get loaded. Whole groups of passengers are boarding now. My thoughts remain in Winnipeg, where I heard the last wishes to be well, where we shook hands for the last time, and where the last tears were shed. All my loved ones have disappeared, but I will never forget them. Words fail me. I can't describe everything I have experienced in the last little while. There are experiences in life that one simply wishes not to describe. They lose their sacred quality when one talks about them. Many Bible passages were read to me when I left. These continue to echo in my mind. They will go with me on the way. In times of stress, such as we experience now, Bible passages have a particular meaning. I'll cherish them when loneliness grips me. I will use them when Satan challenges me and when I get worried. God's word shall be a light on the narrow path on which I am now embarking.

I continue to remember the past year in Canada. We learned to know so many dear people. I call out to all my dear brothers and sisters from aboard the ship: "Be well!" You have shared so deeply with us in our experiences in Africa when we were with you. Now we want to share with you some of the difficulties so that you can help us carry the burdens. Our brothers and sisters must experience a lot of inner conflict to terminate the mission field early! Given the difficult and unpredictable circumstances on the mission field, we decided to separate. My wife, Anna Bartsch, and the children remain in Canada. I am traveling to Africa alone to help.

When we separated for a year in 1934 we thought that was the most extreme thing the Lord could ask of us. Now we need to live through that experience again. On the other hand we are thankful that the Lord considers us worthy to make an offering for His cause. That is why we want to build on that foundation and trust in the Lord. Naturally speaking, we are easily inclined to "throw the rifle into the ditch," because nothing is going as we expected. But we cannot do that and it is not the right perspective to take for the service we are called to. The Lord has plans for His work and wants to use us to fulfill those plans. Oh, that we had more skills and that we could be more faithful.

Finally, I ask all those of you who pray to also remember our brothers in the Africa Mission Committee. It has not been easy for them to advise us. Please support them because so much depends on the kind of support we have when we get into trouble. May the Lord reward you with love and faithfulness, just as you have shown it to me. I know that I am being carried by "praying hands." I would not travel without such support.

Lenzmanns and Katherine Harder Leave Bololo: A Report by Karl Kramer[48]

I greet you with a Psalm: "We want to do great deeds with God. He will suppress our enemy."

The Lenzmanns and Katherine Harder left the Mission Station on August 4, 1939. The two sick women were carried

---
[48] *Der kleine Africa Bote*, September 1939.

on bamboo stretchers. The government doctor for the district had the path to the river cleared so it was passable. We tried to get whatever transportation was possible. We tried to arrange for automobile transportation. We looked at riverboat schedules. We even considered air travel. Nothing worked, so finally, through faith in God we set out on foot. When we got to Djongo Sanga we rented a large dugout canoe that belonged to a businessman. The two children were laid down at the bottom while the two stretchers hung over the water on either side. In addition we had a number of packages of clothing and supplies. It was 2 PM and the sun was very hot but we had to go because it would take us about 6-7 hours, paddling upstream to get to Lodi. Eight men paddled: One steered the huge dugout. The going was slow. We considered what we would do in Lodi. There were many mosquitoes. Everything gets dark after an hour. There was terrible weather ahead. There was no place to land or find shelter. As the storm drew closer we pulled in to shore. Everyone prayed that the Lord would let the storm pass. The Africans in our group ran into the forest and took off all their clothes or whatever they had on. The patients remained on their stretchers. We covered them with sleeping bags and rain coats. The children continued to lie under the stretchers, crying. They felt cramped underneath because we covered the patients with all the raincoats. In spite of it all, we remained in good spirits. The storm let up after about a half hour.

Shortly after that we got started again. We saw a commercial ship on the river. It came to pick us up. The government doctor contacted a captain of a riverboat. All were African. The riverboat stopped in the middle of the river and picked us up. The boat had a small cabin for our patients. The ship's crew had cleaned it out for us. The ship returned to Djongo Sanga, from where we had left at 2 PM. We were to be in Port Francqui in two days but because of the dry weather, the river was very low and riverboats could be hung up on sand banks for days.

I said my goodbyes and made my way back to Bololo at night. I saw another storm approaching. It is always horrifying because the storms are so violent.

Things have settled down at the Mission Station. My relationship with the indigenous people is better. They don't seem to be so oppositional. The workers returned to cut trees. Huge trees lie all over the place and await the fire that will destroy them. When the rainy season returns I will plant banana trees and other fruit trees.

We are all well at the Mission Station.

The Kramers

I Leave Europe August 12, 1939

I have only a few more hours left in Europe. I leave tomorrow at 8 AM. The airplane that will take me to Algiers is supposed to be the fastest in the world. It is called *Savoia Maarchetti* and flies about 400 Kilometers (250 miles) per hour. I will write about the trip later. My travel here on the *Empress Britain* went very well. It took five days to get here. I received my visa in a few hours. I received a warm welcome at the Rorton Mission.

Since I was close to Wiedenest, Germany, I took the opportunity to spend a few days there. A conference had just finished. A Bible study course for youth workers followed so I participated in that. I spoke to the group in the evening about the necessity of mission work. I was happy to meet so many leaders of youth. We need such people to provide the foundation for missions. I realized, too, how easy it would be to destroy something in people's lives that later could never be rectified. But the Lord gave me His blessing as I described the mission work in Africa. I noticed this particularly when, next day, at my departure, a prayer meeting was set aside to pray for the mission work in Africa. I believe the foundation for the Africa mission work is as firm as it is in Canada.

God's word has been particularly important to me in these days of loneliness.

The "clear living stream of water" continued to heal the pain and sorrow of my separation from the ones I love. The Psalms are particularly important to me. To be a servant of God is also linked to suffering. My biggest concern is that I be of service to my brothers and sisters.

No price is too high,
No road too hard,
To spread His fire,
Among the people of the world.
Greetings from your lonely but confident brother,
Henry Bartsch.

From Hotel Aletti Alger

Just a few lines now that I am on the African continent again. The flight was very fast. I left Brussels at 9:30 this morning. I arrived in Africa at 2:20 PM. August 13. I wouldn't believe it if I hadn't experienced it. It was so quick. I got up this morning at 6 o'clock and had my morning devotions, as usual, and entrusted myself to the One who has all control in heaven and on earth. The sky also lies in the realm of His control. I become quiet and peaceful when I realize that I am sustained by the hand of God. I read Psalm 42 today.

> *"As a heart longs for flowing streams,*
> *so longs my soul for thee, O God."*

My host brought me breakfast and wished me a good trip.

When I arrived at the airport, I expected a huge crowd of people. But only a Portuguese newlywed couple showed up. Before I entered the "big bird," I walked around this thing several times. A dead and lifeless thing! I'm to trust it? Others do, so why can't I? But I have entrusted myself to someone greater, a living being that sustains everything with His mighty arms. People must have a lot of faith in such inanimate objects to entrust their lives to them. I notice that the pilot has a talisman, a little monkey, dangling in front of him. I guess he needs a God too. This is heathenism in Europe.

The trip was wonderful. The sun shone in Brussels. I could see the memorials and cathedrals from above. I couldn't get enough of the sights. Trains crawled along their tracks but one could only see the smoke belching from the engine. We were so high that we could no longer distinguish cars or people. The fields are light green and the forests are dark green. One seldom sees a straight path.

We flew over France: Cities, fields, gardens and forests. One picture is more beautiful than the other. I never thought that the world was so beautiful! Everything looks different from above. We need to climb higher if we want to see God and recognize His might. We crossed the Mediterranean Sea. This is even more beautiful. I think of the disciples when they were up on the mountain and said to Jesus: "This is wonderful. Let us stay here." How wonderful it will be when we will leave the earth. Our trip with our Lord will even be more wonderful. Soon we will be united with our Lord Jesus. I want to be there. Instead of the roar of motors I will hear heavenly music.

But now, back to reality. Below we now see steep mountains and ravines. We see no life. Everything is stark and dead. It would be terrible to be down there. And what if one of the motors fails? What will happen then? How will the talisman help then? I'm amazed at the kinds of things people make for themselves. No, our Lord does not let the airplane drop here. In Canada and in Germany hundreds of people pray for my safety.

We see the big ocean and then the beautiful city of Marseilles. (But there is a lot of sin in a port city.) How will the plane land? I see the wheels drop down, we touch down, taxi at about 100 miles an hour. We come to a stop, get out and get ready to get our lunch. It is 11 AM. Radios and electrical equipment are confiscated. We are not allowed to take pictures. Stringent measures are being put in place. They are anticipating war. God can prevent it. We few passengers sit down to lunch. They speak no English, the Portuguese speak no French. We leave in a hour after refueling.

The flight over the Mediterranean is wonderful. Sea and sky seem to blend into one. We come to Algiers. We are to stay there overnight. The people are brown children of Islam. A bus comes to pick us up and takes us to one of nicest hotels in the city. Tomorrow we leave for Gabo. This plane will return to Europe from there and we take another one.

This is Sunday. You will all be going to church. I have never been so close to the Lord on a Sunday, as today. This has been the most wonderful ride of my life. How will I be able to ride on a kipoy in the land of the Dengese? It will take me four days to get to Bololo, if I get baggage carriers. How I wish I could say with Paul, "I can be high and I can be low. I can be skilled in all things."

From your very thankful brother, Henry Bartsch.

Letter from Gabo

We just landed in Gabo. Today we flew for eight hours over the terrifying Sahara Desert. Yesterday I sent a letter describing the beauty of the earth. Today the opposite is true. No life was noticeable. In addition, the flight was rocky but I did not get airsick, though the "nattering" of the engines can drive one crazy.

We landed at Reggan, an oasis with a few palm trees, in the middle of the desert. We had lunch. There are a few white people there and about forty blacks. I don't know how they get the gasoline to a place like this. It was hot: 117 degrees Fahrenheit. I've never experienced such heat. The French have built a hotel made of cement and rocks. One could not touch the outside walls because of the heat. We were served food, everything was pure African, barely edible. Then we boarded the plane for Gabo, which we were to reach in four hours. In the meantime, the plane had become unbearably hot. It cooled down once we reached a high altitude. We had to fly high enough to fly over the sandstorm.

When I looked up I could see the blue heavens. When I looked down I could only see the terrible desert. Nothing can live there. We passed a little lake and then a small stream, the Niger River. It begins so small. We began to see some green and then some little villages.

Gabo is a native village on the Niger River. There are roads for vehicles to travel, though they are not very good. There is also a hotel and a post office in Gabo. As I arrived at the hotel, a truckload of drunken whites arrived as well. How shamefully the whites behave. The blacks look very similar to the ones we know from the Congo. Whites have imposed their culture on these people. A Jesuit priest enters. I took a walk downtown but now am waiting on dinner. I left Brussels eighteen hours ago. Now I am in the middle of Africa. When I walk into town, the naked boys crowd around me, as they did in Dengese. I cannot speak to these people but soon I will arrive at my destination.

Tomorrow we take a different plane. My, how I fell in love with that beautiful "Maarchetti!" It was very faithful and took us through some heavy storms. People have learned how to master nature with machines. I hope we have a good ride tomorrow. If the route had not taken us on a detour, I would be in Port Francqui tomorrow. We need to go to Leopoldville first.

I Arrive in Leopoldville August 18, 1939

I arrived in Leopoldville at 5 PM last night. Everything went well. The Lenzmanns and Katherine Harder arrived here on August 14. Both Sisters Lenzmann and Harder are in the hospital. They leave for Belgium today. Their condition is serious but we know that the Lord can help them. I met Brother Lenzmann unexpectedly on the street. We talked at length about the situation at the mission. Although I am very lonely, I can see that it is best that, given the situation, I am heading there. They leave for Matadi today and I leave for Port Francqui.

I'm in Bololo, August 25

Greetings from Bololo! I arrived at 5:30. At Port Francqui I was fortunate to catch a riverboat freighter to Djongo Beach. That took three days. I walked from Djongo Beach to Bololo. I met some men from Bololo at Djongo Beach who greeted me very warmly. One of them immediately took my things and went off to Bololo with them. The heat was unbearable. It was 1:30 PM and I had a hard time walking. I could not send any direct message to the Kramers from Port Francqui. In Djongo Beach people greeted me in the friendliest manner. All the women asked about Mrs. Bartsch and the children, whose names they remembered. The one black man ran ahead of me and soon there were hundreds of little children and grownup people surrounding me. It was the noise I remembered from earlier times.

Many students also came and greeted me. How I pitied them. I knew so many of them by name. They had told me so much of their inner life. They have gone to the village. We know the background to that. One of our boys was speechless. Today he stood in front of me for a long time and looked at me. The memories of the past came back. I felt like crying at the sight of my students. In the village, the women stood in front of me and would not let me go further. "We want to look at you," they said. How wonderful it would have been for Anna and the children to have been here.

The welcome I received from the natives felt so good. I had pictured it differently. I was flooded with eagerness to work with these people. But under the present circumstances, I could not institute any kind of order or discipline. We will wait with that. I see no need to quit work among the Dengese people, but we may need to transfer to another place from which we can travel easier.

Brother Kramer came to greet me in the village. When I got to the mission station, everyone was very warm and kind. Margaret Siemens takes care of the four adopted children. The buildings are dilapidated and require repair.

A number of boys came from the village. They are so unhappy. I remembered the experiences I had had with them. They had been so happy about the forgiveness of their sins. And we believed them. And now? Who can help them? The powers of darkness are so great.

I get very lonely for my loved ones at home. But since we do not know what our immediate plans are, I am glad that they stayed back. Our Lord knows what is best for us. We will trust Him to bring us together again.

Editor's Note: Lenzmanns Arrive in Winnipeg[49]

On October 9, the Lenzmanns arrived in Winnipeg, Manitoba. Sister Lenzmann, who we thought was laid up in bed, stepped from the train with a smile on her face.

Brother Lenzmann reported that the trip had gone well from Matadi to Antwerp, Belgium. They arrived September 2, the day before Belgium declared war on Germany. Amazingly, they were able to obtain passage on a ship to New York within a few days. Katherine Harder took the train to Reedley, California, her home, and the Lenzmanns took the train to Winnipeg. They, and everyone, wondered why the Lord had called them back so quickly. Hadn't they heard the call of God in the first place? What was God trying to say to them about all of the trouble they had been through?

---

[49] *Der kleine Africa Bote*, November 1939.

Chapter 9

Obstacles and Isolation
1940

Conditions in Bololo

Everything is about the same here. The classes continue. The students are fairly punctual. The 35 girls in the school do better than the boys. If possible, we will continue classes till May. No students came from other villages. The difficulty is the food. Our gardens were just beginning to produce when wild boars and elephants wrecked them. Nevertheless, I allowed the people to cut more forest to set up new gardens. We need to give the people work to do.

Brother Kramer and a fellow teacher conducted classes in a neighboring village. A total of 17 students came. As happy as that news is, we tell ourselves that we do not want to work only with children because, when they get older, the village absorbs them or the Catholic priest tries to get them to come to his church. Everything must change if we are to remain here. And we trust in our Lord. He can change matters so that the adults are converted from their ways and we can do church work.

I am often very lonely. I counted on a three-month absence from my family. Now it is seven months. Letters take up to eighteen weeks to get here. I want to leave everything in the Lord's hands and not worry. He'll make it all well. Thank God, I am physically well and happy in the Lord.

I have nothing new to report from Bololo. We have conducted school now for seven months. The children from Bololo came happily. The girls do much better than the boys. Sister Kramer commented today that the girls are so different since they have attended school. That is encouraging. We have a very good mission with the few workers and the students.

The war in Europe has resulted in greater freedom for the people of central Africa. But that is not to their benefit. The Belgian authorities no longer require students to go to school. As a result, almost all the students attending the Catholic school have fled. Our students don't know about the change in law as yet, but when they do, they are likely to leave too. Then again, we have never forced any students to attend our school. The parents continue to bring the students, including the 40 girls.

As I indicated earlier, Brother and Sister Kramer have taken over the work of evangelism in the villages. This is very important work because it involves the parents, which then encourages them to send their children.

Africa Mission Board's Attempt to Send the Bartsch Family Back to Africa

We want to let friends of the Africa Mission in Bololo know that the Lord is leading us along paths that we don't understand. We are not restless because we are confident that our master does not make mistakes, even if He lets us wait and answers us differently than we expect.

We prepared for Mrs. Bartsch, her four children and Susie Brucks to go to Africa. In fact we applied for a visa from the Belgian Embassy. With this in hand, they were to leave New York July 3, 1940, on a Dutch ship. The plan was for them to go to Capetown, South Africa, and then take the train from there to the Congo. This is a long way around, but travel through Europe is not possible. But God's thoughts are not our thoughts as we have experienced. The political events have made it

Karl, Erna, Arthur, Lydia.

impossible for the trip to occur now. So we have had to postpone it. There were two reasons: The Belgian Embassy did not grant permission to enter the Congo; and the danger of traveling on a Dutch ship is too great at this time. We, in the Africa Mission Board, cannot responsibly send these two sisters and four little children on such a long trip. We continue to pray and wait to see if the circumstances will change so that they can leave without danger and less concern. It is not an easy thing for Brother and Sister Bartsch to be separated like this. They need our prayer.

A Year after Separation from My Family

I greet you with Revelation 3:8 and Psalm 118:19. Revelation reads, "I know all about you; and now have opened a door in front of you that nobody will be able to close—I know that though you are strong, you have kept my commandments and not disowned my name." Psalm 118 reads, "Open the gates of virtue to me, I will come in and give thanks to Yahweh."

These are the words that our Lord gave me this morning. Immediately after that I had so many trials at work that these promises were put to the test. Thank God, the promises were reaffirmed, as in the past. Since the Word of God has shown itself to be a safe haven for the believers, we cling to it and are not put to shame.

When this letter arrives in America, it will be one year since I said goodbye to my loved ones. When I left, we thought of three

Mother and us four in Winnipeg.

months till I would be reunited with my loved ones. Now it has taken this long. The separation from loved ones would hardly be bearable if I were to consider only my natural desires. In spite of the loneliness, time has not seemed interminable. The Lord has arranged change from routine even here in the wilderness. He can replace a lot, but not all things. I hope to greet my loved ones here soon. Then a new test will arise for the Peniel Mission.

School began in the second week of the New Year. About 120 students arrived from Bololo and neighboring villages. We have difficulty with children from other villages because they do not get enough to eat. A month and a half ago I gave up on the children from other villages and focused exclusively on the children of Bololo. There were between 70 and 80 children. Half of them are girls ages 8 to 10 and the rest are boys of about the same age. Four of the teachers who had taught for us before have committed themselves to teach again. They have been a big help. If I were left alone with these children, I would soon lose my patience at their slow progress.

We need local help in the yard, the gardens and on the field. At the school, children are taught to read and write, do arithmetic, sing, study catechism, and Bible stories. Students are in classes for about three-and-a-half to four hours per day. They learn Psalms by heart in the morning and evening services through choral recitation. In this way we instruct the native children in God's word and believe that in the appropriate time, the seed will grow. We saw this after I returned from our trip to Canada; the seed we are sowing is alive.

I am disappointed that the boys, who attended the school in the early days, pay so little attention to the Word of God. Every so often I talk to them about their experiences. All of them have confessed that they are unhappy in their present situation. The others, who never met God, do not seem to be as unhappy with their situation. Someday the light of God will break through again to those who have fallen away. The Spirit of God is active and finds connection in the soul of these boys. It is our duty to sow the seed. The Lord will harvest in His own time.

Travel to Lodi to Negotiate with the Commissioner

On March 18 I closed the school for an undisclosed time. I went to Lodi where I wanted to meet the commissioner. I wanted to talk to him about events that were affecting our mission. I found the commissioner to be very sympathetic to our work. A few days later the commissioner came to Bololo with the King and made arrangements that are to the benefit of the mission, although the King was hostile. I believe the Catholics have influenced him.

Our former state official, Mr. Winandi, has not been replaced. He left the service because of the war in Europe. The temporary replacements in Dekese are very friendly to us and do what they can to help us. On orders of the commissioner, one state official is assigned to live in Bololo. That will make the work of the mission easier.

After the commissioner and King Ikongo-Samu left here, I drove to Port Francqui to buy groceries and other things. I had to take the bike to Bolombo, a distance of about 55 km. My belongings were sent off a few days ago. Since the road to Bolombo had been cleared of undergrowth, I could ride rather quickly. Someone had felled trees over the streams, so they were easy to cross. In fact, I didn't have to take off my shoes once on the trip. The roads are cleared once a year. I came to Bolombo early on April 4 to get the automobile ready to catch the ferry across the Sankuru River the next morning. When the ferry came the next morning, the vehicle would not start. Every effort I made to start the engine failed. After an hour I realized that the engine had short-circuited. The fuse was burned out, and I had no reserve. So I replaced the fuse with a wire for the trip so I could proceed. The ride across the Sankuru takes an hour. At the other side, at Lodi, the rope holding the ferry to the dock tore just as I was driving off. The back wheels hung over the water. If the bumper had not caught on to a log, my vehicle and I would have been caught up in the flowing river. The Lord had His hand in this. He protected me. "The angel of the Lord encamps around those who fear Him." I thought of this later and thanked Him.

In Lodi, I met Dr. Davlo, a government doctor whom I knew from before. He insisted I have dinner with him. As usual, when I am a guest in a person's house, I bowed my head and prayed in silence. When I looked up I noticed that Dr. Davlo also bowed his head and prayed. I felt so comfortable with that. Dr. Davlo is Catholic but deeply pious in his own way. It is hard to find people like this among the younger generation. But they do exist.

The trip to Port Francqui went well. I spent Sunday in Bulape and then returned to Bololo.

Starting up School Again

I called my little sheep back to school on April 15, and now the noise and activity at the mission has begun again. I would like to keep the students here till the end of May. The dry season begins then. The dry season is good for travel because the heavy rains in the rainy season can disrupt travel. God willing, I want to visit the Baptist mission in Boschwe. It is a difficult trip to get there. I will need to take the kipoy, although I could take the riverboat. We'll start school again in September if the Lord does not have another plan for us. We pray for His leading in the work that he has entrusted to us. From the depths of my soul I thank all of those who carry us in their prayers. I am also very grateful for the opportunity to take part in the work among African people.

Isolated after the Kramers' Exile to Luebo in May

I am left alone in Bololo. Brother and Sister Kramer left for Luebo on May 20.[50] They took the most important things along. Now the big house with all that stuff is empty. I had to

---

[50] Germany and Belgium declared war in early September 1939. The Kramers were German nationals living in Belgian territory, Belgian Congo, and so were considered to be enemies of the Belgian State. Consequently Belgian authorities compelled them to leave the mission and be placed under Belgian detention. They were transferred to Luebo and placed under house arrest.

close the school. The children were obedient and worked hard. They have brought me a lot of joy. I am almost sorry to have let the children leave, but the dry season began about fourteen days ago. It is difficult to keep their attention when that occurs. After all, they have attended regularly since September, and it is not good to become too strict with them. Teachers, as well as students, come to the morning worship sessions. The girls are good students. There is really a big difference between the school children and the children from the villages. I believe we will experience a lot of happiness in the Dengese territory, if the Lord gives us opportunity to continue work here.

I was all alone at the mission for eight days. The students and the workers were gone. Everyone escaped to the primeval forest. The stillness at the mission was unbearable. I decided to take the trips I owe to others and see how they are doing.

When I consider the dangers of international travel, particularly travel to South Africa, I think of the mines spread by the warring powers. In spite of my tremendous loneliness for my family, I do not want them to travel till the storm has settled. I am healthy and strong, encouraged and hopeful. But I am not a blind optimist. For times like this, the Lord has given me the special gift to see things as they are, to be a realist. I see how people go to extremes and so lose their inner sense of calm. How I wish my wife were by my side to talk through and pray through everything. But I must do it alone. Sometime in the future, the Lord will answer my question: "Why?"

My Visit to the Kramers in Luebo in July

In my previous letter I wrote that Brother and Sister Kramer went to Luebo. They arrived in Luebo where I visited them twice. They, as well as the children are sickly, since they have poor housing. I invite you to pray that their health returns soon.

I went back to Kafumba again where I received a very warm welcome. On the way I stopped off at several mission stations and was thrilled to see the Lord's work develop. On the way back I left the vehicle in Lodi, and a riverboat took me to Djongo Beach free of charge. I walked back to our place in the heat of the day, as I had done many times before.

Conditions in Bololo after My Return

The buildings and property in Bololo were undisturbed. The animals had suffered terribly. The cat died. I barely entered the house when I was told that the cat was dead. Djema had ordered the watchmen to put the dead cat in the water barrel and had poured water over it, so that the ants and other wild animals would not eat it up. He did this to convince me that it had really died.

The garden suffered considerably in my absence. Tomatoes, lettuce, onions, and carrots, are plentiful and more than I need but the cucumbers are all dried up, and the Kramers' garden is all dry.

This is the middle of the dry season. There is no way in which we can conduct school or church services. What I always feared is now a reality: I am alone at the Mission. The silence is eerie. None of the service staff is here at night. Every so often, jackals howl. They disappear when I scream at them. I do not have a gun. I have been lonely like this for several days. If I didn't have good books and the radio, I would become very bored. But these good friends always teach me something new.

My yard and house have much to be desired, but it is still not as messy as some Canadian bachelor homes I know. I have a very satisfactory cook and house servant. But it is difficult to teach him any new dishes because his experiences are too limited. I often cook my own meals. Today I baked bread; it turned out OK! I bought a lot of food staples before the Kramers left, so I thought I had too much. But now that the price of food supplies has skyrocketed, I am quite happy to have purchased all the goods.

I am healthy. I have not had a fever. I continue to sleep well and have no dreams. Even my loneliness cannot change that.

The work among the Dengese people has not changed much. The old folks always stay. The services among the Yakima are decidedly different. I plan to take a trip through Yakima villages during this dry season. Sometimes large crowds of people show up for services here in Bololo. Sometimes no one shows up. As long as Ikongo-Samu remains the King, things will be difficult here. But we live in a period of time when things can change very quickly. A time can come when there can be a breakthrough of the gospel in this Dengese territory, as it occurred in Mukedi twenty years ago.

On my return from a trip away, I heard that our Governor Liegenis had died. Apparently he suffered little before he died. He died of pneumonia. I would have liked to see him once more. He helped us a lot in recent times. He was an honest friend of the Mission. It would be so much easier to work among the people if they were not as free as birds. They only have to pay the government 24 francs (taxes) a year. Who would want to allow himself to be yoked when he can be free? Nevertheless, I have great hope for these people.

My cook has just arrived and wants to prepare supper. I have eaten quite a bit of meat recently. There is also more than enough milk. The Kramers' children could have such good milk here. Too bad they are not here. The weather is very pleasant. The trees are in flower or hang heavy with fruit. The fruit will be ripe in a month or so. When the Lenzmanns were here, they planted a bush that has spread out considerably. It blossoms throughout the year. The sun shines through the blossoms and adds to the wonderful beauty.

Stay well till we meet again.

My Loneliness (Notes from a Private Letter in July)

I heard a few days ago that my family cannot come at this time. I would have been very anxious had I learned that they had begun the trip at this time. But I would have been doubly happy had they landed here. One must submit to the unavoidable. I am glad that my loved ones live in Canada where they are safe. The war is not likely to come there. It's hard for me to judge how much I am suffering in these difficult times. Since I risked doing the Lord's will to come here alone and to stay here, the Lord will also provide the grace to manage better. Sometimes I imagine that I would get sick. Who would care for me or hand me necessities to stay alive? Thank God, I am healthy, have a good appetite, and can sleep well. All of this is very important in the Congo. At home we do not appreciate it as much as we do here.

Well, I hope that the Lord will give me my health and give me the opportunity to see my loved ones again soon. Our natural life also comes from the Lord, so we should affirm our natural life. I notice, in particular, how much I miss spiritual friendship. To be with the Lord alone are blessed times, times that I did not understand previously. I would also like to learn to be thankful for everything. I just cannot develop the inner spiritual friendship that I need with the local black people.

At present there are very few people at the mission. Everything is dark at night in the village. Beginning tomorrow, the workers and the teachers with their wives are expected to be back at the mission, where they will live. The school will not begin this month. It's almost impossible to teach school during the dry season. We are not getting the rain this year that we had expected. Eight workers and I are repairing the roofs of the buildings. After that we want to burn down the felled trees to prepare the field for the rainy season.

My house helper left three days ago to see his wounded brother and has not yet returned. I don't have another one in reserve, and so I have to do everything alone in the house. That is difficult for me.

Last Wednesday, the government official, D'have, with his pretty wife visited me. I offered up everything that I had to appropriately welcome them. His wife is a very refined woman; while I was away, she baked some bread for me. She also wants me to come to their house as long as my help is away. It is important to take advantage of every opportunity that decent people offer us. D'haves travel to Bisajngandu tomorrow. They plan to return in a week and hope to build a house here in Bololo. I hope our work will be easier when they return.

The government official and his wife returned after lunch to hear the news from Luebo. I'm not sure if they'll stay overnight. I don't really like it, when I don't have enough help in the house. There are workers outside, but all they can do for me is to make fire in the oven and get water. I do have one man, Djema Bokfundu, but he doesn't seem to be learning very well, so he is not much help. He doesn't have a wife but he says he has one in mind. When he brings me his complaints about getting a wife, I simply say, "I don't have a wife either." This connects me with him. The Dengese people can identify with me and my grief on this one topic.

On the short wave radio I hear a German program each week entitled, "Homeland." People, mostly soldiers, who are scattered all over the world, are contacted in this way. The purpose is to encourage them with appropriate songs. I've had many a tear in the quiet while listening to these songs as women, separated from their husbands, speak to their lonely men abroad. Children also speak in such heartfelt ways to their fathers. This cuts me deeply. As I listened to these broadcasts, I imagined my wife and children, but their voices are hard to remember. How much grief and how much separation the war has brought! In a week, it'll be a year since I said goodbye to my family. On the one hand it seems like a very long time. On the other hand, time seems to have run by so quickly.

With hearty greetings your lonely, H. G. Bartsch.

My Thoughts on the Dengese People

I have let the students and a number of the workers have holidays since June. I made a number of trips with my car and want to make a number of other ones by foot, with kipoy and with my bike.

It is very dry here now. This is particularly difficult this year. It is hot and windy during the day; at night, foggy and cold. It's a perfect temperature to catch a cold.

I repaired some of the houses with the rest of the workers and hacked down part of the forest to prepare the fields for manioc. Then we burned the part of the forest that has been hacked down. It burns white powder. The bushes burn down to the roots. Everyone loves these fires.

The women and their daughters go down to the river to fish. The men take the boys to hunt wild animals. They often stay overnight. The surprising thing is that the people are always without fish and meat in spite of all the hunting and fishing that they do. In fact, they become desperately hungry. They don't know how to plan ahead. Rather they seem to be motivated by their immediate needs, as animals are.

It's particularly difficult for missionaries during this dry season to have gatherings. It is barely possible to meet with the elderly, the sick and the crippled. It is easier to travel during the dry season, because then the heavy rains with thunder and lightning are absent. I plan to make a trip with several of the teachers in August to some of the nearby villages. I will probably take my bike, since it's very difficult during this time to get men to carry me.

Oh, when will the time come when these "Esau" children will be able to work properly! I can only get help when I pay a high price. When a neighboring mission program began, the missionaries were too hard on the people. The people therefore left and sought out another Protestant mission. Today the opposite seems to be true. As soon as the people do some work, they run to the Governor or to the King and accuse the mission of being too hard on them. If one evaluates the work of a Negro by European standards, he really doesn't deserve the salt after the day's labor. My patience is often exhausted when I need to get something done. It's almost unbelievable how little work a grown man can do during the day; to get a load of firewood takes a whole day. I am looking at an example of this right now. Nevertheless, I must have patience. The Governor also warns us not to give the local people too much work. I think about the words of Hans Grimm, "If there is too little work, people cannot be either well or healthy." These words carry a lot of meaning. That's why we want to hope that these wild people will have better days, where they can accomplish more and where it is possible for them to do so.

With hearty greetings from your lonely friend and brother in Africa, H. G. Bartsch

Turmoil in the Dengese Region

Dear brother, I received your most welcome letter of July 1 on the fifth of September. Many thanks for the kind words that you expressed. Airmail takes about as much time as the regular mail. The main thing is that I received word from you. I want to tell you how I have been doing in the last year. I will write to different members of the committee or to members of my family. Of course I can't tell you about everything, but I hope I can get some things across.

I'm glad that you received the notice that Brother and Sister Kramer had to leave Bololo. You now know the situation I am in.[51] The situation changes daily. It is as changeable as the weather. Sometimes there is brilliant sunshine in the next day after the darkest clouds. But for now, I am left alone here. Normally it would be easier for me, but now I can hardly make any settled plans for the future. Following the mysterious and sudden death of the Belgian commissioner in June, everything seems to be in turmoil here. He was on the way to Bololo and wanted to establish greater order in this district. Then one night I heard that he was dead. I don't know the cause of his death. In any case, the blacks are quite happy, and the drums are beating loudly. The new commissioner, Mr. Sand from Luebo, arrived in this territory three weeks ago. I invited him to come to Bololo again. Mr. Sand is traveling around it with the King in this district. I will hold off making trips myself, because I really want to meet Mr. Sand.

I haven't started school now for a number of reasons. For one thing, it is very difficult to keep order under the present conditions. Some mean and mischievous men get some of the

---

[51] Brother and Sister Kramer were German citizens and so "enemies" of the Belgian state.

younger students to beat up on other students. This occurs even during class periods. Oppositional students shoot their bows and arrows at their teachers. It is difficult to establish order. The worship services are also disrupted so that it's impossible to conduct them in peace. They sometimes take the wives of trusted teachers and missionaries, and no one holds them accountable. We hear that adult missionaries and their children are killed, and there is no place to complain. The young men who served me faithfully and stood by me do not know what to do. They are shamed in the villages and often beaten. They beat one of the young men a few days ago with a club and broke his teeth. The perpetrator should pay a penalty when something like this happens. But we missionaries are without rights.

One young man lost two of his children. They were both murdered. This is because he did not go along with what the people in the village wanted him to do. Basongo, a very lovely young man, will not get a wife if he stays here. Nevertheless, he stays in hopes that the mission also gets rights as in other places. Another student came to me one Sunday to ask me for advice as to which mission he should escape to with his wife. He wants to keep her and she also wants to stay with him, but her relatives want to take her away from him. "So, where shall we go?" He is a dead man if somebody from the village should even suspect that he came to see me. I advised him to wait.

The young girls in the school are molested, but no one seems to care about such things. This is heathenism. When will the night end? Oh, please pray that the light will come to this darkness!

Often the question arises in my mind, and may in your minds as well. "Why do so few of the old students come back to the mission?" This question was answered for me by the governor here in Bololo. I sat next to him as people came and paid their dues. Some of the former students came and brought their money. Everyone had to pay. It struck me that many had changed their names from the ones that they had had at the mission.

This is the explanation. A commissioner, Mr. Cheney, returned to his position while we were away in 1938. Mr. Cheney opposed our mission so he levied a heavy tax on the children of our school. Some of the older students had to pay back taxes for two years. When these students did not have the money, some foul men from the village sought to bring them back to the old customs. To make them dependent on the people of the village, the village helped to pay for those who could not pay, and in that way, they became slaves of the village and needed to listen to the authorities in the village. Their names changed. In such ways, the Word of God has been trampled upon. All of this is happening now during this time of war, where Europe is being judged by the terror of war. Nevertheless, I want to do whatever I can to be free to God and people. In the next letter maybe I can give a better description of what is going on here.

One pastor wrote that the Mennonites must be experiencing a special kind of grace. "When the devil does everything to disturb their work, the spirit of God gives them a special witness." That can comfort us in this situation.

When I write about such difficult matters, it does not mean that the people here are personally antagonistic. I must say that when people meet me, generally, they are friendly and seem eager to interact with me. But the administration of Dengese does not want the people to come under the influence of the Word of God and does not want them to become Christians. I don't know how long the enemy will succeed in keeping the spirit of God from these people. I know that He has the entire world situation in His hands.

I am physically well. I have enough to live on. Nature is beautiful, and the yard is comfortably well kept. The rain now comes during the day with strong thunderstorms. The air is clear and clean.

I began work at the mission station again. If, as the commissioner says nothing can change here, then I'll commit myself to travel and conduct free, open meetings and seek to do personal work. Things shall change here soon, I hope. "We have to fight on, as it's ordered for us to do. And we will win through Jesus Christ our Lord."

With warm greetings and blessings, your H. G. Bartsch.
The following book summary was submitted by H. G. Bartsch. It's a book written by Tiele-Winkler, regarding her call to the mission field in 1905. Apparently, Ms. Winkler went to a mission program in England, where she discovered that people in foreign countries were suffering. She felt the call of God and wrote the book, Thoughts of the Living God. *She describes how she was struck by the needs of heathen people in foreign countries. She describes how she argued with God and said, "I have nothing to give." The response was, "Give what you can." She describes how she was impressed by particular hymns, and was reminded again not to be disobedient, but to do the will of God. She gave her gifts on the offering plate and gave her life to do mission work.*

There are Signs of Progress in Bololo but I Am Lonely[52]

Everything at the station is in full swing. The King brought many students with him. It appears to me, that the King has changed his mind. Time will tell. Most of the students that were with me in 1935 to 1938 are back at school. The previous teachers are also here and work very energetically. Most of the students also live here where I take care of them. I seek to enforce the previous regulations, as well as I can. The commissioner has also been a positive influence here. I can feel it right away in my work. My prayer is that the schoolwork and this year will go smoothly.

There are also a number of young girls who have come to school. At first they were like "wildcats." Now the 75 girls that are at the Mission seem to enjoy learning. The girls are here till noon and again in the calm of the evening. After the evening gathering, I allow them to go into the village. That is better. They have to work for some hours during each day. Today they had to plant manioc. Some of the teachers are very helpful to me in getting the work done.

---

[52] *Der kleine Africa Bote*, March 1941.

The work with the sick has suffered a lot. It's hard to keep order in the care for the sick when the government does not help very much. There are few doctors here, and consequently, they are very expensive. For example, a man who was very badly burned could not be admitted to our clinic because he required special services and hospital admission. I sent the caregivers with the sick man to Decca, where he could see a good doctor and get proper treatment. Later on, I discovered that they didn't take the man to the hospital in Decca. In fact, they took him to the village, where they put him into a hut. He died several days later. It's just very hard to realize how poorly the local people treat their sick people. When peace arrives and the government establishes a sense of order, there will be much work to be done with the sick. This is particularly so among the women.

In the future, I see a blossoming mission field. Even if I do not see the fruits of that in the future, I want to be thankful that it has been possible to maintain the mission. The Catholic priests trumpet their success in being able to disrupt the work in Bololo. But the commissioner told me in the presence of the priests in Bolombo that he has given us freedom to work in the whole Dengese province.

The lonely life is very difficult for me. You know how much I want to be among people. Even though I have a lot of people around me, I so long to see white people. I know, however, that the Lord has determined my path. So I want to crucify my flesh and become quiet before Him. I will enclose a song that has meant a lot to me.

> *I want to be quiet, Lord, I want to be still.*
> *Deep down in my heart, I want to be still!*
> *I won't say yes, I won't say no,*
> *I won't wish for great things, nor wish for things small.*
> *I'll just be quiet; I'll quiet down and be still!*
>
> *Oh God, you see that I want to be quiet;*
> *Still when my joy beams its light,*
> *Still when the cross brings me pain,*

Whether I laugh, or whether I cry,
Deep down inside, oh Lord, I long to be quiet and still.
Quiet me down, oh God, quiet me down.
Still me as gold is still in a smelter's fire;
Still me, so You can cleanse me of the dross,
Till your image shines through me;
Please help me Lord, to be quiet and still.
Thank you, God, I can be quiet now.
I can rest faithfully in your will,
He guides me quietly in and out,
He leads me into heaven itself,
I am blessed! He leads me to quiet down.

The Work Is Going Well but I am Lonely for My Family

Hearty greetings to you from Micah, Chapter 7, verse eight.

"Do not gloat over me, my enemy:
though I have fallen, I shall rise;
though I live in darkness,
The Lord is my light."

This is the verse that came to me one morning when I was rather depressed. This morning, the Lord gave me the verse from Genesis, chapter 32, verse 12:

"I will do well with you. I will make you prosper."

The morning worship service has just ended. The church was almost full. Many students attended. First Mr. Mpila, and then I, spoke. Everything is done in the way we always did it. Singing leaves a lot to be desired. The old songs sound pretty good if people stay in tune. They're not too many new songs that have been developed. I guess all that remains for the future. I am happy when we can find the "old tracks" again. Even the students from Bololo are fairly punctual. The students from the other villages remain, if we have food available. I'm just grateful that things are going well. I am tired with many tasks to do. The heat, walking back and forth to the various places, taking care of everything makes me tired.

The hardest thing is to maintain control of the workload of the blacks. They do very little work. I was surprised that I was able to get them back to the work after being away for so long. This past week, I worked with the students on Brother Kramer's house. Now, it even looks livable. We have rented the land again from the state. We need to pay rent for the land, though not for our own houses.

According to the last report, the Kramers are well. They live in a separate house in Luebo. Sadly, we are not able to purchase any more items for them from Europe. They asked me to visit them. It's very hard for me to get away because of the many duties that I have here. The cook has just arrived with food. I need to eat while the food is still hot.

The teachers that I have bring me much joy. The classes with the girls are going well.

I hear that the shipping lanes to New York are open. I don't know what happened to the first ship. I was getting excited about the fact that my loved ones might be taking this ship soon. I was restless about it, too. Later on we will see why everything has come about, as it should. Whether we see each other again, on this side of life, or whether we meet in at the Crystal City later, only the Lord knows. When you read these lines, it will probably be Christmas there. If the Lord has determined that I am to remain in this isolation and loneliness, then I want to be quiet and accept that. In recent times, I've learned a lot from the prophet Jeremiah. That has strengthened me in my work for the Master. I feel it even more than ever before, that the caring prayer of you people has enabled me to do this. Often in the late evening I walk along a path through the woods with the full moon shining, and speak to the One who lives beyond the stars about the mission to the Dengese people and about my loved ones. It's then that I hear the words, "I will do well with you . . . . there will be no plague at your door . . . . I will show you my salvation." So many promises then pass through my mind. And I say, "It's worth it for me to be here!"

Since October 1, I have been meeting with 25 of the best students in the afternoon. The instruction of this group has gone well.

I am Lonely on a Sunday Morning

I want to visit with you again as I write you a few lines. It's 9:30 Sunday morning. The worship services just ended. There's quite a bit of noise outside and many people are milling about. Meat has arrived from the forest, and so it is being dealt out to the people. It's not easy to parcel out an animal to so many people. It's particularly disturbing on a Sunday morning.

Despite all the noise, my thoughts raced to those whom I love. My loneliness is particularly severe on a Sunday morning. I recognize that this is a very unsafe time. I definitely expected peace to arrive this year. War has expanded. It is going in all directions. The war seems to be getting closer to the Congo. How, when, and where the Lord will bring me together with my loved ones I must leave in His hands.

I learned from the radio that shipping lanes between the Congo and New York have been set up. I don't know what happened to the first ship. It appears to me that the oceans are very unsafe at this time. Nevertheless, I am happy that the Lord is the captain and that He will direct His path, according to His loving will.

I've not heard from the Kramers for some time. I should actually go and visit them. But, because I'm alone, it's hard to get away. The work that I'm doing has been going well for the past three months. The students come and learn and the teachers are active. The people from the village remain distant. It's harder and harder to get material things here. Business travel is difficult. Nature is just wonderful. It rained at night, and now everything flowers as in spring. I am well. I don't have my help in the home today, so I must prepare my food myself. I read and pray a lot, and think about how the work will go. Life is so abnormal. And I also worry about my loved ones.

With hearty greetings. I wish you well, H. G. Bartsch.

I Get Frustrated in My Work

Everything is going well here in Bololo, according to the African tempo. A person could lose his patience at the slow progress in the classroom if there weren't black help. Presently I work with eight teachers in the school. In the afternoon I give extra classes in the elementary subjects. A short while ago we began classes in the afternoon. The Dengese complain a lot, especially at this time. I would like to, but I can't silence these dear children. After they've been sitting in class their energy explodes as they leave the building after 4 1/2 hours. It becomes hard on my nerves.

Later I went to the Kramers' old house to do repair work. I got the students to bring me 7-foot-long sticks. I used these to build a fence around the building. I've used these to build a fence to house dogs, cats, goats and chickens. With all the noise and all the activity around, I often think about Strauss songs and that comforts me. The Kramers' house is located in a very beautiful spot. I've often thought of living there myself. It makes a big difference where one lives.

> *"And even if you live in troubled times,*
> *Find a home that suits you; not in the dark,*
> *No, at the edge where you can have*
> *A view of the big valley."*

There Is Trouble in the Lives of My Dear Teachers

I'm heavily involved in my work and don't know how I can take off several days to visit the Kramers. All the teachers are of great help. But I can't leave any of them alone. When I do, everything goes topsy-turvy. One of the people that I trust a lot is Ngunga, but he has a very troubled wife. He is very good to me but she whines and cries and acts like a little child. One evening she gave him nothing to eat. After that he beat her very hard. So she went into the village, screaming loudly. He remained quiet and calm, and even came to the evening worship service. When she came back to their dwelling, she lay in her bed and slept soundly.

Mpembe Rdedji's wife was very faithful in the worship gatherings. He often came to my window in the evening with his wife, and remained for a long time. Recently, however, I missed her in the worship services and on the campus of the school. When I asked him where his wife was, he said, "In the village. She's gone fishing." One morning she came out of the village to the Mission, painted with red paint. She had a number of charms hung around her neck. She did not come to the morning worship service, but stayed in her dwelling and sat by the fire. Later on, she became very loud with the other women and the other school children. When Mpembe came to her, she took a burning stick and stuck it into his middle. She had been sent by the village to get the women and the young girls and boys back into village life. Her husband came and told me all of this. Now she sits in the village, and he's here at the school where he does well. This morning, he spoke about Moses' call from the Lord to build the Ark of the Lord. I was pleased with his sermon.

Basongo is a very lovely young lad. I really like him. He's faithful and pious. And many of the other students are really very nice, too.

Lupenki just announced that the doctor is coming. I went to meet the doctor and made arrangements for him. He stayed from ten o'clock in the morning till three o'clock in the afternoon. It was a real refreshing time for me to talk to such an intelligent man in my native language. I did have a bit of a problem over lunch, though. I had sent my cook away for the day, so I had to cook for myself. It went okay, and I noticed that the doctor felt very comfortable and spontaneous. Tomorrow the governor is also supposed to come. So that's how I get refreshed intellectually. However, I am left alone to take care of my spiritual welfare.

The doctor was in real danger with the Yalimas people. The governor sent soldiers and brought 40 men back to Dekese. Neither the governor, the doctor, nor business people seemed to be able to do anything with these wild people. It really is a miracle that I can do what I am doing. I become more thankful for that every day. I want to do what I can.

I am well and can eat and sleep well. I have not taken any quinine for four months now. And there are also very few mosquitoes this year in Bololo, compared to terrible times with them last year. Recently there was a snake in the dining room. When that happens, the blacks become very anxious and agitated.

I Experience Some Replenishing Events in Difficult Circumstances

Because there's an opportunity to send letters tomorrow, I want to add a few lines to what I've already written. It's nine o'clock in the morning here. The children are finished cleaning the campus, and now everything is quiet at the mission station. Only the turtledoves and the larks sing at my window! Everything is quiet and dark in nature. Only my alarm clock ticks away in the big living room. I've been staying at the Kramers' house for the past few days. It's a wonderful place to view the west from here.

I just came from being with the Governor D'Have at the train station. He lives about three kilometers from us. He's a good worker, and is able to get the local people to do the work. Although we think very differently about some questions, it's refreshing for me when we get together. I'm still not sure whether having the governor so close to our mission station will be a blessing.

A week ago the government-appointed doctor, Dr. De-Mupe, came to visit. He's a young 25 to 30-year-old man. He was my guest several times. He speaks German very well and is highly intelligent. He was very polite, as was Dr. Pili, but he's much more practical. I was pleased with his social and religious outlooks. Added to that was his humility, and his freedom to be himself. He's coming to Bololo again next week. The situation for a doctor in this district is very dissatisfying. He can only help individuals, but he cannot provide a healing context for them. He can't isolate the sick from the others. And so others contract the disease. We're seeing a lot of leprosy here now.

At school, everything is going at a slow pace, as is the custom in Africa. We have about 180 students. How we will feed these students is a critical question. The field and what we had cleared has been trampled on by an elephant. I do not have any bread for the children this whole week. Sometimes I really wonder how they can come to school when they don't have enough food. Well, I can't really pity them, because then many of them would run away. The teachers are always at their jobs and are good about it.

Yesterday I had a big surprise. All the students really rejoiced with me when the postman came and brought two packages, and a lot of mail from overseas. The jubilation of the children did not seem to want to end, even though they had received nothing for themselves. The children behave twice as well when I am happy. I can notice this in the class and also at work. They're much quieter. That's a pointer for me in the work of the mission. The work is so multifaceted. Often I really don't know what to do. But the Lord can work through our weaknesses or our mistakes.

Here in Bololo everything is going according to its usual plan. The children are very punctual. The others do not come as quickly, unless they get food. The Word of God has been shared with many people here, and this Godly seed will bear fruit in its own time. That's actually the only comfort of doing work in the school, though it often seems to go too slow for me. I should also spend more time with students outside of school hours. But I'm alone. How I miss my dear wife in this work. I can't describe how much I miss her.

The second Christmas that I've been separated from my loved ones is arriving. I pray that the Lord will strengthen me in this. He can set everything right. I don't know where I'll be this Christmas period. But I would love to be together with some other people for close fellowship. I find it absolutely necessary for my heart, for my mind, and for my feeling of well-being.

Otherwise, I am well. I have a hearty appetite. I sleep well and have no fever. My headaches return periodically. There are few mosquitoes here this year. Maybe that's because I have the yard cleaned almost every day. I recently planted a banana garden but the elephant tore everything apart. When the rain comes the field will be rejuvenated and restored. The fruit trees are in full bloom. The trees are green, and the palm leaves wave at me. Who will enjoy all of this?

Everything is going well and as usual in the school. We have few interruptions; only one, a student ran away and came back. That makes it difficult to continue in a smooth way. But we accept that which we cannot change. Yesterday, the warthogs came silently and destroyed our whole garden. This morning, all the boys want to go and set up traps to catch them. They are heroes when they come back from such an adventure. They are all born hunters.

The governor is still here. The houses that he is having built will be ready fairly soon. He's actually getting very tired of the Dengese people because they treat him so badly. Of the 260 able-bodied men in Bololo, he was only able to recruit about 50 percent to do the work. They gave him three or four different names for the same person and asked him to go and find these people. Such obstacles often try the patience of us foreigners.

I just received a letter from Brother Kramer. They had a little boy born to them, on November 5. His name is Ernst.

I am healthy, and wish you all good health, without my headaches.

I am Concerned for the Kramers and Experience a Fortuitous Event

Much has happened since I wrote you. I've been away from Bololo for almost 2 weeks. My reason for doing that was that I received a letter from the Kramers telling me that a little son was born to them on November 5. They live in Luebo. On the same day that their son was born, Belgian government officials wanted to move them to Elizabethville. But because of the circumstances of the new birth, that trip was postponed. Because the letter was dated three weeks previously, I thought that our dear sisters and brothers had already moved to the new location. I certainly had to go and visit them. Here in Bololo, everything was going well and in high gear. I wanted very much to end the school year without any disruption. In addition to the letter from the Kramers, I received a letter from you, requesting that I visit the Kramers in their loneliness and to see whether I could help them. After thoughtful prayer, I decided to close the school and make my way to Luebo or maybe even Elizabethville. I am not comfortable leaving the teachers with the students without my presence.

On December 5th I drove to the train station, where I could catch a train from the south to Port Francqui. I wanted to phone Luebo to find out whether the Kramers were still in Luebo or whether they had been transferred to Elizabethville. Regretfully, the telephone system was not working. And I couldn't discover anything. So I decided to travel to Port Francqui first, to buy the necessary goods for the school, to then come back to Dombiyongo, then on to Luebo or maybe even travel right on to Elizabethville. After I had done my necessary business, I traveled off again. I don't feel good about the distance I'll have to travel. I don't know whether it's 100, 200, 400, or even 1000 km.

My car broke down about 60 km after Port Francqui: The motor didn't get enough gasoline. I stopped the car in the middle of the road at the hottest time of the day and searched for the cause of the problem. Suddenly a car came from the opposite direction, towards me. He had to stop, because there is no other way around. A gentleman stepped out of the car and asked if he could be of help to me. ("Good advice is better than 80 quiet workers.") We blew air through the gasoline tubes, and the blockage was spewed out. It only took us a few minutes, after we discovered the problem. So I thanked this stranger and asked him what he was actually doing here. "My name is Fisher, and I am the director of the company in this district." After we discussed conditions a little more he told me that Brother and Sister Kramer were still in Luebo. The remainder of the trip was very easy because I now knew that they were in Luebo.

When I arrived in Luebo, I was greeted in a very warm and friendly way by government officials. They said that I had come almost as though I had been called to come. At my request, Brother and Sister Kramer were free to go with me. There were only a few formalities that they had to complete. This was done very quickly after which I went to Brother and Sister Kramers' home. Their happiness at being able to see me again and the clarification of their situation was very great. They began to pack immediately.

This was Saturday. On Sunday, December 8, I brought the Kramers back to their home in which they had lived so long. We read God's Word together, and thanked the Lord from our hearts for His leading in our lives. On Monday, we delayed going to Bololo, since the Kramers needed to have dental work done. The dentist had just returned from his vacation and was available. We stayed for another three days. With many good wishes from the missionaries and the government officials we left Luebo. On December 12 we came to Lodi. On December 14, I was able to bring everybody over the Sankuru River. We stayed overnight again and on Sunday, at nine o'clock, we made our way to Bololo with all of our things. That was the most difficult part, but it also went very well and we were happy to have overcome the obstacles. Aside from the little boy, Ernst, we are all well.

These are the important experiences that I had in early December. If I were to write about the experiences that the Kramers had, I would probably have to fill a whole book. For now, it's important to know that the Lord is in control and guides the little ship that carries His children. He hears our prayers and for that we want to thank Him. The Word of God that has been with me in the last little while is from Psalm 126. For those who have prayed for us and with us, I call out, read this Psalm and thank God for His wonderful answers to our prayers!

"May those who sow in tears
Reap with shouts of joy."

I am healthy and happy in the Lord. I'm also happy that the Lord has given me the opportunity to have a large number of students in school. Many a seed has been planted in the students and will bring fruit in its own time. Oh, how I wish I could experience that in my lifetime, before the night falls. Evening has come, the sun has set. Often, I look at the unripe harvest, and I'm sad about the fact that I can do so little. The power of the evil one is very great, but the Lord is with us. The nations are preparing for the last battle, but we pray, "Give peace, Lord. Let peace reign!"

With greetings to you and all those who belong to you our worthy readers of *Der kleine Africa Bote*.

Your lonely fellow worker,
H. G. Bartsch

At the End of the Year: Hope and Confidence Though the Outlook Is Bleak[53]

Brother and Sister Kramer are now at the mission station. Except for little Ernst, everyone is healthy and well. There's also a lot of goat's milk. We need to use powdered milk for the children. We will need to see how to arrange our lives here at the mission station in the next little while.

We have begun classes and that has been in place now for some time. Many people gathered here at Christmas. Because of my trip to Luebo at the beginning of the month, many other preparations for the Christmas Festival were not completed. Everything was different. We also didn't have the presents that we had had in other years.

Some of our men from Bololo have gone to the City of Dekese to get roofing material. I guess they will experience the New Year and the festivities over there. After the New Year, I want to go to Dekese to discuss matters with the government officials. If I can arrange it, I want to travel to the northern villages.

Although the outlook for the mission is not good, I am not without hope nor am I discouraged. We will have to make some changes in our thoughts about our plans if we do not want to run aimlessly. The issue has to do with new relationships. As you saw in my previous letter, I could work with little interruption with a large number of students. Seeds that have been planted in

---

[53] *Der kleine Africa Bote*, April 1941.

the young hearts will grow in their own time. I had many joys and tears of sadness in the planting of the seed. I fought many battles and heavy moods, but always the Lord was my comfort and my help. He has carried me through and will also carry me through to see my loved ones. He is with me and remains with us "till the end of the world."

― Chapter 10 ―

Obstacles and Fatigue
1941-1942[54]

Travel to Dekese and Kole

I am sorry that it took me so long to answer your letter. Many things have happened in the past few days. Since I've been on travels, I haven't heard anything about the political life of our time. We do not hear about the world events in the jungles of Africa, nor in the villages. After Brother and Sister Kramer returned to Bololo, my plan was to pursue my previous intent to visit Kole. There are many villages along the Lukene River, and I want to preach the word to these people there. I first went to Dekese. I met with a government official there, but I can't really promise any results from that visit. The government officials made many promises, but we'll have to wait to see which promises are kept. I was well received by other government officials and by Dr. DeMnynk. It was good for us to eat together on Sunday. I felt good about the warm reception by the government officials. I felt like I was at home with the doctor. Then on January 13 I took a ride on the motor scooter to Jafa. After that I used my bicycle and had several helpers to carry my things. But the people who had come with me from Bololo went back home.

Now I've been on the road for five days. It was difficult to travel because nobody has worked on the road. Mountains, valleys, streams, swamps, and overgrown underbrush made it very difficult for me and for those who were assisting me. Thankfully we arrived at our destination before the heavy rains came. It is Sunday today; I wanted to be at the mission station at Kole, but I can't go any further today. The bridge over a small but

---

[54] *Der kleine Africa Bote*, April 1941.

turbulent stream to this village has been damaged. Maybe I'll get across it tomorrow.

There is a road from Bolombo to here. I left my car in Bolombo. I didn't take the car because I didn't have gasoline. Besides, I didn't really want to travel through desert territory, where there were no villages. There are supposed to be a number of villages on the road that I will take now.

It's a beautiful morning. There's a new government house on an embankment on the road about a half a kilometer from the village. Birds are singing beautifully in the nearby woods. There are little gray birds that resemble the nightingale and they sing just as beautifully. Drums are beating in the village. The boys who came along with me went down to the village after the morning worship service. We want to have another meeting this evening. People are back so work on the bridge will proceed. That's why I have time to write right now.

On this trip, I am accompanied by four teachers and one student: Ngunga, Basongo, Mipila, Boto, and Bokiri. These wonderful men have been a great help to me with the singing and the speaking. They became somewhat depressed in the villages when the Catholic opposition was evident. Nevertheless, many men and women and children came to our meetings. When possible, they also taught a song or a Bible verse. Many of our meetings were very encouraging and will not remain fruitless. Basongo was full of enthusiasm when it was his turn to speak. He speaks loudly, earnestly and very clearly. He makes a good impression on the listeners, which is not always the case when I speak or when some of the other teachers speak.

I was in Dekese on Sunday. Most of the government officials came to church. I wanted to remain rather unobtrusive, so that I didn't stir up any dust. Then, suddenly, a soldier came up to me and asked if I would lead the Protestant meeting. What should I do? I said yes, and in a few minutes, the whole veranda was full of men and women from various occupations. In particular, there were a lot of soldiers present. We sang several songs in the Dengese language. We prayed, and then sang songs in the Baluba, Botatelle, and other dialects. Then it was my turn to speak. Which language should I use? I spoke in Kikongo, and everyone understood. I told the story of Zachaeus and made applications. At the close, many men and women took part in the prayer. The singing would not stop. I was ashamed at my lack of faith; they asked me to begin a mission program in Dekese. As the government officials left the church, they took an offering to which most people contributed. This is the fruit other missionaries planted before us. We benefit from that.

We had no difficulty gathering people together in all the villages along the Lukene River. Often children and women came to greet us before we arrived at the village. The men appeared when they realized that we didn't need any more baggage carriers. In Langa, the last village of the Dengese border, people could not stop rejoicing when I got on my bicycle and rode into town. We preached to the people about the living Word of Jesus and moved on.

I arrived in Kole, where I stayed for two days. I received many a blessing here. Everyone is very warm and kind. Yesterday they had a baptism of nine persons. The men who came with me also attended. Tomorrow, I want to return back to Bololo. I am thankful that I'm healthy and happy in the Lord. Tonight we will have a farewell. I didn't expect so much love from the people that I've met.

Your brother in the Lord, H. G. Bartsch

February Report of the Meeting of the Directors of the African Mission

1. There was general optimism about the mission program.

2. The treasurer, Brother DeFehr, points out that the financial situation looks good. God has always provided enough funds for the needs as we became aware of them.

3. Brother F. C. Thiesen, the secretary, reported that he is having difficulty getting enough responses from the congregations.

4. The word from the mission field is rather sparse. The last letters that have been received were written in October. At that time, Brother Bartsch indicated that the school is in full swing with both boys and girls.

5. The Kramers are presently living in Luebo.

6. Travel to the Belgian Congo by ship is very difficult at this time. So it's not a good idea for us to send Mrs. Bartsch, her children, and Ms. Brooks.

The readers will want to know what the committee has decided about the future of the work in Africa. The following decisions were made:

1. The secretary was instructed to make every effort to get visas for Ms. Brooks and Mrs. Bartsch with her children. We don't know how much time this will take, but we expect that it will occur in several months.

2. We decided to get in touch with the International Red Cross in Ottawa to see how we might contact Brother Bartsch as quickly as possible.

3. If the war should move to the Congo, mission work would likely need to stop for a short time. In that case we would hand over the mission program to a neighboring mission station. If the work becomes too difficult, we want Brother Bartsch to know that he has our full support to return home. That decision will need to be made in the future.

4. It is our intention to keep Brother Bartsch fully informed about these kinds of decisions and that he has our full support in making the decision to stay or to return home, depending on how the Lord leads him. We want to pray for him that the Lord give him clarity of thought. It is not easy to sort through all these questions, while he is doing full-time work.

5. The message to Brother Bartsch is that if things worsen and he decides to return home, that he set up support for the people in the mission program as much as possible. One possibility is to ask the neighboring Presbyterian mission to maintain the program that has been started.

6. The committee also decided to extend the executive committee authority for another year.

We close the committee meeting with prayer for the missionaries and for the work that has already been done.

H. H. Janzen

A Family Letter

My dear Anna and children,

It's April 1. It's been several weeks since I wrote to you last. My travels and various other hindrances kept me from writing sooner. It's also not possible to send letters as easily as it was before. I understand that many letters don't even reach their destination. Nevertheless, I need to keep writing to keep the connection between you and me.

Since Brother and Sister Kramer are back in Bololo, nearly every job has been taken away from us at the mission station. It's not possible to change anything in the near future. But people in Luebo and Lusambo have sought to encourage me and advised me to have patience. Recently, I made a trip to Lusambo to meet with the governor of the province. I'm satisfied with the friendliness and warmth with which I was received. We have men in high places that understand our situation.

The people in the village are the same as always, and are not antagonistic. But they have discovered a way to keep the children away from us. Also, there are very few adults that come to the worship service. In those villages where the Catholics do not have a representative, people are very friendly and come eagerly to our worship services. I experience that on my travels all the time. At present, Brother Kramer is in charge of the school. The school is very small at this time.

The Belgians have put King Ikongo-Samu in a Luebo jail. He could not get along with the authorities. At my last visit in Luebo, I spoke on his behalf, and now he is set free. I expect his attitude towards the mission in Bololo will be quite different than it has been when he returns in April. So things change here. In Lusambo, I received the right to install teachers in the various villages.

Brother and Sister Kramer and their oldest two children are healthy. The baby, who was always somewhat sickly, died on February 26 after severe illnesses. I am well and am happy in the Lord.

Travel across the ocean is always getting more dangerous. So I cannot advise you to come here at this time. I greet everyone that prays for us.

Your praying and lonely husband,
H. G. Bartsch

The Voice of God Regarding the Zam Zam

My husband left for Africa in August 1939. A month later, September 3, Great Britain and Canada declared war on Germany. World War II had begun. It changed everything: All our plans for becoming a united family. The Committee considered sending us (myself and our four children) in early 1940 but decided not to because too many allied ships were being sunk in the Atlantic.

By June 1941, we again made plans to go to Africa. The Committee bought tickets on an Egyptian ship, the Sam-Sam[55] *to take us to Cape Town, South Africa. From there we could take the train to the Belgian Congo. Many other civilians were registered to sail on it. It was to leave Halifax, travel south to Buenos Aires, then cut across the Atlantic to the Congo. We were excited to be reunited as a family. Karl was 4 1/2, Arthur almost 8, Lydia 10, and Erna almost 12.*

I worried about schooling for the children. There would be no white friends. Henry was concerned about this too. Suddenly it became very clear to me. "I CANNOT GO." I rushed out to

Sam Sam lists heavily to port.

---

[55] Mother spells the name of the ship Sam-Sam. *Time-Life* spells it Zam Zam.

tell Franz Thiessen, Secretary of the Africa Committee. He was stunned. I cancelled my tickets and felt at peace.

Within several weeks I heard on the radio that the Zam-Zam *had been torpedoed by a German warship. The Germans knew that missionaries had been registered on the top decks, but that the deep holds were filled with ammunition. They off-loaded the civilians, sank the ship, and took the passengers to camps in occupied France. What a different life that would have been for us and our children.*

But the story does not end there. A month later I received a letter from Henry dated July 13, 1941. In it he wrote that he heard the news of the sinking of the Zam Zam *on the shortwave radio. He expressed how happy he was that he had sent a telegram telling me not to come. The telegram never did arrive. The Spirit of God had warned me not to come and it was good that I listened to that voice.*

A Note in the *Africa Bote*

The situation at the mission requires that the Kramers and Br. Bartsch remain at the mission station. So the reunion of Br. Bartsch and his family is postponed again. This is very hard on them. Brother Bartsch reports: "At one time, I answered the question about whether my family should come here. I sent a telegram. I could never feel settled about bringing the family to this place. The travel is too dangerous. I always counted on a peace agreement that would be made soon. Now everything looks even grimmer. I can't solve the problem with our children from here. All of the children wish that I were back in Canada. It feels too long for me to be away from the children for such a long time. But what I think is this. Sister Bartsch should remain out there in Canada, at least temporarily. As soon as I am not absolutely required to be here, without the program falling apart, I could leave Brother and Sister Kramer in charge of the program here. And I could come to Canada to resolve family difficulties and make arrangements with my wife to come back to the Dengese district."

Attack on the Zam Zam

The attack on the Zam Zam *came without warning. A passenger at the rail watched the* Atlantis *approach and suspected nothing. Elevating a half-dozen 5.9–inch guns and a 75mm cannon, the* Atlantis *fired at the* Zam Zam, *and hit amidships below the waterline. Ignoring frantic signals of surrender, the raider pounded the* Zam Zam *for ten minutes. The crippled* Zam Zam *heeled to port but managed to stay afloat. Passengers overfilled the lifeboats and then were picked up by the German raider.*[56]

German raider, Atlantis.

July 1941: Africa Committee Notes on Conditions in Bololo

In the past month, we've only received very little information from Brother Bartsch. This is understandable given the world conditions. In his previous report, our dear brother told us that the work at the school is being hindered very much by Catholics. Nevertheless Br. Kramer is working with a smaller number of students. On the other hand, the mission has obtained the right to appoint teachers in various villages. This is good news and a sign that the Lord's in charge of his work. This came about because Br. Bartsch took a trip to Leopoldville, the capital of the Belgian Congo. He did this to talk to the highest authorities to clarify the role of the mission and to make arrangements so that the mission would be least disturbed. He was received very

---

[56] The pictures were taken by *LIFE*'s David Scherman from a lifeboat just after the attack.

A PHANTOM RAIDER'S UNLIKELY TARGET

In April 1941 the rickety Egyptian liner Zamzam steamed down through the South Atlantic, bound from New York to South Africa and Egypt with a motley complement of European refugees, American missionary families, young volunteer ambulance drivers, North Carolina tobaccomen and French-Canadian priests. It was eight months before America's entry into the War, and the 138 Americans and 202 other passengers were about to become unwitting participants—and pawns—in the Battle of the Atlantic.

Five days out of Recife, Brazil, her last port of call before Cape Town, the Zamzam's British captain picked up the distress call of a Norwegian ship being chased by a German raider. Alarmed, the Zamzam changed her course abruptly, veering sharply to the south. But next morning the horizon was empty, and the ship resumed her leisurely passage toward Cape Town.

Shortly after midnight on April 16, the Zamzam steamed into the path of the notorious German raider *Atlantis*, which was traveling disguised as the Norwegian cargo ship *Tamesis*. The Zamzam was completely blacked out, a procedure that was not normally followed by ships of neutral nations. Moreover, her profile was identical to that of sister ships that had served as troop carriers for Great Britain in World War I and had subsequently been converted into Royal Navy Auxiliary cruisers.

Mistaking the liner for one of these warships, the *Atlantis* stalked her and, just before dawn, struck. Mortally wounded by shelling, the Zamzam began sinking as bewildered passengers and panicking Egyptian crewmen abandoned her. After being picked up by the raider, the Zamzammers were transferred to the German freighter *Dresden* for a wild, zigzagging 33-day ride into the North Atlantic. Among the passengers were LIFE photographer David E. Scherman and FORTUNE editor Charles J. V. Murphy, who had boarded the Zamzam at Recife on their way to assignments in Africa. With his camera, Scherman made a record of the passengers' strange odyssey, from the moment he boarded the Zamzam to disembarkation in Occupied France.

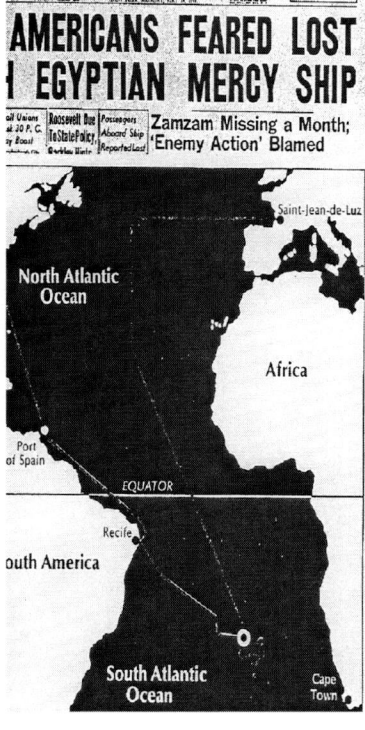

Headlines announce the disappearance of the Zamzam in 1941. The map traces the journey of the liner's "missing" passengers—from South America and on to the spot in the South Atlantic where transferred from the sinking ship to the raider and then to a freighter, which circled indecisively for eight days before finally heading north. The freighter veered a bit, on hearing that a British convoy was near, then turned east for Saint-Jean-de-Luz in Occupied France.

A TARDY ARRIVAL IN OCCUPIED FRANCE

On May 21, 30 days after the *Zamzam* had been scheduled to arrive in Cape Town, the *Dresden* steamed into Saint-Jean-de-Luz, France. The timing was vital: the previous day the British Admiralty had announced that the *Zamzam* was a month overdue and presumed sunk. Another incident like the World War I sinking of the *Lusitania* seemed to be in the making.

Then Berlin coolly announced that, far from being harmed, the Americans were all alive and well in a French resort close to Biarritz, awaiting repatriation. Evidently, Berlin had kept the Zamzammers at sea so that it could top the news of the sinking. The *Zamzam* had been sunk, claimed Berlin, because she carried "contraband"—steel rails for the North African front.

After interrogation, the Americans were freed. Some Europeans were interned; the rest were repatriated.

The Germans took most of Scherman's films to censor in Berlin, but he managed to hide four rolls in a tube of toothpaste, a tube of shaving cream and two boxes of surgical gauze that were carried for him in a missionary doctor's bag until their train reached neutral Portugal.

Murphy and Scherman flew from Lisbon to New York, where LIFE published the photographs, among them Scherman's surreptitious picture of the *Atlantis* (page 27). Displayed in the wardroom of every British warship, this photograph enabled the cruiser H.M.S. *Devonshire* to identify the raider six months later, despite her *Tamesis* disguise, and sink her. In December, only days before America entered the War, Berlin inexplicably released the rest of Scherman's 1,500 photographs, and LIFE published the whole saga of the *Zamzam*.

A final touch was added to the mystery of the *Zamzam* one year later when Scherman photographed Anthony Eden on an assignment for LIFE. The British statesman remarked cryptically over tea: "You chaps on the *Zamzam* were quite a disappointment to us. We expected that incident to bring America into the War."

warmly, and there was great interest and good wishes for his work. We do not have full results of this visit.

Br. Bartsch received the impression that the Kramers would have to go under house arrest again, and then he would be the only white man at the mission station. The Lord is taking our dear brother and his family through heavy times. So it's important for us to plead the Lord, on his behalf, at the throne of God. The Lord can do wonders, as He has often shown in the past. He will make all well. We must continue faithfully in our prayers and believe in his good work. We also want to pray for the Kramers in their situation. It certainly is a heavy burden for them to bear. May God grant grace, that all the sacrifice that is being done will not be in vain! Rather pray that it might bear fruit.

A Letter to Constituents from Anna Bartsch

Dear friends of the mission!

I'm happy to send you a greeting from Isaiah 62, verses six and seven. At this time, I am concerned about the thoughts that my husband expressed in the April letter of this year. I want to share those thoughts with you.

He writes that in his visit with the governor, he has received permission to place teachers in the various villages. This is a great benefit for the mission and means that the mission can expand. I want to write a few things about that situation.

In the same letter, Brother Bartsch reports that the work in Bololo has been shrunk through the cunning opposition of various groups. There are only a few students there. Brother Kramer teaches those classes. Many of you may think that the work has been disrupted. But no, the Lord has opened up new doors so the good news can be spread out into wider circles. It must be like the time of the early Christian church, as Stephan was stoned, and as Saul threatened the early disciples with murder. The disciples scattered into other places and preached the word, and many souls were saved. Previously, we were not allowed to put teachers in different villages. The local Catholic priest was allowed to drive out such teachers. This has changed. The Lord has now opened up new doors and given the right for teachers to be placed in various villages. They're no longer permitted to be driven out of those villages if there is no other teacher in that village. Little, new lights are beginning to glow in various places. The teachers are able to connect the word with their practice. The missionary travels from one teacher to the other and visits each in his own place. Since we did not have that possibility previously, I want to report to you that we are doing what other mission programs have been able to do. Now we are able to carry out such a program in the Dengese District.

Who are the teachers? It's not advisable to set the standards too high. Otherwise you won't have grasp of who the teachers are. These are men who came to the mission as little boys. They learned to read, write, and calculate numbers, but most importantly, they became acquainted with God's Word. Through the Word of God, they came to a personal understanding of the true God, and put off their heathen ways, and have taken on Christianity. Their stance in life is easily seen in the way in which they present themselves: They dress, that is, they wear shirts and pants. And if it's possible they also wear a hat. The people have the idea that Christ and clothing go together. At another mission station, I asked the believing girl whether a different girl, who caught my attention, had been saved. She answered, "You can see, she has no clothes on." This understanding of Christianity was rather strange to us at first, but after various experiences, we have learned the importance of clothing. The teachers like to show their dignity by carrying a notebook, a book, and having a pencil behind the ear. At the mission station, they were held to standards of cleanliness and punctuality.

In their relationships between one another, they show themselves to be different from the others by their pleasant impression on people. They conduct themselves honorably and with respect to the white person, they are friendly and give appropriate answers. Certainly a lot of this is simply training, but usually just simply training does not last long. We have a lot of examples of that. But when God's Word has genuinely changed the person's life, if his thinking and feeling and will have changed, then the face expresses that kind of state of mind. A face that has been marred by fear soon turns into a radiant expression in the eyes and a peaceful look.

Oh, dear brothers and sisters, you should really see the changes in people's lives! Even an unbelieving government official expressed his wonder about the changes in people's lives. He said when he meets children from the mission station, whether in a village or on the road with other children, whether they are dressed as the others are or not he was able to distinguish those who had the kind of facial expressions that I'm talking about. We, too, have noticed these changes and praise God for His grace that has rescued them. The worst sinners become children of God.

How does the teacher work? He comes into the village with his wife and/or family, makes himself comfortable, and builds a house. He receives support from the mission, till he can support himself or till, after several years, a local community supports him. It's just amazing; he is to be a witness of word and deed and for the local people of the Congo, the deed comes first.

- *First he must show who he is. Then they will pay attention to what he says. They test them and watch him and find out that he is very different from the others.*
- *He does not steal, but pays for everything that he gets.*
- *He does not lie.*
- *He does not curse and doesn't participate in things that are typical of others in the village. He has the power to withstand all of that.*
- *He remains with his wife and with his children in the home. His wife is also quiet and works carefully for the welfare of her house and her children.*
- *She prepares the food at the right time. The heathen women only do that when they've had good food.*

The local people talk a lot about the white missionaries and the way in which they relate with each other. And if it is very different than their own style, they excuse themselves by saying that these are white people. But now, when their own teachers live in the way described above, then they begin to pay attention and notice and think about it. This is what persuaded our dear teacher, Ngunga, to become a Christian. Certainly there are many temptations and problems to take one away from Christianity. And so, I want to take this opportunity to remind all of you to pray for these Christians. The heathen customs are very strong, and these teachers are so alone and so inexperienced.

If the teacher remains faithful, he wins. People come to his fire in the evening and listen to him. During the day, he seeks to contact children and elders in the village. This usually occurs under the shade of a huge tree. Wherever it is possible, he holds classes. He seeks to invite people to the worship service on Sunday morning. It's very important for them when they see a book in his hand. They hear him read and sing. Singing the gospel is a great help for the mission. In that way, truths are recorded in the brain and reemerge at another time. The Negro loves to sing. And so, the teacher seeks to sow the seed in his own great weakness and in a totally heathen village that has been untouched by the gospel.

The missionary who seeks to evangelize travels through the villages. He has it much easier now. He is able to come to the villages to hold worship meetings, etc. And the visit is very important for the teacher. Everything is discussed. Problems are identified. Sometimes he needs to correct the teacher or to comfort him. Sometimes he needs to encourage him and to take part in the joy and in the suffering of the teacher. Every so often, all the teachers gather together for a conference at the mission station. There's much joy and much blessing. This is what we learned that the other mission programs do. We met teachers in various villages from different mission stations and have been very pleased when they have been friendly and have invited us to participate in their program. My husband has had many such opportunities, and we have been astounded at how eagerly these teachers have offered themselves to God.

And now about our teachers! Where are they? "Do you have teachers?" One of the sisters with whom I shared this joyful news asked me that question. I became quiet and sad. "If we only had trained 20 or 30 teachers now, as some other missionary mission programs have!" Now the Lord is giving us the possibility *of placing such teachers. Who are teachers? They are youngsters that eight years ago came to our school as 10- or 15-year-olds. We prepared them for various services. They attended our schools. They learned to read, to write, and some other things, but mostly they learned about God's Word in the catechism, in the Psalms and in the biblical stories. They probably don't compare to the well-trained teachers of other missions, because they had many interruptions in their training. But they have recognized that they are sinners, and they have cried over their condition. They found forgiveness in the blood of Christ and have found peace. They have confessed their past misdeeds and straightened out their lives. They even confessed and corrected those things that no one knows about, and for which they will receive punishment when they confess them. They've experienced the presence of the Lord in their need and in their sickness. He has answered them when they were hungry. And when they called upon him, he satisfied them. The Lord has often heard them wonderfully.*

They had to demonstrate their new faith in spite of mockery and beatings from those who were in their own families. The families have kept food from them, and also kept them from having wives, because they have become Christians. For those who had wives, families try to break up marriages. We are witnesses of all of this and of a lot more. It's not surprising, therefore, that they would collapse, and even lose their minds under such pressure. They killed two of the children of one of the teachers. These poor brothers have often run away from the mission station, but they often could not stand staying away. They always came back. Their lives are often threatened. But the Lord has not allowed one of them to be killed. They stand there. In one of my last letters from my husband, he reports that they have brought him much joy. Most of them now have wives, and that is an answer to prayer. Regrettably, many of these wives have not had much training and make it rather difficult for their men. But the Lord can change them.

I want to say one more thing about these teachers; that is, that they have a concern for their own people. Many times they have come to Brother Bartsch's window and have opened up their hearts to him. They have asked and discussed with each other how their whole tribe could become Christian in the quickest possible way. "Can you make arrangements with the government officials? Can he do it by force? What do your people with whom you write all the time, what do they say? Is it really true that all those who do not know God are lost? Why don't you practice the mission with greater zeal?" Such questions cut through our hearts. When they stand there with such big eyes, and see that we can't really answer such questions and that this does not happen on a one-time basis. They count on you at home with the power that you have through your God.

I want to alert all the watchmen whom God has called to be concerned about the Dengese tribe about the great possibilities of the spread of the mission. This new possibility has expanded the scope of the mission immeasurably. Let us take these events as an opportunity. In Revelations 3, verse eight, it says. "See, I have given you an open door, and no one can close it, because you have the power."

For His honor, your fellow worker,
Anna Bartsch

I want to close with the letter from one of the teachers that he sent me in the last few days. I present it in translation to show how they think and write.

Mama Mpembe, (This is the name that our teachers gave to me, Anna Bartsch)

Here's a letter for you. I wrote last month, don't you answer? I'm very unhappy at the mission, but only because of your absence. I'm very sad. We often see Lusangaye (name given to H. G. Bartsch) looking very sad. May God send you to us! But we do not want Lusangaye to leave us. All the teachers love him very much, but may Jesus send you here. Just come. Dear mother, we pray a lot for you and yearn to see you. Please pray for us too and come soon. We want to from our hearts.

My best greetings, I am your Ngunga Djoi.

You'll see dear brothers and sisters how the poor people of Dengese feel. Please pray that the Lord will open the doors, and we can go again.

News About the Mission in the Summer of 1941

Br. Bartsch wrote a private letter on June 20, 1941, to say that he and Brother and Sister Kramer are in good spirits. The Kramers are very thankful for the intercession that Br. Bartsch made at the highest government level so that they could return to Bololo. Br. Bartsch writes "Our situation seems brighter. In the new school year, everything will go back to normal."

In the meantime, hold the banner high of the African mission program. Encourage people to pray, for volunteer missionaries. We will have great mission opportunities in the near future. The Lord is with us.

The concern is not over general obstacles, but over local obstacles, about which we can do little. My big concern was the danger for you on the high seas, and so I advised that my family not come. The whole world is now fighting for domination. Even little states are caught up in this battle. There are attempts to destroy or disrupt small mission stations. Demonic forces will seek to destroy all spiritual efforts by putting everything under one administrative roof. If the government can control spiritual development, that will happen! Nevertheless, modernism and excessive spirituality have no influence on me. We cannot achieve our spiritual growth unless we offer ourselves to sacrifice and suffer.

The Kramers and their children are well and happy.

We're always happy when we hear that the brothers and sisters in the field are encouraged. When they know the situation in the field and the possibilities of the mission program there, then we want to stand by their side and pray for them. "The prayer of the righteous will be rewarded, if it is prayed in sincerity."

One sentence in a letter from Br. Bartsch is of particular interest to us. He asks that each of us pray to encourage others to become missionaries. It is clear to us how great the power of prayer is. When two or three pray together, prayer becomes very powerful. But when a whole large number of people pray together it is even more powerful. God be thanked that there are so many people who are praying for the mission work in Africa. May the Lord bless them!

Events on the Mission in the Summer of 1941[57]

Dear beloved friends of the mission!
Greetings with Habakkuk 2:20.

*"The Lord is in His holy temple,
Let all the earth keep silent before Him."*

In the last little while I had the great joy of receiving a whole number of letters. Some of them had been written in October and November of last year. I thank all of you for your comfort and your love that I could detect in the letters that you wrote. I would like to write in greater detail about some of the things that I'm experiencing, in fact, I would like even more to explain things, face-to-face.

The Kramers' Child Is Ill and Dies

In January, I made a big trip to the villages that lie along the Lukene River. The Lord blessed this trip in that he gave me a lot of joy as I spoke to people. When I arrived at the mission at Kole, I had been away from Bololo for three weeks. Everything looked very sad when I came home again. Most of the people stayed away from the mission. Only a gang of boys hung around the yard. The evil one was active to disrupt the work of the mission. Added to that, Brother and Sister Kramer's baby got

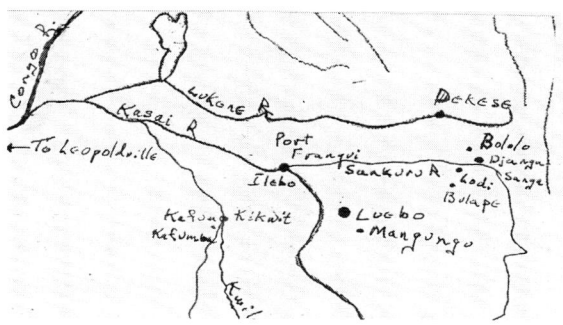

[57] *Der kleine Africa Bote*, August 1941.

weaker and sicker. It looked as though the little child could not live and could not die. It felt as though the waves would swallow us up, but the Lord Jesus was in the boat. He only slept. Since the doctor was very far away, we could not contact him. So we decided that we would see Dr. Stirrud. We hoped to get to Luebo. We heard that Dr. Stirrud was traveling at this time. In the middle of February, Sister Kramer, the sick baby and I left for Luebo. The car had not been driven for a long time, and the tires were not very good. Along the way, about 40 km from the city, two of the tires broke. Since the inner tubes were also broken, we had to overnight on the way; the poor child suffered terribly. But the Lord helped, and we arrived in Luebo a day later. Luckily, Dr. Stirrud was in Luebo, but he had planned to travel out the next day. He could diagnose the illness of the child, and he could give advice, but he couldn't actually be much help. On the way back to Bololo, we had trouble with the tires again, at great expense. On the last day we had to travel in the hammock with carriers. The pathway was overgrown and the bridges over the river were swept away. While in Luebo, we have prayed the Lord to take the little patient child, and on February 26 our prayers were heard. We buried the little child near Brother and Sister Kramer's house. It's the first seed on our field, which looks forward to the resurrection. Although the parents are very sad, all are thankful that the sick child is free of his pain, and that he is received by the One who will give him back to the parents.

The King Is Imprisoned and I Help Get Him Released

In March, I made a trip to Lusambo, the provincial capital, where I wanted to present our situation to the Belgian governor. He was very understanding. Our Catholic opposition, which has turned King Ikongo-Samu against us, has really hindered our mission. Now it so happened that the government official had personally experienced terrible things from the King. So he had the King jailed and sent away. People who have been put in jail like that usually do not return but are put to work at other places. But since the King was only in a personal conflict with the government official, and the tribe cannot be without a King, I stopped off at the Governor's office in Lusambo, and pleaded on the King's behalf.

It was successful. In the middle of April, Mr. Sand brought the King back to Dekese and installed him in his previous role as King. The King appreciated my intercession on his behalf, and seems to have changed his mind about us. When I went to visit him last week I was very well received, in a royal way. Everything seems to have turned out well. Fairly soon, the King will come to Bololo, and then he needs to show me that he is a friend of the mission. The people's attitude is much better since his return.

We Get Permission to Place Itinerant Teachers in Villages

The teachers of the Mission are much encouraged and want to be installed as teachers in the neighboring villages. The Governor has given us permission to install these teachers. But we will have to wait and see how the Catholic mission reacts to this. I want to open the school in Bolombo again. When the King comes, everything should be in readiness.

For various reasons, the trip to Leopoldville became more urgent.[58] So, on April 9, I drove off to Port Francqui, and from there took a ship to Leopoldville. I wanted to talk to various people there about protection and support for our work. There were many issues that had been distorted. It was very fortunate that I could meet with the Governor and the consul to discuss these matters. But the end result of all this discussion, and decisions made did not comfort me and so I drove back to Bololo somewhat concerned.

Recently I got a letter from Luebo saying that Brother and Sister Kramer are permitted to stay here in Bololo. This is a result of my visit with the Governor. So, happily, without knowing about it, I was at the right place at the right time. We're grateful to the Lord for having intervened in such a wonderful way.

With greetings and thankfulness to all of you from the one who is alone. Your brother and fellow worker, H. G. Bartsch.

---

[58] My father speaks vaguely about his purpose for going to Leopoldville because he does not want to write publicly about political matters related to the Kramer's German nationality.

Mid summer 1941: How I Feel Here Now

It's Sunday again today. We have only a very small gathering today. The dry season has come again, and the people of the village are mostly absent. In about an hour, I want to meet with several others in a small Bible study. I want to use this hour to write to you. I can't really tell you how I feel or how things look to me. But I do want to let you look into my life a little bit.

I continue to live in the same house where I used to live and with my few possessions. It's quiet here, often too quiet and calm! But I need to get over that too. I used to take my meals at the Kramers' table. At my house I had Bokiri, a boy from the school, who helped me. His year is over and he has left. I didn't have enough for him to do, and when boys don't have enough to do, they do all kinds of mischief. My plan, of course, this year was to travel a lot. Next month, I want to travel to the north.

I am healthy and happy in the Lord. The love I experience is more than I deserve. Brother and Sister Kramer love me a lot, and the dear sister takes care of me. How would it have been, had I come here with the children? There's no school for the older children. Dr. Stirrud wants to send his children to the USA. But that isn't possible now. The school in Lubondai, in spite of the large number of students, has only two female teachers. The institution is overcrowded and leaves a lot to be desired as far as the training of children. I was very happy when I realized that you were not on the Zam Zam. It was after very serious and heavy thought, that I sent a telegram off to you.[59] I praise the Lord for further leading in this matter. If we are in a position to be led by the Spirit then the outcomes will also be good. And we will thank Him that He is so good that He leads so wonderfully.

Everything is well at the Kramers'; the children are healthy and very loving. It appears to me that many of the letters that I sent did not arrive. It is my impression that the war will last for a long time yet. That's why I long so badly to see you. Please

---

[59] He did not know at this time that mother had not recieved the telegram and that the Lord had led in ways even more marvelous than he imagined.

greet the brothers in the committee, the people in the church and all those who love me.

H. G. Bartsch

I Met with Government Officials and with Father Alphonse

> I greet all of you with I Tim. 2:2.
> *"Pray for authorities*
> *So that we may be able to live*
> *Religious and reverent lives in peace and quiet."*

A few days ago I came back from a three-week trip to the north. When I returned I found many letters from my home country. Many thanks. I often feel very guilty for not having written more. In retrospect, I feel bad that I'm not able to describe the situation in greater detail. I often imagine that my letters will be screened here by people who are not friendly to us. That's why I don't or can't write often and in greater detail. For these reasons, I have not written to the *Africa Bote*. Our situation in Bololo remains the same, and I don't want to always write about myself or my travels. Nevertheless, because of the suspicions I feel, I will write about the trip that I've taken.

A transition in Dekese took place at the end of September. We had waited for it for a long time. The transition occurred between the head government officials of the province. The former head was not very friendly to Protestant missions. Before he left his office he came to visit us at Bololo. I just happened to be traveling to Port Francqui with one government official in the automobile. On the way to Bolombo, I met the government official who was leaving office. Dr. DeMyck was with me, and served as translator. We discussed everything that he has done for the mission. When he asked what else he could do for the mission. I sidestepped any help that he might offer. In my absence, he had built a Catholic school very near to Bololo.

I wanted very much to see the new government official. Since I could not find carriers, I took my bicycle to Bolombo. From Bolombo, I wanted to take the car to Dekese. Actually, we really need safer storage for the automobile. People break into the car. I just can't go on like this. In Dekese, I met the new administrator, whose name was Talmann. He received me very kindly. First we had dinner together, and then I responded to the saying, "Speak so that I may see!" My impressions of him improved considerably as we spent time together. I developed courage and confidence.

The road to Djia was finished in September. This was a gigantic accomplishment. Monsieur Talmann was the first to travel on this road. He advised me strongly to take it. Since the future of our mission lies in the north, I allowed myself to be persuaded to take the trip to the north. I wanted to see some of the northern villages that surrounded Djia. I had one concern: I was not prepared for this visit. Nevertheless, I left the next morning. The trip took only four hours, when usually it would take four days by kipoy. What an advantage it is to have a car in this time when the costs are not considered! The way to the north is very mountainous and has many turns. Nevertheless, the V-8 went 30, 40, 50 and 60 kph.

In Djia, Mr. Valats had 500 black men on the road to the east. Mr. Valats was grateful for the time that he had spent with us in Bololo and wondered how to repay us. Now he built a shade for the automobile, and I prepared to go into the villages the next day. The spring on the car missed a bolt, and so the springs were

Automobile road under construction.

somewhat distorted. Since I couldn't make arrangements to fix the automobile, I just let it go. I went farther north and hoped that the automobile problems would resolve themselves later. I continued the journey on the next day with four carriers of the possessions I had along with one person to carry the bike. It was supposed to take five hours to get to Isanja, the next government city or town. I got there much sooner than that with the bike. The government official gave me good advice to travel through villages at the northern boundary of the district. I learned to know Father Alphonse. At lunchtime and dinnertime in Dekese I had had long conversations with this Catholic priest. He noticed that my bike was not in order, went into the house and repaired it for me. Under circumstances like this, one may appreciate the loving acts of another person. This opened up a friendly conversation for a later point of time.

Difficulties I Face on My Travels in the North

In the villages along the northern boundary I had many opportunities to preach God's Word. I really enjoyed that. People came very eagerly, were very attentive, and learned verses and songs from the choir. I was very happy when some of them could give me back the meaning of the words that I had spoken. There are about 2000 children who could go to the school in those eight villages. The villages are not very far apart and are easily reached by bicycle. The older folks invited me to come and stay there. When I reached the last village, I held a service with them. I was led to go to the neighboring mission station. I wanted to see whether people there could help me with the difficult situation we were experiencing in Bololo. So I risked making this difficult trip on behalf of the mission. According to the government official, the trip should take about six hours. After having something to eat we set off at 11 o'clock. I thought, I'll be there by nightfall. But our experience was different. We had to go through a newly forested area. We had to climb, crawl, and jump, so that we were totally drenched in sweat. All this occurred around midday. And besides, it was very hot and humid. The tropical sun was directly overhead.

At last we got past the brush and arrived in the cool forest just as a very violent storm approached us. We hadn't traveled for an hour when lightning and thunder surrounded and scared us. The storm brought driving rain. In fact, it rained so hard that I had to take shelter behind a very large tree. That was no help. I couldn't lose any more time. Since water flooded everything, the path had become a stream, so I put on my boots and marched forward. Soon we arrived at the Luilaka River. The stream had become a mighty river, and we were afraid to cross it. In fact the water was so high that only a few of the standing markers were visible to indicate where the crossing was. "How shall we get across?" Then I noticed a vine about half a foot under water. It was tied to a tree and stretched across the stream. "So this is where people cross," we told ourselves. "What other people can do, I can do," I said. One cannot be cowardly in Africa; otherwise, one must always return after going halfway. I went ahead and held on to the vine, very tightly. My heart was pounding. As the water reached under my arm pits, I noticed a firm foundation under my feet. A large tree had been the bridge during the dry season. This tree is so waterlogged that it was not driven away by the high water caused by the storm. So the crossing went better than it had seemed at the beginning. We all crossed the stream, soaking wet. We didn't have time to get dry. It was getting to be two o'clock. We had to go on. For two hours, we traveled from one swamp to another. Then we noticed that we had gone astray! Nobody knew the way. Travel through the woods was very difficult. We reached some people before sundown. They were very surprised to see a white man in their district.

Since it was after sundown, we should have stopped there for the night. But the people wanted to get rid of the white man, and told us that it was not very far to the Boko-Monkoto Road, where there was a village where we could stay overnight. Realizing that we were close to a village, we went forward with a lot more courage. It got darker quickly, and the path, as before, was hardly passable. We began to lose our way. We began to bump into things, to trip, to fall. But then suddenly we arrived at the road. It was well kept, but there were no cars. I could've used the bicycle on this road. But my bike carrier remained behind and had lost his way in the darkness. I had to wait for my belongings to arrive. The luggage carriers had also remained behind. I lit the lantern and sent two of my carriers to find the lad who had carried the bike. Eventually we all got together again. It was midnight.

The moon came up. We could have marched forward on the road, but all the men were so tired because of all the day's events that we decided to stay in the woods overnight. My clothes clung to my body, partly because of crossing the river, and partly because of sweat. The metal suitcases had remained dry. I changed clothes, set up my field bed, got something to eat, and lay down to rest. The moon shone kindly through the trees, and I was comforted. I began to say, "Dear moon, you travel so silently through the evening clouds," and then I turned to the One who is above the moon and above the stars, and I had nothing to complain about. I was only thankful. The Lord has said, "He will show you the best way to go." This was the way for me to go, because it had been determined by God's plan. I became quiet and calm. In spite of the pain in my feet, I fell asleep.

The morning sun greeted me when I awoke. We packed our things and went forward. After an hour we arrived at the village that the people in the previous village had told us about. The village's name was Nkiri. I looked for a place where I could shower and have a warm breakfast. The people of the village brought me fire, water and eggs. They said that the way to the east should be easier than the previous trip. So I left my help in this village and went ahead on my bike.

The way was indeed better than I had expected. The only problem was that the mountains were very steep. So I couldn't really ride my bike all the time. At about 12 o'clock, I came to the mission Boka.

The dear people here have placed themselves in the middle of the forest. You cannot find a piece of prairie land anywhere. Only two women are at the station at present. Other missionaries with their children were in the next village. Someone sent for them and they came the next day. I actually only wanted to stay there for one day, but Brother Bisse offered to come back with me to repair my vehicle if I would just stay another day longer. I decided to stay for another day.

On October 9th Brother Bisse and I began to make our way back to Dengese, along with six carriers. We found a better route to travel than we had taken before. Besides I was doubly happy because I had company. We left early in the morning. I was very peaceful, because I had given Bisse command of the group. We got back to the river. On this path there were markers. We didn't cross the river when we came to it, but we sent men to try to find a better crossing. After a short while, they found a better crossing, approximately 500 meters away.

It turned out that this crossing was 100% worse than my previous crossing. The cable was barely visible. There were only parts of the bridge remaining. It was 12 o'clock. We had no time to lose. To cross the river, we cut down a tree with our knives. Some of the men had to get the vines to hang on to. We wanted to make the crossing safer so that we could also hold on to the things that we had brought along. All of this took a lot of time. We cut a tree down with our knives. The tree fell into the water the way we wanted it to, but it was pushed down by the mighty stream. Good advice was hard to get. The men came with the vines. Brother Bisse crossed to the other side, swimming part of the way, and holding on to the vines as well as he could. Then he tied new vines across the stream, and we were ready for the crossing. It's hard to describe how all this went and we didn't have cameras to take pictures of all this. We all arrived safely at the other side. And all our belongings came across. Our trunks were no longer waterproof, but that's only an aside. Even our lanterns had filled with water that had to be poured out. To illustrate what danger we were in, I might mention the fact that the vines we used to cross the river tore after we got across. The Lord let us get into great danger. But He didn't allow us to sink. "For He commands His angels to take care of you that they shelter you on the way."

After we arrived on the other shore, we allowed the carriers to go on ahead with our things, so that we did not need to wait for the belongings to arrive when we arrived at the next village. It was 4:30 PM when we arrived at Isanga-Njali. We couldn't travel through the swamp land very quickly. When we finally arrived on higher ground, the sun began to set. It got darker quickly, and there was no life in the lanterns. Everything got soaked in the stream. Mr. Bisse thought that the village was close by, and so he advised me to take one assistant to go on ahead. He would wait for the bicycle carrier to arrive. I went. It got dark. It got dark so quickly that we couldn't see where we were going. Now our wandering group was divided into six subgroups. It was a troublesome situation. There were heavy clouds in the sky. We could see nothing. I was wet and tired. To sit down was to be eaten by the ants. To go ahead was to trip over some fallen branches or to walk into a tree. To keep from freezing, I had to keep moving, but that tired me out even more.

At midnight, we had a terrific thundershower. It felt as though we were in an airplane bombardment. But we were not hit by lightning. Nor was a tree hit. A heavy downpour followed and lasted till morning. Only then could we dare to move forward. In about an hour, we were in view of the outlying fields of Isanga-Njali. So we assumed that the village was not far off. We met our assistants, who were carrying our belongings. They followed us. Everything was quiet in the village. Everybody was still asleep. I went to the guest hut. I got into bed. I wanted to lie down quickly, but then I realized that the metal suitcases had not been waterproof. Brother Bisse came soon. His group had been in the lead when the rain appeared so one of his men had been able to start a fire. They had been able to warm themselves and had been able to drive the insects away. We dried our things when the sun came up. We healed our wounds and filled our bellies. We stayed for two days at this place, because we were so tired. We healed the sick and preached the gospel with a lot of joy.

Brother Bisse told us that the assistant who had carried our bike in the dark through the woods had thrown away the wheel. Apparently a poisonous snake had bitten into the tire of the wheel and the tail of the snake hit the back of the assistant. At that point, he threw the tire away and killed the snake. In Dejia, as Brother Bisse began to repair the spring on the automobile, and as he came up from under the auto, I advised him to take the papers away which he had laid under the automobile. I suggested he put a blanket underneath. As an assistant removed the papers, he discovered a very small but very poisonous snake under the papers. Brother Bisse had lain on that spot for over an hour. Psalm 91, verse 13 was partially fulfilled here. Brother Bisse was of great service with my automobile. He also took apart the rear springs and put in a new plate. All of this took a lot of time, because we had so few tools. I'll write about the trip by car later.

Greetings. Your Henry Bartsch

The Following Comes out of a Private Letter

We haven't had any school in the past few weeks during the dry season. We hope to begin again soon. This is our prayer and our hope to provide the children with hope. We also hope that the chief will visit us in the next few days. At present, the teachers and their families live at the mission station.

We have dealt with burns and injuries in our work among the sick. The people from the village are clearing new fields, and often wound themselves in the process. The burns come from the situations in their homes where they make a fire and fall asleep. Often little children get too close to the fire or fall into the glowing ashes. In the last few days a mother came with her little infant. The child's wounds could be healed.

A Note from the Kramers

Brother Bartsch traveled much of this year. Presently he is here again. We pray constantly for peace in our time so that normal relationships can be established again.

On the practical side of things, we have started a garden. To buy food is very expensive, and many of the foods are not available. With a lot of work, we are able to grow some things for our own welfare. The soil is mostly sand, and so plants do not grow well. But we have had good cucumbers and tomatoes. We want be thankful to the Lord for that.

We also notice the Lord's presence in our daily protection. A short while ago, in the early morning a large snake was on our veranda. I called the other teachers, and they came very quickly, but as soon as they saw the huge snake, they took off. They left me alone. At a dangerous moment our little daughter opened the door to see what all the noise was about. The snake charged at the door, but my wife was able to grab my daughter from behind and shut the door. Shortly after that I was able to strike the snake and kill it. The snake was about 6 1/2 feet long. . . .

With hearty greetings,
M. and K. Kramer

A Report from the Editor of *Der kleine Africa Bote*, November 1941

We've received very few letters from Brother Bartsch. What we know is that he and the Kramers and children are healthy and well. We know that they've been instructed to share only personal stories because of the war situation. So we have received very little information from them.

Regrettably, we have not received any further word from our mission field in the past month. We are eagerly awaiting such word and pray that the Lord may soon provide us news. We also pray that Sister Bartsch will be comforted with word from her husband.

When we think about our brothers and sisters in Bololo, we need to recognize again and again how well the Lord has led them. In spite of the separation that they've experienced, they are grateful to God. We're also happy that the Kramers have been able to return to Bololo. The instruction has continued at the school, and work was done to fight against the evil powers against them. Brother Bartsch has taken a lot of time to travel around. The obstacles that stood against the mission have been removed. The Lord has done this. The King changed his mind about helping the mission. Here at home, Sister Bartsch and Sister Brooks are waiting patiently until the doors open for them to go back. Although there were many obstacles to sending money to the missionaries, we have always been able to arrange for such a transfer. They've always received the funds. Here at home, there is growing interest in the work of the mission as indicated by the letters and by the many gifts. We always say that the Lord has provided for the work in the darkest jungles to continue. And so we invite all of you to continue to pray and to give. Shouldn't we really be very thankful? Let us continue to be grateful.

There's a dark cloud hanging over the mission programs. There's a report in the December issue of the Zionsbote *that governments, such as the Belgian Congo, are prohibiting mission programs from outside the country. The prohibition is based on an assumption that mission programs are not a necessity. We, of course, ask what can be more of a necessity than to save people from their sin? Please pray that the way will be open to us and the mission program can continue. The Lord will hear this prayer, if it is His desire to do so.*

The steering committee

A Private Note: Conditions are Bleak Here in Early January 1942

. . . . concerning our situation here. I can share with you that it isn't possible to do mission work when we are blocked in every way from doing it. The Catholics are using the world crisis as an excuse to rile up the local population. My travel in the various villages has purpose only if our mission work can be done.

When I returned from the furlough last year, and everybody seemed to do what I wished, I took it as God's leading, and was hopeful that I could work with Brother and Sister Kramer at the mission station. However, now everything has been turned around. I continue to believe that the Lord has His hand in the whole matter. We want to trust him, even though things go differently than we expected.

In Bolombo, about a day's travel from Bololo, I received the land lease agreement. The setting is very pleasant. We can build everything at that place that we need. Initially, I have contracted to have three houses built. One of these is for the white people. I will pay the taxes for the new land and also for the houses in Bololo. But I will not build new ones here. I want to keep the doors open in the future for our work here in Bololo. God has wonderful people here in this region.

We want to arrange everything in the next few days. Since the situation here has become almost unbearable we want to seek to bring Brother and Sister Kramer to another place. Then I want to come home. The government people in Dekese, the doctor, the King, the heads of the villages, the teachers, and the Dengese people love me very much. They will be very disappointed if/when I should go away. But I can do nothing more here. Please pray for us.

I don't know what I will do if I can't cross the ocean. You know about the dangers in crossing the oceans, as well as I do. Brother and Sister Kramer are well and always mention that I should greet you from them.

Hearty greetings to all who pray for us.
Your inner-connected,
H. G. Bartsch

— Chapter 11 —

Return and Reflections
1942

The Africa Committee Considers Possible Closure of the Mission

From the reports, you know that Brother Bartsch has now been away from his family for three years. His family lives here in Winnipeg and have been well looked after. The world situation indicates that we cannot send the family to Africa at this time. From the letters of Brother Bartsch we sense that he is happy in his work and happy about the fact that his family is safe here.

At our last meeting, about a year ago, we decided to send a letter to Brother Bartsch and give him the freedom to decide whether he should return here or stay, depending on his own inner direction. We will support him whatever he decides. Of course, till now he has not returned, although we can see in his letters that he has considered it a number of times. He is concerned about the situation for the Kramers, and for the belongings of the mission station, and above all, he is concerned about the mission program. We need to renew our commitment to him, that he feel free to decide what he needs to do. We have written him to this effect.

We are particularly thankful to the Lord for the assurance that many people who have prayed for the work in Africa continue to support it with financial support. In fact, the support has not shrunk, but has gotten larger and bigger. One indication of this is that the treasury of the mission has grown. But there are always expenses for the work. And there are so many letters and verbal indications of support for the work and for this we are very thankful. We give thanks to all those who have prayed and offered support in our churches for the work that is being done in Africa. May God reward you!

But let us not get tired. We want to continue to pray and to work and to give, and in due time, we will receive the blessing.

Someone may ask in these days, "What good is it to pray and to give when the doors for the work in Africa seem to be closing tighter and tighter? Maybe we should quit the work." So we want to share with you that we have discussed these issues at our recent meeting. We've talked about the events of the world and also on the mission field and have decided that we want to spread the gospel throughout the world in Africa. Rather than feel discouraged as we look into the future, we are encouraged and believe very firmly that the work of the Lord will continue in Africa. We pray that there will be many victories there. We don't know when and how this will happen, but we trust that the Lord will care for the mission. And we've decided to allow Him to use us wherever he demands it of us. Many things are not clear to us. And we look for answers for the many questions that stir our hearts. For us, persistent questions rise up that don't leave us and for which we do not have answers.

The Henry Bartsch family in Winnipeg, 1943, before their move to B.C.

Brother Bartsch Has Returned in May 1942

We have waited a long time for word from Bololo. Recently we received the word that Brother Bartsch has arrived in Florida safely. This news stirred the greatest happiness among his family. And also for those who have prayed for him and who have now received the answer to their prayers. According to the telegram, we expected to meet Brother Bartsch on May 26 in Winnipeg. Many people were expected to be at the train station to greet him there. Then, without notice, we were told that Brother Bartsch had arrived late in the evening on Monday. It was a real surprise for the family and friends but everyone was very happy that the long-awaited moment had arrived, where the family could be reunited. It feels like a miracle. The Lord has protected Brother Bartsch. The Lord be honored for this! He has done well.

The Lord willing, there will be greetings for Brother Bartsch at the Mennonite Brethren Church in North Winnipeg. We expect very many people.

June 1942: My Return to Canada and Reflections on the Status of the Mission

Our dear brothers and sisters and friends of the Africa mission.

In the past 14 days since I've been in Canada, I have received many congratulations and wishes for my well-being. I really can't answer each of the letters directly, so I take the opportunity to thank everyone through the *Der kleine Africa Bote*. I have been particularly impressed with the power of prayer in the past few years since I've been separated from my family. The Lord has heard our prayers wonderfully. He has kept me safe on the trip, He has kept me healthy while I was in Africa, and He has brought me back to my own family. In the light of the circumstances in the world today, this is a miracle before our eyes. We see through these events that the Lord is mighty and has His hand on the rudder. It surely brings to mind Psalm 46: "God is our refuge and our strength, a very present help in time of trouble."

To all those who have supported us and prayed for us, I say a hearty thank you. For the joy of having our prayers heard, we continue to thank God. From location, I also want to thank those brothers and sisters who have strengthened me through letters. May the Lord reward you for your mission service!

I want to answer a question that has been asked of me by many who have prayed for me. The question is, "What will happen to the mission station now?" Brother and Sister Kramer do not live in Bololo anymore.[60] I have come home. It is not possible to send others there now. That is not to say that the seed that was sown cannot grow. Under such circumstances, the Lord is able to reveal his name in special ways. I take the perspective that He will continue to work among the Dengese people. This situation was not created by human failings, but the Lord has something particular in mind for the work that we have done. In the past few years, we've gone through difficult times in Africa that others have not experienced. Often we have asked ourselves, "What does the Lord want from us?" The only answer that we find now is in Hebrews 12, verses 6 and 11:

> *"The Lord disciplines the one, whom He loves,*
> *And chastises every son whom He receives.*
> *For the moment all discipline seems painful*
> *rather than pleasant;*
> *later it yields the peaceful fruit of righteousness*
> *to those who have been trained by it."*

In the last little while, there were a number of opportunities to spread our work throughout the Dengese region. To the glory of God, I can now say that the authorities acknowledge our work and are very friendly toward the work that we are doing. We were given permission to spread the word through the Dengese region. The King has also altered his orientation towards us in wonderful ways. The government authorities personally invited

---

[60] The Kramers were moved to Luebo again because of their German citizenship. Belgium and Germany were at war. That left dad alone at the school and clinic.

me to accept the license to spread the gospel in the whole region. The mission station is now under the protection of the state. I received a hearty invitation from local people and also from the Government officials in the north to begin the missions program there.

I am writing to the many people who have prayed for a long time for the people of the mission. I'm writing about the great changes that are occurring on the field. When the time comes, we want to reenter the field with more of the courage and strength than I needed on the field. I encourage all of our friends of the Africa mission to continue their eagerness for the mission field in Dengese. We want to renew our strength, find new workers, and gather whatever materials we need to be ready when the signs of peace emerge.

If the Lord wills, we want to visit the many friends of the Africa mission in various places in Canada and in the USA. When we do, we want to share with you in greater detail what the Lord has done for us and with us.

Many people wonder where we will settle for the remainder of the war. Many people have also given us very kind advice. At this point, we have not decided that. We present everything to the Lord and leave the issues at His feet. Our hope is that we can be a blessing to others.

I want to send a very special greeting to those who've worked alongside of us. Please come and visit us or write to us about specific questions that you have about work on the field.

We ask you to pray especially for a small group of men who have committed themselves to be baptized. They are there now without white missionaries. Our fellow workers will understand that better than anyone else. Our Lord, however, is not dependent on human beings or on circumstances. He can protect His children, even in the most difficult circumstances.

Brother A. A. Jansen visited me in the last little while in Bololo. He asked me to pass on greetings to all friends of the Africa mission. He is emotionally very tired and needs to recover.

Brother and Sister Kramer, whom I've visited shortly before I left, greet everyone heartily. They and their children are healthy and under protection by the state. They live in Luebo in the little house and have all the necessities for living.

> We greet you with Psalm 126. We remain connected to you,
> Your fellow workers in the Africa mission.
> H. G. and Anna Bartsch

Welcome to Brother Bartsch from the Executive Committee

May 31 was a happy day for friends of the mission and a special day to give thanks and praise God for preserving Br. Bartsch on his trip home. Guests came from great distances to celebrate his return. Imagine the M. B. Church in Winnipeg! Repeatedly, people asked, "Is Br. Bartsch really here?" But yes, he sat there next to his wife, somewhat strained, but apparently healthy. The face Sister Bartsch presented was one of quiet and a deep sense of peace. Many a person asked, "Are you happy now?" Many have tried to help in whatever way they could to make it possible for her to carry through these difficult times.

There were many introductions and many readings of psalms and praises by various members of the committee and by various ministers. Then Br. Bartsch stepped to the podium to thank God for His gracious guiding in his family. Then he greeted the large gathering and told several stories about his travel home. He pointed out that there were two goals in his mission: The first was to win the souls of the native people, and, secondly, to train ministers there. "Even difficulties draw us closer to the Lord," he said, "and therefore they are to our advantage. And always, while we were out on the field, we experienced the strong support of the many people at home who were praying for us. This was enormously important for us in the difficult times that we faced."

Br. Bartsch passed on greetings from Brother and Sister Kramer and the young Christians on the field. Brother and Sister Kramer live in Luebo in an adequate little house. The Belgian state has taken responsibility for their care.

Br. Bartsch compared his experiences to the apostle Paul in Lystra. He said that the Lord had plans for everyone. He said the plan in Dengese was to bring the good news to the people. This is what we wanted to do in Dengese, but the way of carrying out the mission was different than we had anticipated. We had anticipated building up the station, the mission station, and then from the central point spread the gospel to the villages. But the Lord destroyed the wonderful plans of many workers, schools and hospitals. Our workers had to leave the field, one after another, till Br. Bartsch was the only one left. This meant that he had to give up his plans to build up the school. Then he began to realize that the good news of the gospel could be preached in many parts of Dengese region. He had to travel. And it gave him great joy that the good news of the gospel could emerge. The apostle Paul was supposed to become a god in the city of Lystra, but the Lord allowed Paul to be stoned in that city. Br. Bartsch reported that he experienced similar events. Even though he wasn't stoned, he did experience many very difficult circumstances. But that was from the Lord. The danger is that the people are inclined to convert themselves to the missionary, to make him a god, as soon as he finds the Lord. Then it's often not easy for the missionary to turn the person away from himself to direct him to the Lord Jesus. The Lord helps in this circumstance as well.

King Ikongo-Samu created a lot of problems for him. There were many attempts to win him over from his ways, but none of them were successful. Then the Lord provided the opportunity to rescue the King from jail when he was in particular need. That changed things. The King became a genuine friend of the mission and sought to express his gratitude by supporting what the mission was doing. Nevertheless the Catholics succeeded, for a while, to turn him away from support of the mission and that created new problems.

And how does the mission station look now? Have you closed the mission? These are questions many people ask. No, the mission program has not been closed. The mission program is presently in a fallow stage, as so many mission programs are. Shortly before coming back home, Br. Bartsch had the joy of baptizing six young men. He tested their faith for a whole year and watched how they lived. There were tears of joy on his cheeks as Brother Bartsch reported about the baptism of these young men. When somebody has accepted the good news of the gospel, he needs to also take the step into baptism. The baptism took place in a water hole that had been the place of fear of "evil spirits." The candidates had overcome all their fears and recognized that Jesus Christ is stronger than the evil spirits. The Dengese region is a very rich field. And even though it's lying fallow now, in its own time it will bring forth much fruit.

It's a sad thing, that among many missionaries, patriotism is higher than their faith in Christ.[61] As children of God, we need to follow the advice of our master, which says, "Love your enemies!"

Repeatedly Br. Bartsch emphasized how much the love of the children of God had encircled him. In a very moving tone, he encouraged people not to lose their faith for the work and to continue to pray for the people in Africa. The Lord has not yet closed the door to His work in Africa. The work of the mission is not yet over. He said, however, that he could no longer work there alone. That is why he came back. He thanked the congregation again for their full support and for the support of his family.

My Last Days on the Mission Field and My Views on Doing Mission Work

In the interests of the mission at Bololo, I want to share some experiences that I had in the last few years. I hope the war will end soon, and there will be new energy for the work that places these experiences in the past. We have already done much at the mission. We could have done many things better if we had had more workers. Jesus prays, "Pray that the Lord of the harvest sends workers to the field." Because of the shortage of workers, we could not have worked the Dengese field region any better than we did. For the mission station to be successful, we needed enough foreign workers to manage it.

---

[61] The Kramers, who were German citizens, were not accepted at mission stations by countries who were at war with Germany.

If we had been able to establish a number of outposts early on, our conflict with the Catholics would have been spared. We had to cram ourselves into one particular mission. We managed that sufficiently with the resources that we had. The government official in Dekese encouraged us several times to send out more foreign workers. This is not so easily done, as every missionary knows. It is simply not so easy to manage the mission station without appropriate manpower. It is not enough to have a good will and a warm heart to be effective. Even the best missionary can drop out of the mission for various reasons leaving that particular branch of the mission to suffer. For example, the Lord can give a brother or sister all the necessary gifts to teach, he or she also needs to win the trust of students. That's when a strong Christian influence begins. It can bring much blessing. The work is done with love and enjoyment, both by the teacher and by the students.

But when, all of a sudden, something happens, when that teacher gets sick or has to travel or even dies, the school faces a dilemma. What should we do with the school then? If a substitute teacher is not available, the school must close and the students must travel back to their own hometowns. Then they come under the influence of the local villages again and lose what they have learned in the school. If after a year and a day, another foreign teacher is appointed he may even teach the same material as the previous one, and may in fact be better than the previous one, but he needs to build the trust with the same students again. Some have moved away, others have become lost in despair; others have grown past the age of attending school. Or, the students may have learned from a local teacher how to do the devil's work. That's why there should be several teachers at a school who work together in teaching at the school at the same time. If there are several teachers present, then the above tragedy in the school does not need to be repeated. Even if some people lose their strength, the work of this school continues and becomes the basis of a future church.

We believe we have become acquainted with the importance of training students to become leaders. So we pray that God will call out teachers in this land for his service. We're not looking for highly-educated teachers but for those who have the talent to teach and to love the children.

In the Dengese, we had very good teachers. We were very thankful for that. They however got sick, and had to leave the work that they loved. We couldn't find replacements. I've often greeted my former students and talked to them about Jesus. I have then been very thankful that the lessons that they learned at school had penetrated the depth of their being. When I met individuals on the paths or in the village, I often asked the question, "Do you remember the time that you spent at the mission?" A smile crosses their black faces, and the word "Yes" crosses their lips. Most of the students then also add, "But I don't have that peace anymore." I ask, "Do you continue to pray?" "Yes," they say, "when I get into trouble." "Does God hear you then?" "Yes, He always hears me," is the answer.

Many of the former students, who have gone astray, have passed away. So, when I speak to former students about eternity, the experience is very different than when I speak to people who have not gone to the school. The seed that has been planted in the school in these young people will bear fruit in its own time. Even when many of these children at Bololo go back to their sinful ways, the Lord can speak to them, which is often not the case with the others who have not gone to school. Finite human beings must bring the message of the crucified one into the darkest nights of heathenism and teach people about their living Christ. Then the Spirit of God begins to work. I've often been asked here at home why I haven't baptized those who have experienced conversion. To that I can say that we put less weight on the baptism than on the consistent Christian life. Many of the Africans get the impression that baptism is the high point of the life of faith. Many so-called Christians coast after that. They stop taking their life seriously because they wear the badge of Christianity through baptism.

Nevertheless, before I left Africa, I did baptize six of our former students. Since their conversion, they have become adults and have shown consistent Christian character. At first, I only wanted to baptize one of those students, because this one student had demonstrated his commitment by his behavior over the period of time. One day, shortly before I was to leave, Basongo came to me, looked me in the face lovingly, and became very quiet. If it had been another student, I would've thought that he came to me to get something. But not Basongo. He cannot make requests like so many others can. This young man stood before me, and waited. We talked about various things about the mission, and about some other stories from the villages, etc. Then I asked Basongo to come closer and to sit down. I asked him to consider baptism. When he heard about baptism, it's as though his face shone. He had wanted to be baptized a long time ago. But he didn't have the courage to ask for it.

Basongo went into the villages and shared his joy with other friends. When he told them about his decision to become baptized, others came and requested to be baptized, too. I got the group of six together and agreed that I would baptize them. I called this group together several times and gave them instruction on how to live after being baptized. I will never forget these happy students. It was a particularly moving experience on the evening before baptism. Those who were married brought their wives with them when they declared their confession of faith. All of them sat on the floor in my living room, singing one song after another. Everyone sang with full voice as did the others who were not being baptized. Then they gave their confession of faith. The stories of their conversions were simple and clear. I was impressed again how they reported their conversion, either as a result of preaching or a Bible study or in discussion with other brothers and sisters. They had come into a relationship with our Savior. The one telling the story was peaceful and friendly. This is often in contrast to the experience that I've had here in North America.

March 15, Sunday was a very stormy and rainy day. After church service we went to the water, where many years ago Brother G. Vande-Velde had been baptized. The baptismal candidates had picked this place themselves. When we arrived there, all the women who had wanted to come with us disappeared. Only a few who wanted to see the baptism came. The water in the old baptismal place was too shallow so we had to go closer to the spring, where the water overflowed the bank. A last test of their faith occurred there. The village people believed that those who look into the source of this water will be possessed by evil spirits. As they stepped into the water, none of those who were being baptized expressed any fear. They were all very happy and prayed again as they walked into the water. Then one after another they came towards me and answered my question with a loud yes. I was deeply moved. We went back into the house, and then had the formal acceptance into the church, as we do in North America. We then had a dinner and followed that with a time of prayer.

We don't know if the Lord will give us opportunity to go there again but we pray earnestly that someone will go, and that the Lord will send workers to Bololo.

Greetings from your Brother and Sister, H. G. and Anna Bartsch

Committee Affirmation of the Mission Work

We are happy to learn that Brother Bartsch is healthy, is doing well and is back with his loved ones. At the meeting Brother Bartsch gave several reports about his experiences in the mission field. I also gave a report of my trip to Hillsboro, and my meeting with the mission committee of the conference. After the reports, we made several decisions: We affirmed Bartsch's decision to travel home by air rather than by sea. We were also happy that, in spite of the fact that the mission work at Bololo has been closed temporarily, the word of the cross has been preached in the school and in the villages. We are also grateful that the Lord has provided His blessing for that work. We believe that the promise of our heavenly Father, that His word would not return void, will also be true in the Dengese region. As evidence of this, we have the baptism of the six young men, whom Brother Bartsch baptized shortly before he left. We thank God for these "first fruits" of the work and will continue prayer support for our black brothers.

We affirmed everything that Brother Bartsch did with regard to Brother and Sister Kramer in the Congo. We also

affirmed his decision to arrange for the legal leases on the property in the region of Dengese. It is also our firm sense that the MBE mission program has been entrusted to us by the Lord in the Congo and therefore we are praying for an orderly and a peaceful transition of this mission program to the General Conference of the Mennonite Brethren mission.

In the meantime, Brother and Sister Bartsch will be provided a stipend from the North American MBE mission program made in monthly payments to them. We have asked Brother Bartsch to visit the various congregations, and to provide reports about his work in the field. His travels will be arranged by Brother F. C. Thiessen, the secretary of our board.

We also decided to search for more candidates for the mission field. This is so that when the time comes for the mission field to open, Brother and Sister Bartsch can return with appropriate support. Has the Lord spoken to any of our younger brothers and sisters? If the way should open for missionaries to return will we be ready to send them? We then want to approach the work with greater energy, both financially and in prayer support. We thank God for each of you and wish all of you God's blessing.

H. H. Janzen, Chairman of the Africa Committee

A Reflective Report on a Mission Trip in the Dengese Region

According to Luke, chapter 9, verse six, the disciples traveled around preaching the good news of the kingdom, and healed many people.

One of the most important tasks that the Lord gave to his disciples was to declare the good news as they traveled around. Traveling and spreading the gospel was the central theme. This is an essential message for us here in this land and in heathen lands. It is the simplest means by which we can spread the word of God. Our Lord moved from place to place preaching, talking and healing all who came to him. He taught his disciples to do the same thing, as they traveled around. They did that till they lost their lives. The apostles taught their disciples to do the same thing. This is the basis for us to build the kingdom of God in our mission program.

I've been privileged to take many trips in the Dengese region, and it was always possible for me to preach God's Word. I've received many personal blessings through this work, because I knew that whenever I spoke God's Word, it was God's seed that would eventually grow and bear fruit.

On one of the trips to the region of Dengese, I came through several villages. The people in these villages belonged to the Yalimas tribe. They were very wild, scantily dressed and very much feared by the Basongomenes tribe, even though the Yalimas tribe is much smaller. The Yalimas tribe is much more unified and very active. Superstition and witchcraft are actively practiced here. Almost everybody has some kind of witchcraft symbol around his neck. People are very sensitive to any trespass of the witchcraft's symbols. I don't know many of the witchcraft potions but if one does not follow the regulations, that is, the customs surrounding these potions, people are killed. When a white person enters into the village of this tribe, one experiences a certain amount of trembling. I got the shudders when I walked past a man dancing around a fire, and I saw the glistening spears and the long knives. The shrieks that come from these men sound like they do not come from ordinary human beings. Often these men are somewhat or totally drunk. These events go on till early morning and shrieks sound like raving madness. They're getting ready for the hunt.

It was all very dark when I arrived in the village of Bolombo. Carriers with my things were in the rear. Only my collapsible chair and the kipoy came with me. Although I was hungry and tired, I made my way through the village. My cooking assistant walked behind me very carefully and carried the collapsible chair, always ready to set it down. The men were dancing at the end of the village. The women and children sat by their huts, next to the fire. I went from fire to fire and spoke with the women and the children. It was not a suitable time to spread the word of God. In some cases, the children ran into the huts, because they feared that they would be eaten. I asked one of the women why the children were so frightened. The answer was, "When my child sees a white man close up, he believes he must die." No wonder, when the little ones see a white man, that they are afraid of death.

At one of the huts, an old mother with her younger girl prepared the evening meal and also the meal for the coming day. The old one greeted me in a friendly way when I spoke to her. In the meantime, the younger woman quickly ran into the house. The older woman was very talkative so I stayed a little longer at that particular hut. Since I was tired, I asked my assistant to set up my chair. The boy did that quickly, and I sat beside the fire of this elderly woman. At first she didn't want me to do that but I had walked a long way and was tired. She indicated that it was okay. After a short discussion, I expressed my interest in having a small meeting in this village. At this, the woman got up and began to point out that all the men were at the other end of the village. She said I had better go there and hold a meeting or a worship service. She said that she was alone here at this end of the village, along with a few other people, and besides, she said she didn't understand when I spoke. (The dialect of the Yalimas is a little different than that of the Basongomenes.) The more the old woman pressed me to leave, the more I stayed and decided to wait there till other people would join us and listen. I was not persuaded to go away either with words of attack, or with pleading. Even my young assistant declared to the old woman that I would not go away. The old woman put her hand on her mouth as a sign of her amazement and turned her back to me. Then, suddenly, she shrieked loudly, and I wondered, "What's going on?" When the old woman shrieked several more times, people began to come.

Old people came first. The old men and old women sat down and looked at me through the glow of the fire. After about 10 to 15 people got together, the old woman said, "Now you can speak." When I responded that I could wait until more people came she called out a few more times, and more people came. Soon there were 70, a fairly large crowd of old and young people. The old lady sat down in front of me and wanted to hear.

When I began, everything was very quiet. I asked whether they could understand my speaking. "No" was the answer. "We are Yalimas and don't understand your language." What should I do? I knew that the people understood me, but they wanted to stop me from speaking. I called my young assistant and asked him to tell the creation story. He did that very eagerly, and nobody had reason to say that he couldn't understand. The story was long and often connected to events of the New Testament. The boy was very clear and could tell the story from memory the way he had learned to at school. After he finished I stepped into the role of being the speaker. In the meantime, all of the misunderstandings of my language, or their claims of misunderstanding my language, disappeared and I asked them questions about the stories that the boy had told them. The old woman who had sat with an open mouth answered every question. She recited whole sections of the story of Adam and Eve and the downfall and the expulsion from the Garden of Paradise. This gentle old mother had gotten the entire story correct. I was surprised and very happy that the old people had heard the story and could understand it. The Lord opens the hearts of even such old people.

The elderly woman was so confused about the event that she wanted to have my young assistant and me go to the other end of the village and tell them the story too. In the meantime, it had gotten very late so we decided to end the worship service. We said goodbye to each other. I went into my hut, and the people who had come to hear me went into theirs. Supper was very simple because of the late hour. I was very tired and so I went to sleep. The noise of the dance echoed in my ear, as did the questions and the answers of the old lady. I could not forget them. I thought of the words, "The Lord has opened the heart of this one, so that she had paid attention to what Paul had spoken to her." Yes, among these wild Yalimas, the Lord has called people to the everlasting life. Are we ready to bring them the gospel of Jesus? They will never come to Bololo to hear the word of truth. These people who sit in the darkness invite us to come to them to tell the story of salvation. One must press into their region to share the gospel. That's not possible for everyone, because the roads are bad and are very difficult to traverse. There are also many dangers along the road. It was exactly in this village, where I shared the gospel and where the elderly woman had understood it and become acquainted with Jesus, that Brother Kramer, in one of his travels, almost lost his life. It was a miracle that he got away from the spears of these people. But here with the wild Yalimas, Dengese people called them to everlasting life. Won't you help to carry out such a gospel to these people?

My Last Days in Bololo, Written from Canada

I will never forget the last days that I experienced in Bololo. They were difficult and meaningful. The concern was not only about the work I would leave for an undetermined period of time but also about the care for Brother and Sister Kramer. The care for the Kramers did not turn out to be as easy and as simple as we had originally thought. All the plans that we originally made failed. Our neighboring mission station staff were afraid to have German workers, because they saw what happened at the Bololo mission. Brother and Sister Kramer had the wish to make themselves useful at some mission station and I was also pleased, because it would be better than for them to sit in jail. I've often spoken with the commissar about them. His wish was that the family of the Kramers would be taken care of by Christian people. The Lord has not permitted that for some reason. Then we prayed that the brother and sister could get together with their German kinfolk in Elizabeth. That failed too. The Lord has also not permitted that. With heavy hearts we then determined that Brother and Sister Kramer would have to go to Luebo. The commissar of the district provided Brother and Sister Kramer with a modest little house, where they now live with their children. Brother Kramer receives a stipend from the government and Sister Kramer receives support from our mission. It has also been possible for us to send funds for the Kramers from here.

After the arrangements for Brother and Sister Kramer were complete, I began to liquidate some of our assets in Bololo. It took a lot of time to organize everything. I wondered how my leaving would impact the people from the village and the mission. We could give satisfactory explanations for Brother and Sister Kramer's departure. But all the people in Dengese knew that I was not afraid to live in Bololo as the only white person so when the people at the mission noticed that I was planning for a long trip they then asked me where I was going. When I told them that I was going to find Mama, that is, my wife, and the children, they were quite in agreement. It took about 10 days to load everything. The Kramers' belongings were sent to Luebo, at their request, so as to prevent termites from destroying them. What to do with the living animals was a more difficult question. Except for the chickens, I left everything there. I gave the goats to the watchmen and to their children as payment. I think it was a fair payment. I hope these young boys will take care of these things.

We then celebrated a small baptism in which I baptized six young men. It was a wonderful day. Everyone was very surprised and happy. I had my doubts because there was so much heathen behavior still in them, but when I heard their expressions of faith, I received a great peace to baptize them. The Lord had done his work in these Dengese people and that became very evident to me. The wives of the believing men were also present at the telling of their faith stories. It's questionable as to whether they understood everything that their men said, although they had also heard God's word and they watched the behavior of their men. When we went to the water, the wives followed us till the forest, and then they disappeared. Apparently, getting close to the water was too frightening for them. The other village people also did not come close to the water. Only some of the believers, whom we did not baptize, came to the water and took part in the ceremony.

The high point of the day occurred around the Lord's Supper. We gathered together in my dwelling place in a tight little circle, sang a number of songs, prayed and read God's Word. Then I spoke to the newly baptized people about their commitment to each other and to the Lord Jesus. I underlined the importance of taking responsibility for each other. We took the bread, broke it and ate of it. After the bread, we took the wine–rather than wine we had a plum wine–and drank it. To close, we had prayer.

Then I left for an undetermined time. The village people from Bololo accompanied me way beyond the village.

We waved to each other for a long time. The question arose in my mind. "When will we see each other again?" This leave taking was not supposed to take as long as I had thought it would. Before I left the area, I took a trip to Luebo to see Brother and Sister Kramer. They were very surprised that I came to Luebo. They thought I had left for Leopoldville a long time ago. I stayed in Luebo with the Kramers for several days. Then we said goodbye, not to see each other again during the war. On my trip to Leopoldville on the way to Port Francqui, I stopped at a restaurant to have lunch. I got to the Presbyterian mission at Bulape for the night. Because Dr. Poole was there, and he was such a good friend, it took me a while to leave in the morning. It was arranged by the Lord.

During the night, Brother A. A. Jansen came to the place where I had had lunch and stayed overnight. When he asked how far it was to Bololo to see Brother Bartsch, he received the answer that I was now in the town of Bulape, 20 miles away. He immediately sent me a message to say that he was in Mweka. We stayed there for several days, because I had liquidated property in Bololo. Then we decided that we would travel back to Dengese region again together. We first went to Dekese to see the government official. The new government official greeted us very warmly and invited us to stay. We stayed for a full day at Dekese, where we accepted the hospitality of the government official. He expressed his willingness to support the mission program that we had started in Bololo. I was happy that Brother Jansen had heard that. The next day, the government official (Talmann), Brother Jansen and I went to Bololo. The people in the village were very astonished that I had come back. They had not expected me to return so quickly. Next morning, everyone in the village came to our gathering. They were very responsive when we preached the Word of God to them. Brother Jansen also spoke to them in Kikongo language. When we left on Monday morning, the whole crowd of people from the village accompanied us and wished us a safe journey, and the leaders of the village told us that we must come back again soon.

I often think of the last days and hours at our mission in Bololo. Our prayer goes to them. We were there with our whole soul.

Yours in the Lord,
Henry and Anna Bartsch

Questions About Where We Settle

People have asked where we are planning to settle down. I want to report on how we are doing.

Except for Sister Bartsch, all of us in our family are well. Sister Bartsch developed skin cancer in her last year. After treatment by several skin specialists, the cancer disappeared. Recently, however, this evil disease has returned, and we needed to start treatment again. The doctor is confident that he can cure the cancer. Dr. Davidson is presently on military assignment and returns in February for vacation. He will consult with us about whether he can treat her in Rochester. May the Lord give her full recovery!

On February 12, we experienced another health crisis. Again it was Sister Bartsch who experienced it. While getting on one of the streetcars, Sister Bartsch fell backwards on the ice and broke her right arm in two places. The doctor realigned the bones and put her arm in a sling. So far, everything is in order, and we hope that the arm will heal. This will take about three or four weeks.

We don't understand what our Lord wants to say to us through these events. We know that His ways are right and this difficulty can also be presented before Him.

We ask all friends of the African mission to the pray for our welfare.

I arrived on February 12 at 10:45 and had just entered the house, when Dr. Neufeld brought my wife with her broken arm into the room. All the wonderful plans that we had made fell apart. But we also know that we can thank the Lord even for such events.

Our hearty greeting to all the churches that I have been able to visit in the last little while, and to whom I have brought the Word of life: "The Lord's ways are wonderful. And He will see that they are carried out."

Greetings from the heart, Henry and Anna Bartsch

Committee Report of the Africa Mission Program

On February 19 the directors of the Africa mission program met to make plans for the future.

In May of last year when Br. Bartsch returned from Africa healthy and happy, it was our wish that he visit the various churches that had been supporting him. He has done so. He has visited the churches in Ontario and British Columbia and some of the churches in Manitoba. There are still a number of invitations in Manitoba that he has not yet been able to respond to as well as a number of churches in Alberta and Saskatchewan.

We hear that Br. Kramer is well in Africa.

We asked ourselves the question of what we must do next. If the Lord does not change the world situation, and does not open the doors for us to go back to Africa in the near future, what shall we do? We made a number of decisions that are listed below:

• *If we are not able to serve the field in Africa at the present time, and it lies fallow, the committee was satisfied that we must preach the gospel in many of the Prairie Provinces. We will keep our eye on Africa and the mission program there, but we are asking Br. Bartsch and Brother Lenzmann to visit congregations and preach the gospel here in Canada.*

• *When candidates are selected for the mission in Africa our missionaries will interview them and discuss things with them.*

• *If Sister Katherine Harder continues to work among the blacks of Kansas City, we will support her.*

• *We also decided that Br. H. H. Janzen would work among the Russian people because of his special gifts in that area.*

• *Please pray that the work of God among our own people on this continent continues.*

My Travels in Canada in the Spring of 1943

Dear friends and brothers and sisters of the African mission.[62]

I was able to begin my trip to Alberta on March 13, 1943. Because my wife had broken her arm earlier, I was not able to begin the trip till now. Our earlier plan was for both of us to visit the churches in Alberta, but the children could not remain alone with a caregiver for so long, so I made the trip alone.

In early March, the weather turned sunny and I was happy that my trip would go better than it had in Manitoba, where I traveled in the cold of winter. But the weather turned windy again, and it began to snow on the night on which I planned to begin my trip.

The train was filled with soldiers and their girlfriends. The train was so crowded that in cars, passengers had to sit on the luggage in the aisle. There is chaos on the trains. The air is thick with smoke and the floors were dirty. Beer bottles roll around on the floor with a lot of cigarette butts or discarded papers. It was refreshing for me to get to a train station where I could step outside and inhale fresh air.

The storm became more intense and it snowed more heavily. The train was about an hour late. Several brothers met me in Coaldale and I was welcomed into the home of Brother and Sister Kornelsen. It was a welcome visit. And it was good to visit with B. B. Jantz, a teacher from the old country. We had much to share with each other.

I was able to visit a number of churches in the Alberta region. I thanked the mission committee in Coaldale for their good planning, and for their welcome introduction to the congregations. I thanked the women for their warm welcome in their homes. On April 30 I returned to Winnipeg and met my loved ones. My wife's arm had healed wonderfully. Only the skin cancer in her ear does not seem to disappear. We ask for your continued prayers.

---

[62] *Der kleine Africa Bote*, May 1943.

Farewell to Brother and Sister Bartsch[63]

We met often at the M.B. Church in Winnipeg, North, to thank God for the opportunities and the Lord's goodness to Brother and Sister Bartsch. On July 11 of this year (1943) we met again to celebrate the Bartsch's move to Yarrow, British Columbia, where they have bought their own home. Many true friends of the Africa mission gathered on this evening. There were many mixed feelings. We told ourselves that Brother and Sister Bartsch would be living in B.C., and that, even though the distance between Winnipeg and Yarrow is not so great, it is not likely that we will see each other very often.

There were many brothers present from different parts of the Mennonite Conference. Each of them spoke to Brother and Sister Bartsch and emphasized that "His sheep hear my voice," John 10:27. Brother Thiessen spoke about the many opportunities that the congregation had had to interact with the Bartsches. He also mentioned the many opportunities we have had to thank God for them. God has stood by them and supported them. It is our hope that the way to Africa will open up again for them. The hope is that the work will not disappear.

Sister Bartsch got up then. Deeply moved, she thanked the congregation for many of the blessings that they had received and the love that had had been shown to them. She said it would be impossible to forget her time in Winnipeg while her husband was away. She read Psalm 86:11: "Teach me Lord your way that I walk in your truth; hold my heart to that one thing: That I fear your name." This, she said, was her deepest longing.

In closing Br. Bartsch spoke to the congregation. He spoke from John 11: 26. "He who lives and believes in me will never die." He also thanked the congregation for the many blessings that he has experienced. They believe that the Lord is leading them away from Winnipeg at this time. He expressed the desire that British Columbia not be the end goal, but rather it be Africa. They would much rather go there now but the doors at present are closed, so it's important

---

[63] *Der kleine Africa Bote,* July 1943.

for them to wait. They prayed. In closing we sang, "God be with you till we meet again."

Next morning, the Brother and Sister, with their children, got into their vehicle and left for British Columbia.

The Final Status of the Bololo Mission Program

In order to clarify the status of the Bololo mission, I need to tell you a little bit about the situation of Protestant missions in the Belgian Congo.

There are about 48 Protestant mission programs in the Congo that have about 166 mission stations. In addition, the Roman Catholic Church is very strong, with 79 organized orders, which have 255 mission stations. Since Roman Catholicism is the official state church, it's not surprising that this church receives the support of the state. The Protestant missions have always had to assert their rights. Although the Catholic missions are organized in various orders, fundamentally they are all in agreement with each other, because they all belong to the Catholic Church. The Protestant missions are not so well coordinated. Besides the Mennonite mission programs, there are Baptists, Presbyterians, Methodists, Salvation Army, Pentecostal, Adventist, and many others. Every group wants its special consideration by the government. Of course it is not easy for the government to respond to every group equally which is why the Belgian government has encouraged little mission stations to unite so they do not have to deal with so many different directions and requests.

When Brother and Sister Bartsch went to Africa in 1931, they came upon a station called Kafumba, where A. A. Jansen and some of his coworkers had established a mission. Brother and Sister Jansen were self-supporting on the mission station, but they belonged to the M. B. Mennonite Church. They registered their mission with the government as Mennonites. When Brother and Sister Bartsch left that mission to go to Bololo, they registered, according to law, as Mennonite Brethren. So there were two mission stations in the Belgian Congo that were registered as Mennonite Brethren. Neither of these two mission programs had a conference that was supporting them: Kafumba was self-supporting and Bololo was supported by our Africa Association.

Over the years, the Kafumba mission grew to more than a hundred members. The growth was slower in Bololo. It took several years till the number of young men committed to Christ reached 80 to 83. Brother Bartsch was very careful with these people and wanted to train them in the way of Christ before he baptized them. Shortly before he returned to Canada, he baptized six young men.

The government gave the Kafumba mission a certain advantage, and advised Br. Bartsch to connect with the Kafumba mission. Practically, this was very difficult, since the Kafumba mission did not rely on any outside organization for support. In contrast, the Bololo mission received support from the Africa Association. If Kafumba had wanted to affiliate with the Bololo mission, then the American M. B. mission program would certainly have wanted to support the entire station.

This year, the M. B. churches of North America accepted the Kafumba mission program into its conference, along with all the workers and programs. This meant that it would be very evident that the government of the Belgian Congo would demand that the two mission programs unite. This is completely understandable.

While this was the situation in Africa, the Lord has also prepared the foundation for unification of mission fields in North America. Although the American M. B. Association was an interdenominational group, a number of very dear Brethren and friends of missions of other churches, and many members of the M. B. Mennonite Church of Canada were very supportive of the Kafumba program. In the meantime, the Bololo mission had aroused considerable interest and support in the Canadian Conference of M. B. churches. This was so much the case that the Bololo mission expressed the desire to be supported by the Conference of M. B. Churches of Canada two years ago.

Considering the situation on the mission field and the situation in North America, the directors of the A.M.B. mission decided that the time for unification of the two programs under the General Conference had come. The directors never wanted separate operations, but wanted very much to establish security for the Bololo mission. In the interests of the general mission work, they wanted to recruit workers. The General Conference gave its blessing to transfer the authority of the mission to the North American M. B. churches.

All funds that are designated for the Bololo mission will be directed to the Bololo mission. Under the authority of the General Mennonite Brethren Conference, the management of the Bololo work will continue, as is, till January 1, 1944. Please continue to send your contributions to C. A. DeFehr, who will manage the accounts till January 1, 1944.

Since the mission is being turned over to the General Mennonite Brethren Conference, and since we are preparing for that transfer, we will publish only one more issue of Der kleine Africa Bote.

–F. C. Thiessen, Secretary of the Africa Mission Association

Epilogue

The Influence of My Father's Life on Me

Henry G. Bartsch, my father, died on December 23, 1966. He turned 70 on December 17, two weeks before he died. He preached his last sermon in the Yarrow Church on the previous Sunday. As he and

Mother prepared to attend the children's Christmas Eve Program on the 23rd at the Yarrow Mennonite Brethren Church, he told my mother that he was not feeling well. He went to his study and lay down on the couch. When she came to him he said, "Alles was ich verborben habe, ist nun alles gut." (Everything that I have done amiss, is well, is forgiven.) She asked, "Was sagst du?" (What are you saying?) He quietly departed without another word. The doctor said that he died of a massive brain hemorrhage.

Evelyn and I returned from Eugene, where I attended the University of Oregon. We had two children, James, 6 1/2, and Mark, 2. We found the hearse on the yard, as well as several of his friends in the house. I spent several quiet minutes with him in his study before the undertakers took him from the couch.

My last contact with Dad occurred three months earlier when we left my parents' yard to begin fall term in 1966. As we walked out to the car, the news flashed that President Balthazer

Vervoerd of South Africa had been shot. I said, somewhat impulsively, "Good!" He gently said to me, "Karl nicht so." *(Don't talk like that.)*

After his return from Africa in May 1943, he took Mother and the four of us children (Erna, 12; Lydia, 10; Arthur, 9; and myself, 6) to Yarrow, British Colombia, where we purchased a house and two acres of land. We planted raspberries on the two acres. He spent much of his time visiting and preaching in the churches. We worked on the berry field. In 1948 the bottom dropped out of the market, so we raised chickens, then turkeys, but all of these activities were a substitute for my father's primary mission, which was to be a missionary in Bololo, Belgian Congo.

I recognized the deep yearning both Mother and Father had to be in Africa, especially their tears and hushed comments made to each other when they received letters from their former students. At one point, I saw him standing at the doorway in their bedroom, crying over a letter that they had just received. "Ihr seit ungehorsam," I said, in an arrogant and self-righteous tone of a 7 or 8 year old. *(You are disobedient for not going back to Africa.)* They could not go back because they felt the need to take care of us children and because of unsettled conditions in Africa.

Henry Bartsch and his wife Anna were always referred to as "Missionary Bartsches" by people in Mennonite Brethren circles. In the late 1940s and 1950s, it was an honor to be a missionary. I piggybacked on that status. I showed pictures of Africa in grade 3. Ever since then, as late as the 1990 Mennonite World Conference in Winnipeg, Manitoba, someone would see my name tag and ask if I was "Missionary Bartsch's son." When I indicated that I was, they told me stories that he had told to them in remote Saskatchewan churches in 1936 about the plight of natives in the Belgian Congo. You understand, then, that my early identity was shaped by both the stories he told and the public image of my father.

I did not know my father very well in my growing up years. That is, I did not share personal experiences with him. He *returned from Africa when I was six years old. I didn't recognize him, so I asked my mother if this was really my father. She said, "Yes." I took him by the hand down the stairs to the front porch and called to my friend next door and said, "See, this is my dad."*

During his absence Mother had kept him alive in my mind, through prayer and songs about him such as "My daddy lies over the ocean. My daddy lies over the sea. Oh bring back my daddy to me."

My Father's Influence on Me at the Crossroads of My Life

My father significantly influenced me at a number of crossroads of my life. The first occurred on the evening of New Year's Day, 1946. I was eight years old. I felt a sudden conviction that I needed to be converted. I went to my mother and I told her, "Ich will mich bekehren." She immediately called my father. Mother also called Erna, Lydia, and Arthur and father asked me if I meant what I said. I said, "Yes." He then read me John 3:16. "For God so loved the world. . . ." He asked nothing about a list of "sins" nor did he invite a confession of them. He simply said God loved me. The whole event didn't take more than a half-hour, and I felt very relieved, totally accepted and totally forgiven for those things that I knew I had done wrong.

Father spent the next few years traveling around to churches, talking about the events in Africa. We had to work on the raspberry farm, while he went to speak in churches. At one point, I said that I want to be a returned missionary. It had status and I would not need to pick raspberries.

I must have been about 7 or 8 when he took my brother and me to New Westminster, a distance of about 40 miles from Yarrow, to get some goats. We were desperately poor and I think he thought we could get goats to milk. He took the back seat out of our Willys and we stuck in two goats. They bleated and peed all the way home. The car stank for days. The goats didn't provide milk but they became my pets. At one point or another he also brought home a rabbit and a dog. The rabbit did not survive, but the dog did.

At about that age he also took my brother and me along to climb Vedder Mountain. Two other men had invited him to go and he saw this as an opportunity to take his two sons along. I don't think they appreciated that. In any case we got to the peak, about 3,000 feet and went down the wrong side because the other two men insisted. It was too foggy to tell the difference but Dad and my brother and I knew they were not right.

It was a tradition in Yarrow for elementary and junior high school kids to climb Vedder Mountain on Easter Monday. So when I was 14, my friend Art and I arranged to climb on an Easter Monday with two girls slightly older than us. I asked Mother if I could go. She inquired as to who was going in our group. When I told her, she did not say yes, and said that she would check with my father. He did not talk to me directly, but Mother said that he did not want me to go.

I snuck out of the house at about 5:30 in the morning. I felt guilty but went anyhow. It was a miserably cold day. Clouds hung over the mountain. We couldn't get a fire going to roast the hot dogs. We decided to go down early. I tried to show off; I stumbled, rolled and cut my eyebrow, which bled profusely. I tried to hide it when I walked into the house, but there was no hiding it. Mother looked at it and called Dad who immediately said we needed to go to the hospital to get it sewn up. He didn't utter a condemning word on the 15-mile ride. In fact he was silent on the entire trip, in the waiting room of the hospital and on the return trip home. The silence was not oppressive. It was just there. I felt terrible for having violated his wish for me that day. I wondered if my accident was a punishment for my deception, but neither he nor Mother ever spoke about it again. He seemed to say by his silence, "You'll need to figure something out yourself."

It must have been clear to the leading Brethren in the church that my parents needed a mission. They had raised turkeys to make a living, but were not good at it. So in January 1952, they accepted the positions of superintendent and matron of Bethesda Home, a mental hospital in Vineland, Ontario. Erna was married in May of 1951, Lydia was attending Bible school in Yarrow, and Arthur was in his senior metric year in Chilliwack. I was almost

15 and in the middle of eighth grade, so I went with them to live in the mental hospital in Vineland, Ontario, while the others stayed in Yarrow, British Columbia.

Bethesda Home was located at least a mile from the nearest neighbors. We lived in one of the hospital buildings with patients on the second floor. We ate with the staff, and so I had little private time with my parents. I worked on the farm in the summer of my 15th year, supervised patients while they milked cows in the morning and evening and plowed the fields or mowed hay in the daytime. I often felt lonely in the evening, not knowing anyone and far away from everyone. So I often got my parents' keys to the locked units and played chess and checkers with the men.

My father opened up possibilities for me after that first summer at Bethesda. Although I never talked about failing grade two, my parents knew that it bothered me that I was a year behind my peer group. Unbeknownst to me, my father went to Eden Christian Collegiate to explore the possibility of my taking two grades in one year. This would be grades 9 and 10. He came home, presented the situation to me and asked me what I wanted to do. I accepted. Completing both grades that year significantly affected my view of myself. It was a hard year of tough academic work, since I had to take exams in both grades, but I never regretted it. He opened up a possibility to me that I hadn't even considered.

My father opened up another possibility at the end of my year of grades 9 and 10. As the year came to a close, I began to miss the friends I had made, the school plays I had acted in, and the baseball team I had played on. The prospect of working away from all that on the Bethesda Home farm with mental patients bothered me, but I didn't say anything to Dad about my feelings. We did not talk about such things. A few days after school was over in June, he drove up the Bethesda Home drive with a 1946 Chevy pickup truck. He said that if I wished, I could take that truck across the country, 3000 miles, and we could use the truck on our raspberry farm in British Columbia. I was 16. We arranged for me to go the next day.

I grew up on that trip. Although we spoke little about feelings or personal things, his trust in me to take the trip alone built a bond between father and son that I never forgot. I decided to get baptized while on that trip. That summer my father baptized me in the "Jordan" in Yarrow, B.C. Again, as in the arrangement to take grades 9 and 10 in one year, his sense of who I was, and what life was like for me, led him to open up possibilities for me in ways that I could never have done for myself.

My parents worked at Bethesda home for three years, while I attended high school (Eden Christian Collegiate) and stayed at the dormitory, coming home only on weekends. Needless to say, I didn't get very close to my father during those years. My parents left for British Columbia in January 1955, while I finished my senior year at Eden. I don't recall it bothering me that they missed my graduation.

After I returned to British Columbia in the summer of 1955, I took my senior metric in Chilliwack High School. I was 18. In the meantime, Dad felt called to go to Europe on a mission trip. I lived with Mother. In summer, I got jobs on the pipeline. The next year, 1956, I went to Winnipeg to attend Mennonite Brethren Bible College. I believe my parents were pleased with this, but we never discussed my plans to go into the ministry.

I left the Bible College with more doubts about my faith than I had had when I went in. I never discussed these with my father or mother. I went to the University of British Columbia in Vancouver. I told someone I needed to discover what I believed rather than learn what the church believed. I didn't come home from Vancouver very often that fall, even though it was only about 60 miles.

I think my parents were worried about my faith and possible attachments, but said nothing about it to me until a very icy winter day shortly before Christmas. Roads in Yarrow were icy, no cars drove on that Sunday morning so Dad walked to church alone. Mother stayed home. There were only a few people at church, no choir, but Evelyn Reimer, 16, had come to church. Her voice instructor, Rudy Boshmann, asked her to sing a solo in place of the choir. She did, and Dad was impressed. When he got home he said to mother, "Karl is at the big university and will find some English girl, when there are such wonderful girls here." Mother took it upon herself to write me. She was very careful to *only suggest I consider Evelyn. I didn't reply, but came home the next weekend. I came on a Friday. She had some supper for me and sat at the table, obviously anxious. She said, "Was denkst?" (What do you think?) I played dumb and asked about what. She said, "About what I wrote to you." After stalling a little longer, I said, "Well, I have already asked her to go on a tobogganing day with a group of others." She said, "Gottes wille!" (God's will!) I said, "Can I have the car?" Both my parents learned to know and love Evelyn.*

After graduation from University of British Columbia in 1960, I spent a year in Toronto with Inter Varsity. We got married in 1961. Father officiated and married us. We moved to Manitoba and then in 1962, Evelyn and I went to Korea for three years with the Mennonite Central Committee. I had left home. Although I stopped in at home every so often, and my relationship with my parents was good, my arrows were pointed outward.

Perhaps the last time my father opened up possibilities for me, now us, occurred when we returned from Korea in 1965. We had two children, and I was accepted at the graduate school at the University of Oregon. On the second day that we had returned, Dad asked what we were planning to do. I told him that I planned to go to graduate school and was going to the Canada Bank to see if I could get a Canadian student loan. He invited me to his study and pulled out $1000 in cash. I asked him where he got that from and he said, "The Russian czar." Apparently the Russian czar had seen the revolution coming in 1917, and had sent his niece to Switzerland with some of the crown jewels. Before she died in about 1964, she willed the interest from the czar's money to go to those who had served in his last battles. Because Dad had been a stretcher bearer and had evidence to show for it, he was given a lump sum of $1000 which he could not put into the bank because it would reduce his old age pension. So he gave it to me and I promised to pay it back as soon as I was able to. This $1,000 was a lot of money, perhaps the equivalent of $5000 or $6000 today. It enabled us to get started since we had a net of only $3.00 to our name, with two kids and no money for graduate school.

I didn't realize till that last year that Dad was declining in vigor and spirit. His status was diminished after leaving Bethesda. Although he continued to preach in church occasionally, he looked tired. He passed away the year after we returned from Korea.

What I Learned About My Father Through the Writings I Translated

The translation of my father's writings was a deeply rewarding experience for me. Not only did I learn about the events of his life, but I also learned about the person I had only vaguely known before. The childhood images of his adventurous spirit took on new meaning as he described the events of his life. In this section I summarize what I have learned about my father through his written work. I do this through the lenses I have acquired, partially from my genetic make-up, partially through my early learning in the family and partially through life experiences and professional training as a psychologist.

I reflect on the person my father was in several categories: His temperament, his character, and his identity. Our temperament is our genetic predisposition to think, feel and act in a patterned way so to give stability across situations. Our character consists of the critical choices we make about who we are or will be, what we value, how we seek what we want and manage our fears, how we develop plans, goals and programs for our lives, how we think and cope with challenges we face. The raw material for our character choices are the life situations before us and our temperament predispositions and our prior experience. Our identity consists of our private self-reflections and our public presentation of the person we see ourselves to be. It is how we construe ourselves to be. It is not so much how we act, important as that is, or the reactions of others, but in the ongoing story we try to keep going, made up of our past, as we construe it, and of the future as we see ourselves being. Our narrative identity gives us our unique and continuing sense of the person we see ourselves being.

We are fortunate that my father wrote so many stories about the person he thought himself to be. He didn't share these with me in face to face meetings. Then again, I may not have been ready to receive what he did share then. I summarize below what stands out for me about my father from the translation I have done.

Self-Awareness

In my growing up years in Yarrow and in Vineland, I did not know my father to talk about his personal style. It wasn't done in the communities I grew up in at that time. While I always knew about his deep and abiding faith in God, I didn't know how his faith in God affected his inner life, his thoughts and doubts, his moods and feelings, his conception of himself and others. It is new for me to read how self aware he was of his temperamental style. He describes not only what he does at age 20 in his escapes from the "Reds" and in his 30s in central Africa, but how he thinks and even feels. He "owns" his own style and temperament: He seems proud of his energetic, curious, adventurous, risk-taking style and that he is energized by events and, especially, danger. I see him in a way I had not thought of him before.

Proactive Style[64]

In my growing-up years I never thought of him as proactive. I thought that life happened to him, especially after he returned from the Bethesda Home assignment. I thought of his trip to Europe in 1956 as a desperate attempt to get a hold on life

---

[64] A quote attributed to Teddy Roosevelt comes to mind. I think my father may well have agreed with it. "It is not the critic who counts, not the man who points out how the strong man stumbles, or where the doer of deeds could have done them better. The credit belongs to the man in the arena, whose face is marred by dust and sweat and blood, who strives valiantly . . . . who knows the great enthusiasms, the great devotions, who spends himself in a worthy cause, who at best, knows in the end the triumph of high achievement, and who at the worst, if he fails, at least fails while daring greatly, so that his place shall never be with those cold and timid souls who have never known neither victory nor defeat."

again. But his description of his style in the early 20s and 30s presents a different image. He anticipates events, initiates actions against all kinds of odds, leads effectively so that others join him in his mission, demonstrates competence to overcome obstacles, shapes events and has an impact on events, and gets things done. He eagerly accepts difficult challenges. I think he was alert to what was about to occur next, and sensitive to possibilities for accomplishing his goals. He is optimistic, naturally so by temperament, in situations that most others would consider futile. I am impressed with his energy and with his courage in the face of danger. Courage is doing what you fear. It is walking into the "valley of the shadow of death," reminding oneself not to fear because "thou art with me."

His energetic optimism did not seem to be a blind faith. Blind faith denies or ignores the realities. This style, in excess, would be to take on non-feasible tasks and projects. Were the tasks infeasible? The visa officer in Belgium certainly thought so when he said, "You want to put your head through the wall. You can't do it." His response is humorous. "These walls are pretty hard. I would hurt my head if I tried that. But King David says in the Psalms: 'With my God I can jump over the wall.' That's what I want to do." But when he shared the experience with his wife–my mother–he became very depressed, had doubts and felt discouraged, and said so. Both he and my mother bolstered each other's faith as they waited for seven months for a visa to get to Africa without money to live on. They questioned whether they had heard the voice of God correctly. But they waited and went on anyhow.

Impatient Style

Stylistically, my father had fast pace. He struggled with impatience. He made quick internal connections between signals and reactions. He did not wait or ponder for long when he saw what needed to be done. On one occasion it saved his life, as he describes leaping from a wagon at full gallop with a revolver behind his left ear. Earlier, on the same day, he impulsively rode off into the wheat fields to find the "White" troops only to put himself into real danger. He said it led him to do something "foolish." On another occasion he feels this terrible anguish of God's call while plowing the fields in Saskatchewan, leaves his equipment on the field, rushes in to his wife and says, "If I resist this call of God in my life, I will endanger my salvation."

I didn't know that he was aware of, let alone struggled with the pace aspects of his temperament until I read what he wrote. He notes both its strength and weakness but does not disown his style. After arriving in Belgium in 1931 to get his visa to the Congo, he and my mother and two children had to wait for seven months, rather than the expected seven days. He says he learned two lessons: Humility–a spirit of deference and submission–and patience. "Impatience" is time-related anger. It is a demand that something be different "now." He says, "My impatience, my pace to get things done, would have made me unsuitable to work among the people of Africa. I now know that a European temperament along with a North American pace is the greatest barrier to mission work among the African people. I had to learn to become quiet, to watch and wait. . . . "

How did he learn to become more patient? He says that the refugees our family stayed with in Germany helped him overcome his impatience and spiritual battles. He saw how "they had faced near death and knew from personal experience how the Lord had rescued them." His openness to the presence of God when he relives his near death experiences enabled him to work through his patience issues. They were not resolved once and for all. His impatience reappears again and again in his writings and also in my experience.

Action-Oriented Style

From his 42-year-old perspective in 1938, Dad describes himself as a twenty-year-old who needed to act. He felt confined if he could not act. He could not sit still. He wanted to make an impact on the events of the day and it almost cost him his life. I don't think my father acted out of a need to do his duty as Mr. Braun did. Mr. Braun's duty was to be a mayor, which Henry said he loved to do and which, I might add, suited his personality. For Dad, action was the thing. When Mr. Braun did not choose him to distribute the food, he needed to act in another way. He acted not to serve a purpose for the community or Mr. Braun, but to satisfy his own curiosity, to see what was going on. He seemed to have done it on a whim. He met the Cossack who called him a "crazy kid." He describes his eagerness to be involved in spite of the dangers. Others may have laid back but the idle life was not enough for him, especially when action was possible. He loved risk, excitement, the adrenalin rush of adventure, even if it meant doing something foolish, as he says about himself. This was his natural, probably genetic, temperament style.

Personalities like this are great in a crisis. They are perceptive of events, almost with a sixth sense. They don't pause long when it is possible or necessary to act. And Henry did act when the officer held a revolver to his left ear. The action saved his life. That led to his conversion in the wheat field. But more than that he notes that he told K. Dueck and G. Harder that he committed the rest of his life to the Lord, acknowledging that he did not really know what that meant. What is also of note is that in reviewing this event twenty years later, he experiences the loving presence of God. And because, as he said, "I had life in God, I did not need to be afraid."

Spousal Support

One of the greatest sources of stress for someone with Dad's style is bureaucratic blockage;[65] irrational paper shufflers stifle such a person. It can lead such a person to turn on the person blocking him, to challenge, argue and even fight in rage. What the person does internally with this external blockage is critical. Dad was fortunate to have a spouse who shared deeply

---

[65] Another factor precipitating excess in a style such as his might occur when he is diverted from his felt purpose, as Dad felt in Kafuma.

in his life purpose. She was as committed to the mission as he was. He knew this when he stopped his tractor in the fields of Saskatchewan, ran in to tell his story to his wife, and they jointly decided on God's call. So as not to confuse themselves about that call they jointly decided to tell no one else. But they reaffirmed their joint call. So when they ran into bureaucratic red tape regarding their visa in Belgium, they jointly went to their deepest inner being and found refuge in the call of God in their lives. That process of facing seemingly insurmountable difficulties, whether externally or internally, going to the wellspring supported by scripture passages, and choosing a path other than the one his style would predict, led to a Godly character.

My parents model of waiting on each other, sharing deeply about their feelings and intuitions before going ahead with decisions that affect both of them, has been helpful to Evelyn and me in our 45 years of marriage. My temperament/style is not too dissimilar to my father's. I understand his impatience to get things going. So I feel grateful to see how he and she worked out such stressful moments in their lives together and deepened the Christ-likeness of their characters.

Dad drew considerable strength from his relationship with my mother. I always knew that he loved her, but until I read his letters in this translation, I did not realize how much he missed her. I have sometimes mentioned to people that I only saw my father kiss my mother once, which I simply accepted as "that's the way things are." Elderly people, (those over 50), I thought, do not express affection. But his letters reflect the passion and emotion of desperate loneliness while alone in Africa. Their private letters to each other also express this passion for each other. I did not previously know that this existed. I am impressed with the frequency with which he refers to missing her. He signs his letters, "Your praying and lonely husband."

Response to Traumatic Experiences

Dad's experiences in his escape from the "Reds" and in central Africa certainly qualify as traumatic.[66] Our psychological pores open when we face a personal crisis. A traumatic event has the potential of awakening us to the best in us or it can open us up to utter despair, helplessness and disconnection from others. Dad's writings translated here reflect his struggles with faith, with loneliness, and despair. They also reflect him "owning" of these experiences and finding the resources in God to overcome them. His traumatic experiences in the Congo opened him up to face himself and his identity: "Have you forsaken me, God? Who am I? How do I live my life meaningfully?"

The life threatening events didn't change his temperament. They did not, for example, remove his tendencies to impatience. But they brought him face to face with basic life choices: Confidence in adversities, hope versus despair, perseverance instead of hopelessness, vision of possibilities rather than pessimism, sacrifice of family and spouse for a cause rather than retreat in comfort. Character is formed by such choices.

Dad repeatedly notes the "loving presence of God" even within the traumatic experience. This is the classic trauma treatment approach: A felt exposure or awareness of the traumatic situation with a felt healing resource (God present). Such an experience is deeply centering. The traumatic events are remembered but the sting of the event is lifted. Our psychological pores open whenever we face a personal crisis. We are in a state to be healed of our stylistic or temperamental foibles when we make deep structure choices. The events changed the direction his life was to take.

---

[66] Traumatic stress is a surprising occurrence of piercing intensity that is outside the range of usual human experience. When we experience continued and ongoing demands or expectations that challenge our ability to cope or manage our lives, we face ordinary stress that can cumulate to have the same effect as traumatic stress.

Life Purpose

Central to my father's life was the purpose he found in his faith in God. Perhaps because of the traumatic events of his early 20s, he knew that God had a particular call in his life. For him, as for me, one aspect of the call of God is to become Christ-like; to form a character that reflects the person of Jesus in daily life.

The 1930s were a period of arrogant colonialism in Africa. The British expressed it in South Africa and Northern and Southern Rhodesia (Zambia and Zimbabwe), the Germans expressed it in Tanzania, and the Belgians in the Belgian Congo. Liberation did not come till the 1960s. Black Africans were considered indolent, lazy and distained by white colonialists. There are references to Dad's (European) frustration with getting his African help to get work done. But he also makes some critical choices in his stay as a missionary. He cannot tolerate being on a plantation in Kafumba that uses black labor and then seeks to evangelize the same black people. He speaks with horror at the abuse of blacks in Luebo.

What emerges is his tremendous love for the African, particularly the Dengese people. The response of fear and threat they felt when his party first arrived to one of trust and love they expressed when Dad returned in 1935 is remarkable and speaks to the reciprocal nature of love.

Dad refused to present a "cheap grace, even though it might win him plaudits with the home crowd." He refused to baptize "believers" till he was assured that their character had been transformed. He resisted imposing "Christian rituals" as a substitute for real character change: Integrity, loving care for others including spouses, honesty in dealing with others. A central theme in my father's life was to develop wholesome personal qualities of character and to teach them or elicit them in others.

I believe that Dad's central motivation was the love of God. After the horrendous events on the day he escaped from the "Reds" he says, "God spoke so clearly, was present with us so closely because he loves us so much." Later he said he "felt love for his persecutors. So I prayed for them . . . . faith kept me going, even when I faced dying."

Although God had rescued him so dramatically, he says he did not want to become a preacher or a missionary. So he was totally stunned by the call of God to become a missionary in Africa. This led him to wait for funds, when patience was his personal weakness. He learned to depend on others for money, when he prided himself in his ability to master events. He said he needed to learn humility and to reflect on what God was trying to teach him when his personality tendency was to take charge of events rather than wait for them to come to him.

I always knew that honesty and integrity were important qualities of character that my father valued. He certainly had the skill of putting on a mask when he did not want to show feelings —as when he faked calm as he faced the "Reds" who had just raped the town, or when he walked in to the G.P.U. (secret Soviet police) office to get his exit visa.

He demonstrated his integrity when their visa arrived for them to go to the Belgian Congo, and he needed to leave a deposit of 20,000 francs. A medical doctor whom he had not met sent it to them and asked only a modest interest. He turned it down. He said he could not accept the money because he was not going to make enough to even pay on the interest. He rejected any deception that he might be able to pay it back, even though their entire mission depended on their having the money.

I recall when I was about 11 or 12 when he came home from delivering berries to the berry plant. He looked very sad at the dinner table, and then said that the receiver/inspector of the berries, a non-Mennonite, said, as an aside, that for many Mennonites their expressed faith did not seem to connect to their behavior. How did he come to that conclusion? He said many people put the rotten berries at the bottom of the trays and covered them with good berries. This saddened my father considerably and left an indelible imprint on my mind. When he says in his writings that he could not baptize his students earlier, it was because he did not see consistency in them. Integrity meant consistency between external behavior and an internal state.

One of the most difficult decisions my father, mother and five others faced was leaving Kafumba Mission. He did that, I am convinced out of his sense of integrity. He could not do a "plantation" approach to mission work; mix preaching God's love and salvation while exploiting blacks. So he left the Kafumba Mission for undisclosed regions.

Hope and optimism characterized much of his writings even about events that seemed hopeless. He noted signs that God was leading them in the right direction. I suppose those signs could have been read otherwise: Willy Jantz and his wife leaving shortly after arriving in Bololo, the near death of his pregnant wife, with two little children. Sometimes his optimism and readiness to take on overwhelming tasks seems almost foolhardy.

The departure of Willy Jantz and family must have been a real blow to my parents. I know of other instances when they were hurt and felt hurt by church officials. Never did I hear complaints about other people. Never. They clearly felt the hurt after the Bethesda experience, but I never heard negative statements or complaints about the people. I respect them for that.

Dad got discouraged but he kept on hoping. He begged, "God forgive me for my discouragement and despair. Later I found many children of God in Lodi." He called the mission in Bololo "Peniel," the place of wrestling until a blessing is received and a place in which transformation takes place. His life was based on his faith in God's presence.

His faith was a seamless web linking his character with his concern for people's inner life and spiritual condition, and linking his responses to the condition of the people with whom he worked. "We cannot care for the soul unless we also care for the body of the people". He spent considerable time detailing stories of the awful physical conditions of the Dengese people: Undernourishment, death of infants, and lack of medical care. So even though he did not have a medical doctor available, he set up a clinic to care for men, women and children.

Conclusion

I conclude this epilogue with the same conclusion I had in the Preface:

"Thank you, Dad, for sharing your perspective on life with me and for having lived it so fully. And thank you for writing about your life, the ways God was your very present help in time of trouble. You enrich my life as I read and remember the stories you told. I want to pass them on to your grandchildren and their children, children you have never seen. They need to hear from you. Against all odds, God saved and led you to serve others. May your God be their God! And may they learn to know the God of love in Jesus of Nazareth as you knew him."